Brian Inglis, was an Irish journalist, historian and TV presenter. He was popularly known in Britain as the presenter for All Our Yesterdays. His publications covered a range of topics, including biographies, medicine and the paranormal. Other books by Inglis include *The Forbidden Game: A Social History of Drugs* and *The Story of Ireland*, amongst many others.

PRAISE FOR BRIAN INGLIS:

'Mr. Inglis has given us a brisk, lucid and detailed account.' – Philip Mason, *The Spectator*

'Scholarly and very readable.' – *The Listener*

'A searching examination of one incident in our chequered history which even dyed-in-the-wool Britons will find hard to defend.' – *Yorkshire Post*

Also by Brian Inglis

Poverty and the Industrial Revolution

The Forbidden Game: A Social History of Drugs

All our Yesterdays

The Story of Ireland

Trance: A Natural History of Altered States of Mind

THE OPIUM WAR

BRIAN INGLIS

ENDEAVOURINK

AN ENDEAVOUR INK PAPERBACK

First published by Hodder and Stoughton Limited
in 1976

This paperback edition published in 2017
by Endeavour Ink
Endeavour Ink is an imprint of Endeavour Press Ltd
Endeavour Press, 85-87 Borough High Street,
London, SE1 1NH

ISBN 978-1-911445-92-0

Printed and bound in Great Britain by
Clays Ltd, St Ives plc

CONTENTS

The Life and Work of Brian Inglis

An assessment by Neil Inglis

The life and career of Irish author Brian Inglis (1916-1993) brought him many accolades for his achievements in journalism and broadcasting. His editorship of The Spectator (1959-62) was notable for his nurturance of new talent and the resulting boom in the magazine's circulation. On television, he was a pioneer (on What the Papers Say, starting in 1956; and he went into battle with primitive vote-tallying computers during the Rochdale by-election in 1958). In 1962, Brian took over the reins of All Our Yesterdays, the long-running Granada documentary series that reviewed the events of a quarter century in the past, reaching its glory days in the period 1964-70, when it covered the WWII years.

Henry Fairlie is sometimes credited with coining the term "The Establishment" in the pages of The Spectator, and Inglis was in many ways a quintessential Establishment figure. Yet Brian chafed against such respectability. His investigation of unorthodox healing, *Fringe Medicine* (1962) was considered so controversial that the publisher included a preface by a well-regarded surgeon to reassure anxious readers. On The Spectator, Brian brought in younger writers, often on the political Left (Alan Brien, Bernard Levin); yet in so doing he deliberately overlooked the magazine's historic ties with the Tory Party, an affiliation never forgotten by the magazine's proprietor. Inglis's resignation, soothed by the prospect of a top job in TV, soon followed. Inglis's generous contract with Granada Television allowed him to pursue his own intellectual interests and, when AOY to an end in 1973, Inglis was not sorry to return to full-time writing. Why?

As the host of a top-rated WWII documentary in the 1960s, Inglis was never free to speak his mind. On camera, he was sharing his insights with millions of armchair historians all over the country, for whom the war was a recent and vividly remembered experience. This was neither the time nor the place to shock mainstream audiences with awkward revelations (Inglis could not have mentioned the Ultra/Enigma programs, were he aware of their existence). One day, Brian vowed to slough off these restrictions. A return to freelance status would allow him to be a revisionist historian.

The Story of Ireland (1956) and *The Forbidden Game: A Social History of Drugs* (1975) are witty, densely researched and highly readable, in Inglis's trademark economical style, in which every sentence and every phrase have something important to say. A different aspect of his personality, a disturbing asperity, is evident in *The Opium War* which dates from the same period as *The Forbidden Game* and was palpably inspired by Inglis's researches in connection with the latter title. *The Opium War* is an epic work that resonates to this day, and some effort must be made to understand the author's motivations in pursuing this project. Moreover, this is the publication regarding which the Inglis estate fields the most queries. Inglis regarded the opium trade as an abomination – yet as we have observed, he did not object to drug use per se, or on moral grounds. What, then, were the roots of Brian's anger?

The Opium War (1976)

The story begins in India (a country where Brian spent his early years – his father, Sir Claude Inglis, was a well-regarded hydraulic engineer stationed in Poona and other areas. Inglis Sr. never regarded or treated Irish Catholics or Indians as inferiors.) Opium grown under conditions of great horror was harvested, packed, and shipped to China, with twofold aims; to maximize the flow of revenue to British coffers, and to ensure as much plausible deni-ability as possible for the Crown.

Imagine Inglis as a prosecutor building a case against the British Establishment. Inglis's excoriation of this opium policy is warranted, yet a reader may wish to call for a cross-examination. What, exactly, was the author's own agenda in this matter? Brian's treatment of capitalism and foreign trade is bleak and Dickensian. This is a world of chimney sweeps and child labor, of landlordism and rack-renting, of official rapacity and corruption. Missing from Inglis's account is any sense of the self-correcting capacity of British-style capitalism and the powerful impulses for reform it could and did engender (one thinks of the Quakers and Abolitionism). Likewise absent from *The Opium War* are any references to the many wonderful advances in science and technology in the 1700s and 1800s, which made human life so much better and more bearable (clean water, communications, and electricity, to name a few).

In fact, the reference to electricity provides us with an important clue to Inglis's motivations. Inglis had no time for the Victorian pioneers of science and technology (such as Michael Faraday), because they were too closely identified with efforts to suppress and ridicule Victorian spiritualism, a topic dear to Brian's heart, and covered in exhaustive detail in *Natural and Supernatural* and its sequel, *Science and Parascience* (1978 and 1984). Inglis viewed the paranormal as the single most important under-reported story of his own time. His investigations into psi forces earned him mockery from contemporary sceptics, and he fought fire with fire, shaming his critics in the process. For Inglis, those Victorian rationalists who had mocked the Occult (Faraday and Darwin among them) were cut from the same cloth as the Whitehall mandarins who rationalized

Imperial foreign policy (watch out for Brian's use of the word "suspect" in describing both types of men – a classic Inglis-ism, denoting reprehensible behavior).

If one returns to *The Opium War*, one might argue that the British expedition to punish the Chinese authorities was an Empire's predictable response to a perceived affront. The real surprise would be if London had done nothing. The British action may not have been pretty, it may not have been ethical, decent, or wise – but it was in keeping with the behavior of imperial armies throughout history. The saga of the Chinese opium racket, and its tragic outcome, represented a case study in commodity trade and frontier economics, in an era of limited communications and obsessive official secrecy. This was the kind of case study, unflattering to Great Britain, that was calculated to appeal to a left-leaning economics lecturer in Ireland in the immediate post-war era (and Brian was employed in such a capacity while studying for his PhD at Trinity College Dublin). In fairness, Brian was never a Marxist; he would have had patience for the modern-day practitioners of victimology, and he was always too good a scholar and too widely read to tolerate intellectual laziness. He would be the first to admit that the world in the century of his birth (2016) had changed irrevocably; for countries that once labored under the Imperial yoke (India, Ireland. . . and China) have put the past behind them and enjoyed massive booms. In this, Brian would have found much cause for optimism.

INTRODUCTION

It has happened to me before, and I trust will again, that the research for one book has lured me to write another. Preparing to investigate the history of drugs for *The Forbidden Game*, I happened to pick up the 1840 'China Papers' dealing with the events leading up to the opium war, which must surely be one of the most compulsively readable collections of documents ever published as a Parliamentary Blue Book. From that I went on to read some of the authors who have covered the same ground: from contemporaries like Thomas de Quincey and Samuel Warren down to recent writers, Maurice Collis, Arthur Waley, and Hsin-pao Chang. And one aspect of the subject began increasingly to interest me: what, or who, was the cause of the war?

Not that there is ever a single cause; though there may be an accepted trigger event, like Sarajevo. In the case of the opium war, however, the popular assumption has been that the chief cause, at least, is easily identifiable. As Thomas Arnold complained when he heard that an expeditionary force had been despatched to China, it was 'to maintain smuggling'; and, worse, smuggling which consisted of 'the introduction of a demoralising drug, which the government of China wished to keep out, and which we, for lucre of gain, want to introduce by force, and in this quarrel are going to burn and slay, in the pride of our supposed superiority'. This view, however, has been challenged; not merely by defenders of the government's decision at the time, and apologists for it since, but also (I was surprised to find) by most of the serious students of the period who have written about it during the past fifty years; beginning with David Owen in his diligently researched *British Opium Policy in China and India*, published in the United States in 1934. 'Only in the light of the immediate occasion', Owen concluded, 'can the conflict be called an opium war'; a verdict soon to be echoed by Professor W. C. Costin, and more recently by Maurice Collis and Edgar Holt. American historians of Chinese descent have tended to accept this view. In his *Commissioner Lin and the Opium War*, Hsin-Pao Chang surmised that though it arose over opium, it might just as easily have been the Molasses War if molasses had happened to be the commodity which the British merchants had been determined to sell; and I. C. Y. Hsü, in *The Rise of Modern China*, described opium as 'the immediate, but not the ultimate, cause of the war'.

To pursue this controversy in *The Forbidden Game* would have taken me too far from the book's main theme; and I have gone into it here, instead. All wars have some of their roots far back in history, often in events or trends which at first sight have little or nothing to do with the eventual hostilities; and the opium war is no exception. As it happens, too, the convoluted course which those earlier events took is more absorbing than the actual war itself, which was too one-sided to be of much interest even to military historians and which, I feel, has been too often related to need repetition in any detail.

I have followed current colloquial usage in the spelling of Indian and Chinese names and terms; or, where there is no generally accepted spelling, used the one which seems least likely to cause confusion (for example, the East India Company's Canton agents were usually described as 'Supercargoes', but I have preferred, as some of them did, the term 'Supracargo', which sounds less like a latter-day freightliner). For simplicity, too, I have used the term 'Viceroy' throughout, when referring to the Emperor's representatives in the provinces of China. There were also Governors; but the functions and pronouncements of the two were not kept distinct – certainly not in translations of their edicts. I have modernised old spelling and, where necessary for clarity, grammar and punctuation. One source of confusion, however, or at least of irritation, I have left; the frequent contemporary references to 'England', or 'the English', by which was meant Britain, or the British.

Currency presents a problem. Opium transactions within India, where it was produced, were conducted in rupees; the opium trade, in Spanish dollars; and the revenue derived from opium, in sterling. This is less confusing than it might be, as the rates are easily memorised: £1 = $5 = 10 rupees*. The rupee, however, varied in value between eight and twelve to the pound; and the Spanish dollar frequently had to be bought at a premium, owing to its scarcity. The statistics, therefore, have to be regarded as approximations. But they were approximations, anyway. 'Every statement regarding the quantities of opium consumed in China', the historian Hosea Ballou Morse complained fifty years ago, 'appears to differ from every other statement'; not surprisingly, in view of the fact the drug was contraband. Still, precision happens to be less important than trends; and the available figures, though they may be inexact for any particular year, are a safe enough general guide.

---

*Although it is never easy to make comparison between the value of money at any given date with what it is worth today, a useful rule of thumb is to multiply by ten: £10 being the equivalent of £1 then.

1

THE CHINA
INVESTMENT, 1729-93

There must have been five stages in the development of
man's appreciation of opium, the botanist George Watt
surmised, in his monumental *Dictionary of the Economic
Products of India*. The poppy would first have been admired
as an attractive flower; then, relished as a vegetable (it was
still eaten in India as a salad, 'like lettuce', at the time he
was writing – the 1890s). At some point, it must have
been found that the juice of the poppy could be made
into a refreshing beverage; and consumption of the juice
would have led to the discovery of 'the potent nature of
the inspissated sap'. Only then would it have come to be
taken as a drug.

As a drug, opium was taken for different purposes,
travellers from Europe in the sixteenth and seventeenth
centuries found, in different regions of India. In the Mogul
Empire it was regarded as an intoxicant, and as such

1

reserved for the pleasure of the Court and the aristocracy; arriving in 1608 in the *Hector*, the first ship to visit India under the British flag, William Hawkins was well received – but not by the Emperor who, he gathered, was under the influence. In central India, however, it was in everyday use among all classes; the staple of the coolie and the courier, who ate or drank it in small quantities to provide them with the energy and endurance to carry them through the working day. Rajput warriors took it to calm their nerves before going into battle, so that it became associated with bravery; if a pledge were ratified between two men by eating opium together it was considered inviolable under all circumstances.

When the British East India Company secured trading rights from the Mogul Emperor, early in the seventeenth century, its agents found that although he enforced a strict monopoly, the contractor who managed it for him was willing to sell them opium for export; a welcome concession, because the profit they could make on it helped to pay for the spices they needed from the East Indies. They had known it at home only as a sedative medicine; but in Sumatra, the agent in charge of a British trading station wrote in 1713, it produced

> *very different effects on different constitutions. Some are laid by it into so profound a sleep that the noise of a drum, a cannon or even a scolding woman cannot wake them. Others are reduced to a perfect state of indolence, insensible of pain and possessed with*

such a kind of negative pleasure as renders them regardless of everything. A third sort are downright delirious, sleep with their eyes wide open, and talk a great deal without any design or connection.

Opium had the effect, invaluable for traders, of making hungry where most it satisfied. Those consumers who became addicted to it maintained a rate of demand which seemed proof against price increases. And among the countries where by this time a demand existed was China (as Daniel Defoe knew; Robinson Crusoe twice shipped opium there, because it 'bore a great price among the Chinese'). The impression was to gain ground later that the Chinese must have taken opium from time immemorial; but Chinese scholars have found no reference to it earlier than the eighth century A.D. The opium-bearing poppy was not indigenous there; and the American missionary and diplomat Samuel Wells Williams, whose *The Middle Kingdom* was to be the fullest and fairest of nineteenth-century studies of China, came to the conclusion from his researches that for nearly a thousand years, such imports of opium as there had been were for medical purposes. The Jesuit missionaries who were allowed into the country in the seventeenth century, he pointed out, did not mention it. They surely would have made some comment, if they had encountered it.

Opium came into use as a non-medical drug in China at some time towards the end of the century, in and around

Canton, the port through which most foreign merchantmen traded. Their crews reported that it was smoked there; not eaten, or drunk, as in India. How and where opium was first smoked remains a mystery, but the probability is that it had been tried out in the East Indies, mixed with tobacco (a method reported in use in Java in the 1680s) and introduced by Dutch traders first to Formosa, and later to the mainland. At some stage a way was found to dispense with the tobacco. The opium, Wells Williams explained, was first 'seethed' – simmered in water – and strained several times to remove impurities. The resultant paste was then rendered down to the consistency required, necessitating a loss of about half the original weight, but enabling the purchaser to judge if there had been adulteration. The smoking equipment consisted of a pipe made from a tube of heavy wood, the bowl at the end of it being designed not so much to hold opium, like a tobacco pipe, as to collect the dross. The smoker lay down on a couch, near enough to a lighted lamp to be able to bring the bowl close to the flame.

A pellet of the size of a pea, being taken on the end of a spoon-headed needle, is put upon the hole of the bowl and set on fire at the lamp, and inhaled at one whiff, so that none of the smoke shall be lost. Old smokers will retain the breath a long time, filling the lungs and exhaling the fumes through the nose . . . when the pipe has burned out, the smoker lies listless for a moment while the fumes are dissipating, and then repeats the process until he has spent all his purchase, or taken his prescribed dose.

The effects were first to make the smoker loquacious, and prone to break out into 'boisterous silly merriment'; then, to send him to sleep – but sleep which, Wells Williams felt, gave no refreshment to the addict, only a craving for more.

Reports of the spread of the opium-smoking habit eventually began to disturb the Imperial Court in Pekin; and in 1729 an edict put a ban on its importation, except under licence for medical use. Heavy penalties were imposed for dealing in the drug; offenders were to be sentenced to wear the cangue (an outsize wooden collar, worn like a portable pillory) and to receive up to a hundred strokes of the bamboo. This was disturbing news for the East India Company's Canton agents, the Supracargoes (so-called from the time they had sailed with the Company's ships as its commercial representatives; by tin's time they had settled in Macao). If the Company were detected importing the drug illegally, it would lose its trading rights in China. These rights had not been easily secured, because the earlier attitude of rather condescending benevolence which visitors from the West had encountered when they first reached China in the Middle Ages had changed to suspicion and hostility following the appearance of the Portuguese in the sixteenth century. Their commercial methods were not readily distinguishable from piracy; and when the first English ships reached China under Captain Weddell in 1637 they, too, were suspected of being pirates. As Weddell had resorted to force to overawe the local officials, he had confirmed the prevalent impression that the 'foreign devils', as they came to be popularly known, were not to be trusted. It had been difficult for the East India Company to live down this reputation, particularly as the Manchu emperors were even more worried about the spread of foreign influence in China than their Ming predecessors had been.

But they were also chronically in need of revenue. Because the foreign merchants were prepared to buy Chinese tea and silk, they came to be tolerated, though control on their movements remained strict. They were allowed to settle in Macao, where the Portuguese had acquired squatters' rights, exercising much the same kind of limited authority that a town council today enjoys. And following the decline of Portugal as a maritime power, the East India Company had become commercially dominant there, with the help of a Charter which gave it the monopoly of all British trade with the East. But the Emperor, the Company Supracargoes feared, would withdraw all facilities if he heard that they were defying his new ban on opium. They sent a warning to the Company's Calcutta headquarters not to ship any further consignments. The recommendation was accepted, and apparently observed, though doubtless small amounts continued to be smuggled in. The opium smokers of Canton had to rely on what they could get from the Portuguese through Macao, or on supplies landed by freebooters.

Robert Clive

There matters might have rested indefinitely, with the Company continuing to send only licensed consignments of opium to China, had it not been for an event which was to have a profound effect on the Imperialist era. The Nawab of Bengal, Aliverdi Khan, had retained control over foreign traders by keeping them commercially content and politically impotent in his domains; much the same policy as the Chinese Emperors were following. But when he died in 1756 he was succeeded by Surajah Dowlah, whose hatred for the East India Company and all it stood for prompted him to seize Fort William, the Company's Calcutta headquarters. While he slept off a debauch, over a hundred British subjects were locked up for the night in a twenty-foot-dungeon, 'the Black Hole of Calcutta', and by morning only twenty-three survived. 'The Europeans,' Aliverdi Khan had warned, 'are like a hive of bees, of whose honey you may reap the benefit; but if you disturb their hive they will sting you to death.' On the battlefield of Plassey in 1757 Robert Clive administered the sting which was to prove mortal not only to Surajah Dowlah but to the entire Mogul Empire; and it is at this point that the train of events which brought about the opium war can be seen, by hindsight, to have begun.

They began because the territory was so eminently plunderage. Although the great days of the Empire had departed, Aliverdi Khan had continued to enjoy a revenue which would have been the envy of most European monarchs. Of all the provinces which had been subject to the Moguls, Macaulay was to recollect,

> *the wealthiest was Bengal. No part of India possessed such natural advantages both for agriculture and for commerce. The Ganges, rushing through a hundred channels to the sea, has formed a vast plain of rich mould which, even under the tropical sky, rivals the verdure of an English April. The rice fields yield an increase such as is elsewhere unknown. Spices, sugar, vegetable oils, are produced with marvellous exuberance . . . the tyranny of man had for ages struggled in vain against the overflowing bounty of nature. In spite of the Mussulman despot and the Mahratta freebooter, Bengal was known throughout the East as the garden of Eden.*

The East India Company, which owed much of its prosperity to this source of its trade, had every intention of holding on to it. But how could the necessary security be maintained? Clive was in no doubt that – as he told the Chairman of the Company's Court of Directors, Laurence Sulivan – he could have 'appropriated the whole of the country to the Company and preserved it afterwards'. But the Company, though its army had shown it was capable of such conquest, had no equivalent body of administrators capable of political consolidation. Nor had it any desire to recruit them and pay them. The Company, as Sulivan curtly reminded Clive, was a trading concern, in business for profit. Bengal was to remain independent, under a puppet ruler.

The consequences were disastrous. The Nawab might nominally be on the throne of his forefathers, but it was the Company which had put him there, and alone could keep him there; and this offered the Company's servants, as they styled themselves, an unprecedented opportunity, which they seized the moment Clive returned to England in 1760. They were traders; the great majority of them had only one ambition, to make their fortunes as quickly as possible (the high mortality rate in the East being an additional inducement) before returning to England to buy seats in the country, and if possible in parliament. They had no stake in Bengal's future: on the contrary, funds diverted from their pockets into investment would be wasted.

The man who showed them the way was a young Dutch adventurer who had emigrated to England, and then joined the Company: William Bolts. With some colleagues, he undertook to provide the revenue the Company required to pay its expenses in Bengal, in return for what amounted to a free hand for his group in raising it there; an offer which was welcomed by the Company's management in Calcutta. The method Bolts' group used to raise it, and to enrich themselves in the process, was simple but ingenious. Under the Moguls, the Company had enjoyed the privilege of distributing its imports and exports without having to pay the transit charges imposed by local rulers.

Bolts' group now claimed that this right extended to all produce, including the manufactures, the corn and even the vegetables of Bengal. As a result, the group was able to offer higher prices for local products than the Bengal merchants, who had to pay the local taxes, yet sell them more cheaply; and by this means the merchants were quickly forced out of business. The group then used the virtual monopoly it had acquired of the entire marketing system to compel producers to accept lower prices, and to compel consumers to pay more, the Company's sepoys being called in to persuade anybody who raised objections. The Nawab protested at the way Bolts' agents 'plunder the people, injure and disgrace my servants'; and some of the servants of the Company, shocked at what was being done in its name, added their protests, including Sergeant Brego, in charge of a detachment of the Company's sepoys. Called upon to enforce the local agents' decisions if anybody refused to accept them – he told the Council in Calcutta – 'a flogging or confinement immediately ensues'. But when he tried to intervene, pointing out to the agents that his orders were to see that justice was done, he received menacing notes saying that he would live to regret it. This, he explained, was why he was writing to the authorities; if he was informed against, as had been threatened, he hoped they would realise why. Henry Vansittart, who had taken Clive's place, did realise why; but he was powerless. 'It was Colonel Clive's good fortune,' he remarked, 'to leave India before the Company's treasure

10

was totally exhausted'; there were no funds at his disposal, and most of his colleagues were too busy following Bolts' example to heed his pleas for moderation. Their depredations roused hatred against them, leading in 1763 to a dispute in Patna which culminated in the savage massacre of all the two hundred British subjects in the town.

Although Patna was the centre of the opium industry, opium probably had little responsibility for the crisis. It was not in common use locally, Indian hemp drugs being preferred; and the fact it was primarily bought for export by the Company had protected the Nawab's monopoly. But the industry was to be profoundly affected by what followed. Although Patna was soon re-occupied by the Company's forces, and the Nawab deposed, there could be no question of putting up and propping up another puppet ruler. Clive had to be asked to return, with what amounted to full authority to take over the Nawab's powers and rights, including the opium monopoly. Clive immediately realised the reason for the collapse of the Bengal administration. In his time, as he was to explain, the Company had not been allowed to carry on trade within Bengal, let alone trade free of duty. What the Company was not allowed to do, its servants clearly had no right to do; and the absurdity of a system 'so ruinous to the natives, and so prejudicial to the revenues of the country' was obvious. As he had been given plenary powers, he could bring the spoilation to an end. But to effect reforms, he needed administrators; and if they were not to be corrupted by the pursuit of riches, they would have to be salaried. Where was the money to come from? 'This rich and flourishing kingdom' as Clive himself had described it after Plassey, had been reduced in less than a decade to near penury. Only a few commodities remained which could safely be taxed: salt, tobacco, and betel, because the consumers' dependence upon them ensured that they would continue to be bought in Bengal even if duties increased the price; and opium, because of its established export market. A land tax, it was decided, and duties on salt, tobacco and betel, would provide the revenue to pay for the new administration. To restore some of the profits which had vanished after Plassey, the Company's agents would have to look to opium.

The Patna Group

The source of a war, like the source of a river, may turn out to be not some well-defined spring, but a patch of marshland. The opium war had its origins in the malodorous swamp which Bolts and his crew left in Bengal. Thereafter, the flow of events leading to conflict can be mapped, because opium, for so long only one of the Company's many trading interests, became progressively more essential to its prospects, and even to its survival.

The initial step, and one which to a great extent determined the future, was the transfer of the Nawab's monopoly to a group within the Company. Now, the

Company had the monopoly, and could dictate its own price to competitors – or refuse to allow them to trade in opium at all. Because the opium made from the poppies cultivated in the Bihar region around Patna was more highly esteemed, especially for smoking, than any other, this amounted to making opium an export, as well as an internal monopoly; and the Patna group, as it came to be called, began to look around for more customers. China, with its estimated 300 million inhabitants, was the obvious market; but the Company Supracargoes there were still adamant in their refusal to have anything to do with contraband. There was, however, another way to ship it to China, without involving them. Although the Company held jealously to its monopoly of trade between Britain, India, and the East, it permitted what were described as 'country ships' to operate under its licence. They were useful because they were prepared to take goods on spec-ulative trading voyages, and they were tolerated much as charter companies may be tolerated by a national airline, so long as it can control their competition. How and where they disposed of their goods was no concern of the Company's, as technically the goods ceased to belong to it the moment they were bought and shipped. More opium, therefore, could be produced for sale to the Parsee merchants in Calcutta, and despatched by them in country ships to Macao, without embarrassing the Canton Supracargoes. In 1767, when Clive left India for the last time (ironically, he had himself become an addict; his death seven years later was attributed by his family to the effects of an overdose of laudanum) over 100,000 lb. of opium was brought to Macao illicitly by this means.

The Patna group had some uneasy moments before it established its monopolistic hold. The Dutch did not see why they should pay the inflated prices they were now being charged; nor did the Parsee merchants and the country ship owners, who wanted a larger share of the profits; and they made their grievance known in London. The Court of Directors were aware of the growing strength of the free trade movement, soon to find expression in *The Wealth of Nations*; and they realised that what the Patna group was doing would expose them to criticism, and perhaps legislative intervention to revoke their Charter. In 1769 they issued instructions that the channels of trade should be 'in every respect free and unconstrained', opium being one of the commodities referred to, because any constraint was *contrary to the fundamental principles of trade*. But the members of the Council which Clive had set up in Calcutta knew what to do, now that he was safely out of the way. Although they could not openly reject the Court's ruling, they could negate it for the benefit of their Patna group by means of an innocent-sounding qualification; trade in opium was to be free, subject only to 'such restrictions as the ministers and officers of the Company may think proper to impose for the benefit of the Company and the public'. It would be for the benefit of the Company and the public, the Council decided, that opium production should continue to be controlled; and the control was left in the hands of the group. In theory, free trade had been established for all commodities. In practice, opium remained a tight monopoly.

The system of a monopoly within the monopoly, though, could not be expected to last. The members of the group, probably, neither expected it to last, nor cared whether it did or not. Most of them were busy, like their predecessors, trying to extract what they could from Bengal before they sailed for home; to the alarm of Harry Verelst, who became President of the Council in 1769. Finding himself powerless to interfere in the commercial activities of members of the Company, he sent a warning to Leadenhall Street that the 'prodigious ancient riches' of the Mogul Empire, which had initially attracted, and then for so long sustained, the East India Company, were fast disappearing; unless something were done, the region 'must moulder into ruin'. The Court was only too well aware of the financial disaster looming. Before Plassey, the Company's trading operations in Bengal had brought a flow of between half-a-million and a million pounds a year, in specie, to London. That flow had almost ceased, and would soon be reversed, if affairs in Bengal reached a crisis. In 1769 they did, with a catastrophic famine. By 1772, the once so profitable East India Company could not meet its creditors, and had to be rescued by the government.

Again, as after the Patna massacre, opium was not

responsible for the crisis; but again, the future of the opium trade was to be decided by the change of policy which resulted. The government set up an enquiry; and among those who were ready to give evidence were Verelst, the man of integrity, and Bolts, the buccaneer. Bolts' methods had finally led to proceedings being instituted against him by Verelst in Calcutta; and though with the help of barrack-room legal devices on the one hand, and blackmail and forgery on the other, he had been able to delay retribution, he had eventually been deported. But he brought back to London a fortune of close on a million pounds; and in London, with characteristic effrontery, he published a three-volume work on British India describing what had been happening there, portraying himself as the injured innocent and Verelst by implication as the villain. All branches of Indian commerce, he complained, were monopolies 'of the most cruel and ruinous nature; and so totally corrupted, from every species of abuse, as to be in the last stages of annihilation'. The natives, 'at the mercy of a few men, who divide the spoils of the public among themselves', had looked to Britain for relief – in vain. Now they found themselves 'oppressed beyond conception', so that population and revenue were alike falling.

These allegations had the ring of sincerity; Bolts appears to have been one of those consummate scoundrels, commoner than is generally realised, who managed to convince themselves at all times of their total rectitude.

His *Considerations on Indian affairs* did not, as he had hoped, bring him revenge over those who had been responsible for his deportation; he was to squander his fortune on futile litigation, and had to resume his career as an adventurer, eventually dying in poverty. But at the time they helped to rouse indignation against the Company, and against Verelst, who had to go into exile in France to escape the attentions of litigants; and Verelst's defence in his *View of the rise, progress and present state of the British Government of Bengal,* though it vindicated his own reputation, was an even more scathing indictment of the Company's record in Bengal. The government, which had been trying to escape involvement, was compelled to intervene; and under Lord North's India Act, passed in 1773, a new Council of five members was set up to rule British India (which included Madras and Bombay, though they were regarded as of minor importance) on behalf of the East India Company. One of them was to be, in effect, Governor-General (though he was to have only the casting vote); and the Court of Directors' choice for the post was Warren Hastings.

Warren Hastings

Before Hastings' appointment the opium monopoly's continued existence had not been formally recognised; and the expectation was that it would cease to exist, in deference both to the British government's avowed aims as expressed in the India Act, and to Hastings' own feelings. 'I abhor monopolies' he claimed, 'especially those founded in violence' – as he knew opium had been. He had joined the Company in 1750, at the age of eighteen; and although opportunities to make money had not been neglected, his record compared to most of his colleagues had been eminently respectable. He had been one of those who had warned Vansittart of the consequences of the methods employed by Bolts' agents; he had taken the trouble to learn Urdu; he had listened sympathetically to Indian grievances – too sympathetically, Clive had felt; and for a while he had left the Company's service in despair at its maladministration. Now that he was back, he longed to bring relief to 'an exhausted country'; and that could only come, he realised, by relieving the inhabitants of the excessive burdens which had been imposed on them by taxation and monopoly.

Hastings, though, found himself in the same dilemma as Clive a few years earlier. To provide a just and efficient administration, he must increase the revenue. To put up the land tax or the excise duties would be difficult, in view of the condition of Bengal; and also extremely unpopular. The revenue from opium, by contrast, could be extracted relatively painlessly, as the consumers were foreigners. He knew how profitable the drug could be; in his first year in office he had sold 7,000 lb. on his private account (most of the Company's servants traded in it, if they could afford to, even the Commander-in-Chief of the Company's army).

It would be foolish, Hastings realised, to let so useful a source of revenue slip out of the Company's hands, when it could be farmed out to a contractor, as it had been under the Nawab. He suspected, though, that when the other members of the Council arrived out from England, they would insist on winding up the opium monopoly, supposedly terminated years before. To protect it, he thought of an ingenious excuse. The standard free trade argument against monopoly was that it restricted production.

> *But was not this, in relation to opium, an argument in monopoly's favour? It may be argued that the increase of any production not necessary to life is not an advantage, if some other commodity equally valuable must be given up to make room for it; that it is not a necessary of life but a pernicious article of luxury, which ought not to be permitted but for the purpose of foreign commerce only, and which the wisdom of government should carefully restrain from internal consumption.*

—the first admission that the commodity that the Company would be relying on for part of its revenue was a dangerous drug.

Hastings went on to make a point better calculated to make an impression on the directors, back in Leadenhall Street. If the trade were thrown open, competition would stimulate production; and either the surplus opium would find a market in India, which was undesirable, or the price would fall, which would merely take the profit 'from those few who now solely possess it, and divide it among as many as may choose to share it'; the revenue that otherwise would have come to the Company would simply be dissipated among competing firms. The Court of Directors took the hint. The Patna group, it was decided, would be disbanded, and the opium monopoly farmed out for the Company's benefit to a contractor. Hastings managed, however, to conciliate the group by securing the contract for their former manager, Mir Munheer, and arranging that they would be provided with 'gratuities' in lieu of 'their advantages of trade, from which they interdicted themselves'.

Mir Munheer consequently found himself in much *the* same position in relation to the opium cultivators as the Bolts' group had been in relation to the Bengal peasants in general. Although he was enjoined not to attempt compulsion, the monopoly powers he had been granted enabled him to dictate to the 'ryots' (as the Bengal peasants were known) what price they should receive for their opium. If they were reluctant to grow poppy, he had an inducement for them: they would be advanced sufficient money to buy seed, and hire the labour necessary to prepare the land. But as soon as they had accepted the advance, they found they were in Munheer's debt, liable to be prosecuted if they did not carry out his instructions, and evicted. Soon, angry complaints of oppression were coming in from the poppy-growing regions. These were followed by complaints from the Chinese smokers, now among the Company's best customers, about the decline in the quality of the opium . . . The ryots, in desperation, had been adulterating the drug.

It was just the opportunity that Philip Francis, who had come out to be one of the members of the Council, was hoping for. He was determined to discredit Hastings; and as he enjoyed the support of two other council members, it looked as if his proposal – that the opium monopoly should be wound up – would be accepted. But Hastings proved too clever for him. To Francis's chagrin, his two hitherto faithful backers let themselves be persuaded that opium provided too valuable a source of revenue to lose. He continued to assail the monopoly; the following year he warned the directors in London that Bihar, the main opium-growing area, could only be rescued from its condition of 'universal poverty and depopulation' by throwing open the trade. Again, Hastings outmanoeuvred him, by awarding the opium contract to Francis's friend John Mackenzie – and for a three-year period, ostensibly to give the contractor a better opportunity to come to mutually agreed terms with the cultivators. How Mackenzie availed himself of the opportunity was to be the subject of an outraged remonstrance in 1777, complaining that on a large tract of land where corn was growing, which would have been ready for harvesting in a month's time, the corn had suddenly been cut down, in order that the land might be prepared for the immediate cultivation of poppy. But Francis had been silenced. Mackenzie was left to enjoy the benefits of the Contract for the full term, with a bonus year at the end of it; untroubled except by murmurings from some of the London directors, who suspected that the deal might be designed (as so many Calcutta transactions were) to cream off the profits in India, rather than allow them through to Leadenhall Street.

These suspicions were soon confirmed. By 1780 Hastings' enemies had been scattered, and his position in India appeared secure. But he had to be careful to sustain his Leadenhall Street supporters, now that Francis was back in London, plotting revenge; and the most influential of them, the Irish wheeler-dealer Lawrence Sulivan – Chairman of the Court of Directors, 'the uncrowned king of Leadenhall Street' – was in dire financial trouble, not for the first time. He sent out his son Stephen to India, with a letter suggesting that Hasting might like to put him on the Council, but adding that 'profit more than station must of necessity be our object . . . by your affectionate friendship much more may be done for him out of Council, and how true it is that much is wanted'. Always loyal to his friends, Hastings rallied to Lawrence's support. A new opium contract was due; and as Mackenzie had not been able to provide as much opium as had been hoped, Hastings had an excuse to suggest that some of the government's restrictions on the contractor's freedom of action had been excessive, and that he was therefore proposing to modify the contract's terms. Superintendence of the process of opium manufacture, which had been introduced to try to combat adulteration, had proved irksome; it would be abandoned. The injunction that the ryots must not be coerced into growing poppy would be dropped; instead, the requirement would simply be that the opium was to be procured 'lawfully and reasonably' (which would afford little protection to the ryots; it had recently been laid down that the use of force on behalf of the Company, where the Company deemed it necessary, was justified 'by the customs of the country'). These changes, Hastings admitted, would make it possible for the contractor to use arbitrary and tyrannical methods. The contract, therefore, could not be given to the man who offered to supply opium to the Company at the lowest price. Hastings would himself select a suitable recipient. His choice was the newly arrived Stephen Sulivan. Sulivan, or his father, could not afford to await the new contract's full benefit. He promptly sold it for £20,000; and the purchaser was able to resell it for £20,000 more.

These transactions revealed that opium had become considerably more profitable than anybody had realised – except, presumably, Mackenzie, who for four years had enjoyed the profits. Either Stephen Sulivan's advisers must have grossly underestimated the sum he could obtain by selling the contract, or they had deliberately exploited his ignorance to deceive him. The next time the contract came up, therefore, the Company would be in a position to appropriate the £40,000 difference. Added to the £60,000 profit which it was making on its sales, this would make opium an extremely lucrative source of revenue.

Just how dependent the Company already was on that source was demonstrated in the winter of 1780, when war with the Dutch led to the virtual suspension of trade with the East Indies. Thousands of pounds' worth of stocks of the Company's opium began to build up in its Calcutta warehouses; and file revenue from the trade was severely curtailed. Losses in the Company's fleet from enemy action, too, were heavy; only four out of thirteen ships which were engaged in the China trade managed to reach Canton, and two-thirds of the Company's purchases of tea awaiting them there could not be shipped. But they still had to be paid for. Hastings was compelled to borrow the money, at a high rate of interest; and to find some way to pay it back as soon as possible. It happened that in 1779 one of the country ships had risked taking a consignment of the drug not just to Macao, where it was ordinarily unloaded, but up the river to Whampoa – the port of Canton. Why should the Company not try the same gamble on its own account? When it was put to him, Hastings approved of the plan. Two ships were fitted out and armed, with instructions to sell their cargo of opium wherever they could, but if necessary to bring it to Whampoa, and instruct the Company's Supracargoes to sell it there.

Hastings was aware what this decision might involve. A reminder had been issued not long before by the Calcutta Council that the import of opium into China was prohibited *under the severest penalties – not only loss of life to the guilty person, but extirpation of his family, and the confiscation of the ship or vessel that imports it, which is immediately burnt. We therefore beg you will positively forbid any of our commanders or others receiving it sending it on board for this place – should it happen to be discovered it may be of the utmost consequence to our trade here – and not only to our trade but to our persons. We are here liable to answer for the misdemeanours of any persons who may come as passengers on our ships – also the security merchant of the ship is answerable for the duties on any goods they may bring. Opium brought by them may equally involve us in difficulties, as if brought by the commanders, or any officer belonging to the ships.*

Nonsuch and *Betsy*, Hastings decided, must not be reported as bearing a cargo of opium, 'that being a contraband trade'; they were to pretend to be warships, visiting Canton. *Betsy* was lost, but *Nonsuch* managed to get through to Macao, sailing under French and Spanish colours, with her cargo of 200,000 lb. of opium. The Company's Supracargoes were horrified. Hastings had forgotten, or chosen to ignore, that there was also an imperial ban on armed foreign ships entering the Canton river. His instructions were too explicit to be repudiated; *Nonsuch* had to be restored to the semblance of a merchantman, before proceeding to Whampoa, where her cargo was furtively unloaded.

The alarm of the Supracargoes was understandable.

Since 1759 Canton had been the only port through which trade with China was permitted. Twelve years later, through judicious use of bribery authorised by the Company for the purpose, they had secured what they regarded as a vital concession: the right to reside there. Irksome restrictions were imposed: they could stay only in the winter, the trading season: they had to live in one of the 'factories' (warehouses, part of which were converted into living quarters) in a small ghetto on the river; their movements outside it were severely curtailed; and they were not allowed to bring their wives with them. But they appreciated the reason. 'There is cause for apprehension', the Emperor had warned in 1717, 'lest China may be endangered by collision with the various nations of the West, who come hither from beyond the seas'; and his successors, poorly informed though they were about what went on in the rest of the world, were well aware how his foreboding had been justified by the course of events in other eastern countries, including India, when foreigners had arrived as merchants, established themselves as settlers, and stayed as conquerors. If it became known that the Company was engaged in deliberate law-breaking, the apprehension could be revived, and the concessions might well be withdrawn.

The Supracargoes' only hope was to invoke the assistance of 'the Hong', the group of Chinese merchants who had the monopoly of foreign trade. To be 'in trade', socially speaking, was even less respectable in China than it was in Britain. The Hong merchants were almost as much a class apart as the Jews had once been in Europe. They would suffer severe penalties if detected in dealings in opium. But they would also suffer financially, they realised, if the opium remained unsold, as the Company would not be able to afford to pay for the tea and other goods the Hong had sold to it, which were awaiting shipment from Canton. A buyer for the opium was found, though the amount was so large, and the risks so great, that the price he felt able to offer – $1.50 a lb – was less than it had cost the Company.

The merchant who took the opium was unlikely to have been concerned only to rescue the Company Supracargoes from their predicament. Not that the Hong were sharks; they were 'as respectable men as are commonly found in other parts of the world' – Samuel Shaw, who became a kind of unofficial American Consul in China in the 1780s, reported; 'intelligent, exact accountants, punctual to their engagements'. They were not, by Chinese standards, corrupt. But Chinese standards allowed for what, in the West, was accounted corruption. It was the practice to bend the law by payment to the appropriate authority; usually the Hai-kwan Pu, or Superintendent of Customs. Like the viceroy and other functionaries, the Hoppo (as the British called him) was appointed from Pekin; and he was inadequately paid (he even had to pay to obtain the appointment), on the assumption that he would earn his living by the traditional process of 'squeeze'. For the most part, this was little different from the western habit of tipping waiters or cab drivers. But in China, the civil servant also had to be tipped; and he expected that the gratuity would be proportionate to the value of the service. Smuggling, which was considered no more of a crime in China than it was in England (where the rich bribed, and the poor assaulted, the excise man) was carried on by such means. *Nonsuch's* cargo therefore represented a windfall to all those who benefited, encouraging hopes that more such ventures would follow.

But the experiment was not repeated. When the Court of Directors in London heard what had happened, they wrote angrily to Hastings that it was 'beneath the Company to be engaged in such a clandestine trade; we therefore positively forbid any more opium being sent on the Company's account'. As the venture had been conducted at a loss, repetition was unlikely. Still, the fact that it had been attempted was an indication how important the revenue from the opium monopoly had become. And this meant that there was a strong inducement for the administration to increase the supply, as it proceeded to do by buying Benares opium – formerly not considered to be comparable to the Bihar product, but by this time more in favour owing to Bihar's adulteration – into the monopoly, which was made possible by Hastings' decision in 1780 to annex the territory where the Benares poppy was cultivated. As a result, the Company's revenue from opium almost doubled during his term of office.

It did not occur to Hastings' accusers, when he was

impeached, to denounce him for having deliberately encouraged the production and consumption of a drug which he himself had described as pernicious. On the contrary, one of the points Edmund Burke made was that the Company's servants had 'torn the cloth from the loom, or wrested the scanty portion of rice and salt from the peasant of Bengal, or wrung from him the very opium in which he forgot his oppression and his oppressor'. Hastings was, however, charged with having given Stephen Sulivan the contract on terms which were 'glaringly extravagant and wantonly profuse'. Even Hastings could hardly have denied this, in view of the way it had changed hands, twice over, at so big a profit. He preferred to maintain that he had not known of the secondary transfers, a denial which his biographer Keith Feiling was to accept. In the barely credible event that he did not know of them, Hastings left himself open to another charge; crass incompetence. If he had kept the monopoly in his gift because, as he explained, he had to select a trustworthy recipient, he ought to have made sure that the recipient did not pass it on. But his judges accepted his excuse, and by a majority found him not guilty of the charge.

He was also indicted for sending *Nonsuch* with opium to Canton. Was it a crime, Lord Thurlow asked, for the Governor-General to do, and avow publicly, what the Company's directors had urged him 'by every possible means, to every possible extent', to get done by individual merchants? Hastings had not, in fact, publicly avowed that he was sending opium to Canton. But the impeachment by that time had dragged on for so long that this had been forgotten; and the Lords accepted that what he had done was not a crime.

The final verdict on Hastings' opium policies, however, can only be that they were criminal, in their effects. This is not to deny him credit for what he did, and still more for what he tried to do, for British India. 'Even those who take the most unfavourable view of Hastings', Ramsay Muir claimed, 'will probably acknowledge that the anomalous dominion created by the victories of Clive would have perished of its own rottenness, and left nothing but an evil memory, if the genius and courage of Hastings had not saved it'. Save it he did, but for the East India Company; not for the descendants of the Moguls, let alone for the inhabitants of Bengal. It is impossible to tell what would have happened if British India had 'perished of its own rottenness'. The policies pursued by some other conqueror, or by the Indian rulers themselves, might have had the same dire effects. But as things were it was Hastings, after his enemies had been defeated, who dictated policy until he left India in 1785; and its short-term and long-term effects were alike destructive.

By the time he left, too, the British government had begun to become identified with the policy. It had not escaped the young William Pitt's notice that the East India Company was unfitted to provide a suitable administration for what had become a British colony, in all but name;

and when he became Prime Minister in 1784, he persuaded parliament to accept another India Act, dividing control between the Court of Directors and a Government Board. Its object, he explained, was 'to give to the Crown the power of guiding the politics of India, with as little means of corrupt influence as possible'; his intention being to reassure the Company that though political influence might pass from them, patronage would still be in their hands. They agreed to allow the 'Secret Committee' of three directors to work with and for the Board, which in practice meant working with the Board's President – for nearly twenty years, Pitt's friend Henry Dundas. By this means commercial and political decisions could be kept separate. This, at least, was Pitt's hope. As a disciple of Adam Smith, he was genuinely anxious that his government should not interfere with commerce. But with opium the two were inextricably intermeshed. To the Court of Directors, opium might remain a commodity, making a profit; to the Council in India, and to the government in London, it represented revenue, and as such was of vital concern to whomever should be appointed Governor-General, whether he was the Court's choice (as in theory he remained) or the government's (as in practice he usually was). And when Lord Cornwallis was appointed to succeed Hastings, though he had deliberately been chosen as a man who had had nothing to do with commerce, he found on arrival that opium was one of his main concerns; and a source of constant worry.

Lord Cornwallis

Cornwallis's part in the story, though, is important less for what he did, or tried to do about opium, than for his failure to gain control over the Indian economy in general; a failure which was to consolidate opium's position as vital to the revenue. Although at times Hastings had been dominant in India, at no time had he been in a position to insist upon a policy simply because he felt certain that it would be in the best interests of those concerned – the Company, British India, and Britain. Cornwallis had that opportunity; or at least it appeared he would have it, because he enjoyed the confidence of both Courts – the King's and the Company's – and of the government. His military career, dating from service in the Seven Years War, had been in the category which lies somewhere between respectable and distinguished; and although in the War of American Independence, following his victories at Brandywine and Camden, he had been forced to surrender to Washington at Yorktown, that humiliation had not been held against him; he was known to have denounced the strategy which had led down to it, and which loyalty to superior officers had compelled him to accept. He had, in fact, been asked to go out to India as Hastings' successor in 1781, while still technically a prisoner of war, on parole. When eventually he agreed, with extreme reluctance, to the appointment, he demonstrated his determination to retain his independence by declining to draw the £30,000 a year salary the Company voted him. He was fifty, and set in his ways, but not in his ideas. He knew nothing about India; but he was prepared to learn.

His initial discovery was that the inhabitants of Bengal had been, as he described it, 'advancing hastily into a general state of poverty and wretchedness'. The grossest frauds had been perpetrated under the Hastings administration, he wrote to tell Dundas in the winter of 1786: 'I suspect that even the opium and other contracts, the terms of which appear so advantageous, are not called upon to promote the real interests of the Company'. Uncertain how to proceed, Cornwallis decided to circulate a questionnaire among the Company's agents. What was the condition of the poppy cultivators? Would it be desirable to abandon the monopoly? And if not, should it be farmed out to a contractor, or run by the Company itself, through an agency?

The condition of the poppy cultivators was revealed in the fact that in spite of the 'general state of poverty and wretchedness' which Cornwallis found existed in Bengal, it was impossible to get them to continue producing opium except by compulsion; either legal, as in those districts where it could be claimed that tenancies would be forfeited unless poppy was grown (as the Company's agent was also the magistrate he could lay down, as well as enforce, the law); or financial, through the manipulation of advances in order to get the cultivator into debt and keep him there, so that jail and eviction would face him if he disobeyed. 'Nothing under the amazing increasing price and unlimited demand,' Lt.-Col. Kyd, Secretary of the Military Department, told Cornwallis, 'could possibly have supported the existence of the cultivation of this article under the disgraceful, oppressive and ruinous system under which it has heretofore been conducted.'

The fact that increasing demand from China and the East Indies had raised the price, however, ensured that the answer to Cornwallis's second question – should the monopoly be abandoned? – would have to be in the negative. Whatever the defects of the monopoly system, the revenue from opium had become too valuable to lose. And as the aim of Pitt's India Bill had been to try to separate the administrative and profit-making activities of the Company, the third question also answered itself. The contract system, Cornwallis decided, must be retained, with strict safeguards to prevent its being awarded for corrupt purposes, or exploited to oppress the cultivators. The contract would be given to the man who was prepared to offer the Company opium at the lowest rate, to ensure that there would be no repetition of the Sulivan or Mackenzie episodes. But to protect the cultivators, the price they would receive for their opium would be laid down in advance; they would not be compelled to grow poppy, if they chose not to; and Company agents were no longer to be allowed to combine the functions of plaintiff, prosecutor and magistrate, in the courts. This policy, Cornwallis explained, might mean that the Company would not be able to drive so hard a bargain with the contractor. But the Company would eventually be more than compensated 'by the encouragement which will be given to the ryots to extend the cultivation of the poppy, and by the measures which have been adopted being calculated to promote the general prosperity of the districts in which it was produced'; prosperity which would be reflected in higher revenue from the land tax and other sources.

Had Cornwallis been able to put these principles into practice, events must subsequently have followed a very different course. The Bengal peasants would have found themselves in possession of a disposable income, which they could use to buy goads and services; the economy would have recovered; and the British administration in India would no longer have been compelled to rely on its opium and salt monopolies for its revenue. This had been the intention of Pitt and Dundas, too. Freedom of commerce from state control and from monopolies, they were known to believe, were the foundations of prosperity; and in 1787 the Court of Directors wrote uneasily to Cornwallis asking him to find out all he could about the reasons for the opium monopoly under the Moguls, so that they could be advanced 'as arguments to defend our rights' in any discussion which might arise with the government. When the discussions arose, however, they did not take the form the directors had feared. A new element had entered Pitt's calculations, which was to prove decisive in policy making from this time on: the need to find some way of paying for Britain's supplies of tea.

The rise in the consumption of tea in Britain had been phenomenal. Unknown there until the middle of the seventeenth century, the amounts imported over the next hundred years had remained small; but then they had begun to increase rapidly, from less than one million pounds in the 1730s to over ten million pounds in the early 1780s. Of that amount, however, over half was smuggled in; and in 1784, to check the smugglers, Pitt had reduced the excise duty. The plan worked, but it also greatly stimulated consumption, by bringing tea within the reach of all classes; and by 1789 imports had risen to around twenty million pounds.

Pitt and Dundas became worried; not about the huge increase in consumption, as tea seemed harmless enough, and the import duty brought in valuable revenue, but about how the tea was to be paid for, coming as it did from China, where there had been no comparable increase of demand for foreign goods. 'I am satisfied', Dundas wrote to tell Cornwallis in 1789, 'that by the export of British manufactures and Bengal commodities to China, a sufficient fund will at last be found in China for answering the purposes of the valuable trade which is now carried on' – the tea trade. But the Chinese obstinately refused to buy more of the cotton and woollen goods which British manufacturers were making; and opium was the only Bengal commodity for which the Chinese showed any enthusiasm. Their taste for it presented Cornwallis with the argument the Company needed in favour of the retention of its monopoly, much more effective than any historical parallels from the time of the Moguls. The Company, he was able to point out, was not in a position to carry opium to China in its own ships, because if it were detected in any involvement in contraband that might mean the loss of its privileges, and consequently the collapse of the tea trade. But the Company's Council in Calcutta could dictate to the country ship owners, through its licensing system; thereby ensuring that they took the opium to China, rather than to other markets more conveniently situated. If the Company lost the opium monopoly, the Council would lose this hold over them. Dundas accepted the argument. It was improper, he replied, that the country ships should be allowed to divert the supplies of the drug to the East Indies, 'or to any other place, if it can be rendered subservient to the China investment'.

Whatever lingering doubts there may have been in the minds of Pitt and Dundas about the wisdom of their decision were soon banished by the course taken by the French Revolution, culminating in the outbreak of war in 1793. It became all the more vital that Britain's reserves of bullion should not be reduced by the need to pay for Britons' tea; the more so, because of the additional hazards her shipping would run from enemy action. The revenue from opium, therefore, ceased to be a matter of concern only for the Company, becoming an essential part of the fiscal policy of the British government. Not that Pitt and Dundas were concerned with opium as such. Had the Chinese been prepared to accept rice, or any other Bengal commodity – still better, if they had begun to buy British-manufactured goods – the Company's opium monopoly might have been discarded without a pang. But no other profitable export was available. So the bargain was struck, which ultimately was to have such fateful consequences. The opium monopoly would remain in the Company's hands, provided that the Company ensured that exports of the drug, other than those small amounts customarily sent to the East Indies, were channelled into China.

Lord Macartney

Pitt and Dundas, though, were aware that it would be rash to rely on the commodities of India as the sole security for the China investment. Britain was spending over three million pounds a year on tea, at a time when the state's entire revenue from taxes was only sixteen million pounds. Should anything go wrong in India – and the French, the Dutch and the Portuguese had a common interest in helping any Indian ruler who might decide to turn against the British – there would be trouble, unless the Chinese government could be persuaded to relax its restrictions on foreign trade, and the Chinese people could be persuaded to lose their indifference to British goods. With this in mind, Pitt decided to send a mission to Pekin.

Earlier efforts to establish diplomatic contact had failed; partly because the Emperor did not recognise other monarchs as having any right to parity, so that their representatives could be received only as tributaries; partly because the convention that the foreigners were admitted to China only for purposes of commerce had proved so effective a way of preventing them from doing what they had done in other parts of the world, establishing themselves by conquest. And only rarely had the Chinese authorities acted in a way which could give the British government any pretext for demanding a change in the system. In 1784, however, trouble had arisen when the *Lady Hughes* – one of the country ships engaged in opium smuggling, but conforming to the Chinese usages in the attempt to appear as an honest trader – had fired a ceremonial salute which accidentally killed a Chinese worker in a boat alongside. Although ordinarily the authorities allowed foreigners to bring their own nationals to trial, they reserved homicide for their own courts. They made it clear that unless the culprit (or, as was intimated, 'a servant or some person of less consequence in his place') was handed over, the trading rights which had been granted to British ships would be withdrawn. The Supracargoes, privately assured that trial and acquittal would only be a formality, gave up the gunner; and he was executed. The episode provoked less anger at the time than it would have done (and, in recollection, was to do) half-a-century later; but it provided an excuse for an approach to the

Emperor of China with a request to put the relations between the two countries, including the regulation of their trade, on a less informal footing.

The government chose Lt.-Col, Cathcart to represent his country (his expenses, Dundas was careful to insist, were to be paid by the East India Company, as it would be the beneficiary). Cathcart's instructions were to try to persuade the Chinese to grant to Britain what they allowed to the Portuguese: 'a small tract of ground, or detached island in some more convenient station than Canton'? The Chinese were to be assured that the objective was 'purely commercial, having not even a wish for territory'? In case they were so ill-mannered as to remind Cathcart of the numerous occasions on which the British government had made a similar protestation before and then appropriated the territory, as in India, he was to reassure them with the argument that the situation there had arisen 'almost without our seeking it; from the necessity of defending ourselves against the oppressions of the revolted Nabobs who entered into cabals to our prejudice with other nations of Europe, and disregarded the privileges granted us by different Emperors'.

What if the Chinese brought up the question of opium?

If this subject should come into discussion, it must be handled with the greatest circumspection. It is beyond a doubt that no inconsiderable portion of the opium raised with our Indian territories finds its way to China, where the vicious manners of the people call for

an increasing use of the pernicious drug. But if it should be made
a positive requisition, or an Article of any supposed commercial
Treaty, that we shall not send any opium to China, you must accede
to it, rather than risk any essential benefit by contending for a
liberty in this respect; and the sale of our opium in Bengal must
be left to take its chance in an open market, or to find a consump-
tion in the dispersed and circuitous traffic of the Eastern seas.

—less of a concession to the Chinese than it might sound, because in practice Bengal opium was already taking its chance in the traffic of the Eastern seas. There was no reason to fear that the country ships would be any less capable of smuggling it into China than before.

Cathcart sailed from Spithead in December 1787; but he died on the voyage. After some delay, Lord Macartney was appointed in his place – an indication that the government by this time was attaching more importance to the mission; he was a higher-powered figure, having been Minister at the Court of St. Petersburg, Governor of Madras, and Chief Secretary for Ireland. His instructions were similar to Cathcart's, and on the opium issue identical, except for one small change. The admission that a considerable part of the opium produced in British India was finding its way to China was repeated, but the words 'where the vicious manners of the people call for an increasing use of that pernicious drug' were omitted; either to obviate the risk that the instructions might leak out to the Chinese or, perhaps, because somebody had a twinge of uneasiness about admitting that the commodity on which the British and Indian exchequers were coming to rely was pernicious. The Embassy sailed from Portsmouth on September 26th, 1792; to be greeted with gratifying ceremony when it arrived, almost a year later. Macartney had audiences with the Emperor, as well as negotiations with his ministers both in Pekin and later in Canton, before returning to London – empty-handed. As Peter Auber, Secretary to the Court of Directors, was to describe it, he had been 'received with the utmost politeness, treated with the utmost hospitality, watched with the utmost vigilance, and dismissed with the utmost civility'.

To outward appearances, the foreigners had been courteously but firmly put in their place. But the Emperor was in a less commanding situation than he believed. Although the British request for the formal grant of a tract of land or an island had been rejected, some of the country ships were already enjoying the informal use of an anchorage at Larks Bay, not far from Macao, to avoid paying the harbour dues. The Portuguese had informed on them to the Canton authorities, who in turn had complained to the Company's Supracargoes. The Supracargoes had replied that they had no control over the country ships; and as the Canton authorities made no move against the depot, or the ships which used it, there was a base, at last – insubstantial and, relative to Macao, uncomfortable, but nevertheless a base.

It was not strictly true that the Supracargoes Committee

had no control over the country ships. As the merchants needed the Company's licence to trade in its opium, the Company could have withdrawn it from any of them who refused to obey the Committee's orders. But knowing that the Company could not send opium to China in its own ships, for fear of jeopardising the tea trade, Cornwallis felt that he could not afford to antagonise the merchants. Their behaviour on occasion led to anguished protests from the Committee, that they were every day committing some irregularity of a kind calculated to offend the Chinese authorities, because it 'sets aside their decrees and mortifies their pride', and also because the authorities then sometimes took it out on the Company. When the merchants countered by claiming that the Supracargoes were worried only because they were engaged in smuggling opium themselves, and resented the country ships' competition, Cornwallis had no hesitation in rejecting their accusation; but he felt bound to write to the Supracargoes to warn them that whatever their personal feelings, they must do nothing which would hamper the country ships' operations. The consequences to the Company if they did, he pointed out, was 'too obvious to need a comment: the loss of revenue to our settlement by the non-amount of such export being withheld from you – for it is not to be expected that the Company can be enabled to furnish annually supplies equal to your wants; nor can there be any other mode of furnishing your treasury, than by the commodities of India being sold in China'.

Father and Oppressor

By the time Cornwallis returned to England in 1793, he had gone some way to establishing British rule in India on a more just and efficient footing. But there was still no sign of any return to prosperity in Bengal; and without it, there could be no rescuing the Company from its dependence upon the opium monopoly, with all that it entailed. What had gone wrong?

A young agent of the Company, Henry Thomas Colebrooke, was trying to find out. He had entered its service as a boy of seventeen, in the last months of Hastings' Governor-Generalship, and had been appalled at what he found. The management of affairs was left to 'harpies, no sooner let loose upon the country than they plundered the inhabitants with or without pretences, and, as a price of the sacrifice of every principle of honour, rendered to their employers a small proportion of their ill-gotten pelf'. Even the judiciary had been corrupted; 'justice was dealt out to the highest bidders by the judges, and thieves paid a regular revenue to rob with impunity.' At first, Colebrooke had blamed Hastings. But under Cornwallis, who could not be suspected of condoning corruption, he had come to realise that it was the system which was at fault. Things had improved, he told his father – a former Company man – in a letter written in 1788; but he felt that 'to regulate nations as an article of trade, for the profit which is to be derived, seems a solecism in politics'; and he cited the opium monopoly as one of the worst examples. When Cornwallis's attempts at reform failed, Colebrooke, afflicted by 'the melancholy sense of increasing poverty in Bengal', began to compose a treatise setting out his views on what ought to be done. It was dangerous, he admitted to his father, for any servant of the Company to make the criticisms he felt should be made; he might be regarded as disloyal. But he went ahead with his *Remarks on the Present State of Husbandly and Commerce in Bengal*, and in 1795 a few copies were privately printed in Calcutta.

The *Remarks* presented the first detailed explanation of why Cornwallis's expectations had not been fulfilled. His aim had been to restore to the Bengal peasants a disposable income so that from their spending, commerce and industry could again begin to flourish; this would relieve the administration from its dependence on the land tax and on the salt and opium monopolies, because the load of indirect taxation could be more evenly spread, and more easily borne. But to achieve this, he needed efficient and incorruptible administrators, agents, and tax collectors; and the Company still had no revenue out of which to pay its officials enough to encourage efficiency or incorruptibility. Instead, it had continued to accept tenders for the collection of taxes and the running of monopolies. To enable the successful applicants to fulfil their obligations they had to be vested with the Company's authority, which meant that the peasant had little protection. They had disregarded usage and engagements, 'and imposed taxes at pleasure, which they reinforced by violence and coercion'. The share of the value of the land's produce which cultivators had enjoyed had been drastically reduced; all the more, when the Board of Revenue began to listen to the kind of adventurer who assured them that he could farm the tax still more profitably; 'his proposals are accepted; he rack-rents the estates; the cultivators emigrate; and he leaves the property at a third of its value'.

The poppy cultivators might have been expected to have received some protection from these pressures, because of Cornwallis's insistence that they should not be compelled to grow poppy if they did not want to, and that if they did grow it, they would receive a fixed minimum price for their opium, which the contractor's agents would not be allowed to reduce. But the new regulations were ineffectual. The minimum price was insufficient to induce the ryots to cultivate poppy voluntarily, because it did not sufficiently take into account the amount of work entailed. The ground had to be prepared by ploughing twelve or fifteen times; and thereafter incessantly weeded, manured and watered. Then 'the most tedious occupation of all is the gathering of the opium which, for more than a fortnight, employs several persons in making incisions in each capsule in the evening, and scraping off the exuded juice in the morning'. When the labour involved was taken into consideration, poppy cultivation was little more profitable than growing corn, and more risky, owing to a variety of accidents to which the plant was liable, from insects, wind, hail or unseasonable rain.

If a ryot decided to give up growing poppy, though, invoking Cornwallis's regulation, he would find he could not do so, because owing to the system of payment by advances, he was perennially in the contractor's debt. Should he invoke the law, so would the contractor, who could have him evicted; as Colebrooke sardonically observed, 'a very efficient form of compulsion'. And between them, the tax collector and the opium contractor saw to it that nothing remained to the cultivators and their families except their subsistence. What this meant, Colebrooke illustrated by describing their diet; the average daily consumption of a family of five 'in easy circumstances' was 8 lb. rice, 2 lb. vegetables, and 2½ oz. salt: that was all.

The solution which Colebrooke advocated was the termination of the opium monopoly, and the introduction of free trade. It was the measure of the changes that a decade in office had brought about in the attitudes of Pitt and Dundas that their response, when a copy of the book reached them, was peremptorily to forbid its publication in London; it did not appear there until Dundas had left the India Office. And although his 'disloyalty' did not wreck Colebrooke's career (he went on to become a member of the Council, and the foremost Sanskrit scholar of his time; in the opinion of his contemporary John

Crawfurd, a future Governor of Singapore, 'the greatest of all orientalists'), his findings failed to change the Company's opium policy. It could not be changed because Cornwallis, though he could lay down the law, had not been able to enforce it. Efficient and trustworthy agents and collectors could not be found until Bengal began to become prosperous again, providing the revenue to pay their salaries; but until there were efficient and trustworthy agents, Bengal could not begin to become prosperous again. And when he had tried to reduce the amounts which were being sent to fill the Company's Leadenhall Street coffers, on the argument that Bengal needed a breathing space in which to recover from the earlier depredations, he had been met by implacable resistance.

It could not have been otherwise, because the loyalty of the Court of Directors was primarily to the Company's shareholders. As Macaulay was to recall in his essay on Warren Hastings, written nearly half-a-century later, the directors were guided by the motto of the great predatory families of Teviotdale, 'thou shalt want ere I want'. Not that they were aware of being responsible for any crime:

> *Far from it. Whoever examines their letters at that time will find there many just and humane sentiments, many excellent precepts; in short, an admirable code of political ethics. But every exhortation is modified or nullified by a demand for money. 'Govern leniently, and send more money; practise strict justice and moderation towards neighbouring powers, and send more money'; this is,*

in truth, the sum of almost all the instructions that Hastings ever received from home. Now these instructions, being interpreted, mean simply, 'Be the father and the oppressor of the people; be just and unjust, moderate and rapacious'. The directors dealt with India as the Church, in the good old times, dealt with a heretic. They delivered the victim over to the executioners, with an earnest request that all possible tenderness might be shown.

The directors, Macaulay insisted, were not necessarily hypocritical. Writing so many thousands of miles from where their orders had to be given effect, they might not have realised what the effect would be. But they had often left Hastings with the choice only of which of the two demands to disregard; their moral, or their financial, injunctions. 'He had to consider what disobedience they would most readily pardon; and he correctly judged that the safest course would be to neglect the sermons, and to find the rupees'. Cornwallis, too, had been compelled to find the rupees. He had tried to secure justice for the men who produced them, on the assumption that their flow would be increased in the long run; but the system had eventually defeated him. And he had been unable to suggest any way to change it. Unrestricted private enterprise would simply deprive the administration of its revenue, leaving it helpless even to try to protect the producers. Like so many of his contemporaries, however, Cornwallis thought that giving more power to government would be still more dangerous. 'Left to themselves', he admitted to Dundas, the Company's directors 'could never conduct any branch of the business of his country properly; but he felt their responsibility must be upheld, to provide 'a useful check on the ambitions or corrupt designs of some future minister'. So the system remained. And while it remained, cultivators in Bengal would continue to be compelled to grow poppy not as a cash crop, but for their subsistence; in order to pay for the British administration of their country, and for Britons' China tea.

2

BREAKING THE
MONOPOLY, 1793-1830

Sir John Shore

One threat remained, though, to the opium trade; and under Cornwallis's successor, Sir John Shore, it seemed likely to lead to the collapse of the Company's monopoly, and perhaps even of the Company. Ironically, it was a consequence of one of Cornwallis's expedients to eliminate corruption: his decision that in order to prevent a repetition of the Sulivan affair, the opium contract would be awarded to the merchant who undertook to provide the Company with opium at the lowest price. The consequences became apparent only gradually; but by 1794 the Bengal Board of Trade found that the value of its opium from Bihar was fast declining. The reason was obvious: the producers, as Colebrooke explained, had been driven by desperation to adulterate their product with poppy leaves, stalks, and even with cow dung.

Aware of this risk Cornwallis had attempted to guard against it by an arrangement that had already tacitly been conceded under Hastings; the contractor had been instructed to test supplies and seize, without the need to pay compensation, any opium which had been adulterated. The agreement was that the contractor, though forbidden to sell any consignments of the drug thus seized to the Company, would be permitted to compensate himself by disposing of them locally in Bengal; this having the additional advantage that it would meet the demand there, small but persistent, and consequently put a check on illicit sales. But as Surgeon Fleming, the Company's Inspector of Opium in Calcutta, discovered and reported, the contractor had found an ingenious way to circumvent this regulation. He had secured the contract by offering to collect the Company's opium at a price which was not merely lower than any of his competitors', but which was actually less than the price he was supposed by law to pay the producers for it. The reason he had been able to do so, Fleming explained, was that though he was forbidden to sell opium which the producers had adulterated, there was nothing in his contract to prohibit him from taking the pure opium which he had brought from the producers, adulterating it himself, and selling it to the Company. He had done so; with the result that the quality of Bihar, which hitherto had been regarded as the best, deteriorated so catastrophically that the value of its sales in China was drastically reduced; leaving Benares opium, which earlier had not qualified for sale under the Company's trade mark, because it was considered inferior, fetching the better price in China.*

The country ship owners, and the Parsee merchants who supplied them, seized the opportunity this discovery gave them to resume the campaign against the Company's trade monopoly, in the hope of liberating themselves from its irksome restrictions, and at the same time putting themselves in a position where they could buy opium more cheaply. The Company had been justifying the 300 per cent profit it made on opium on the ground that only a monopoly could ensure the necessarily strict quality control. But that was precisely what it did not ensure, the merchants claimed in a memorandum, because the Company, knowing their customers in China used opium 'merely for the purpose of intoxication', felt quality did not matter. The Company's Calcutta Board of Trade realised the danger. The British government might not care about quality controls, but it was deeply concerned about revenue; and if the merchants could persuade Pitt that the revenue from trading with China would improve if the traffic were thrown open, he might remember his free trade principles. The Board therefore hastened to rebut the charge. They would not even have deigned to notice it, they said

*'Bengal opium' was the term generally used outside India for all varieties including Bihar (Patna) or Benares, produced in the region, much as 'Bordeaux' is for claret. Within the trade, though (again, as with Bordeaux) 'Bengal' tended to mean opium with no pretensions to a Bihar or Benares pedigree. I have used it in the former sense.

had they not heard it stated by persons whose education and situation ought to cause them to reason more justly, and to act upon sounder principles, and they now anticipate it only lest it should be used in Europe; and they bring the case to their own feelings by observing that if a wine merchant were to mix elderjuice or other trash, perhaps in itself not unwholesome, with Port or Bordeaux wine and to pass off the composition as wine, we should on detection reprobate the fraud and not admit his attempting to justify his conduct by saying that there was not any harm done to the consumers by the imposition.

Pitt, though, was not concerned for the Chinese consumers. With the war intensifying – in 1797 Napoleon Bonaparte carried his first major campaign in Italy to its triumphant conclusion, forcing Austria to make peace; and he was rewarded with the command of the forces assembling to invade Britain – the British government's overriding need was to ensure that its revenue was maintained (which meant maintaining the supply of dutiable tea) without any strain on reserves (which meant finding ways to pay for it, other than in specie, in Canton). If the Company could not run the opium business profitably, the business would be taken out of its control. And when, in 1797, the opium revenue fell from almost £200,000 the previous year to £30,000, largely because of Chinese dissatisfaction with the quality of the drug, the Company's monopoly was again in danger.

Shore, however, was well acquainted with the background to the problem; he had been Cornwallis's right-hand-man in Bengal. There was nothing for it, he decided, but to pin the blame on the contract system, and bring the opium monopoly under the direct management of the Council, through a Company agency. By this device the Council could hope to appropriate that share of the profit which the contractor had enjoyed; and, more important, it would be in a position both to supervise and restrict production. By this means, Shore hoped, he would restore the Company's reputation, and enable it to make the most of the renewed demand that could be expected from China when supplies were found to be again of high quality, but in short supply.

The policy of restriction

The policy worked, though not until after some anxious moments. Just before the century ended, an imperial edict indicated that the existence of the opium menace was beginning to be recognised by the Court in Pekin. The 1729 edict had been directed chiefly at a new fashion: the smoking of tobacco had similarly been interdicted, before, but it had none the less gradually come to establish itself in China. The new edict against opium, however, complained of

> the power which this substance communicated to those who partake
> of it, of not closing their eyes for entire nights, and spending them
> in the gratification of impure and sensual desires, whereby their

respective duties and occupations are neglected. When this habit becomes established by frequent repetition, it gains an entire ascendant, and the consumer of opium is not only unable to forbear from its daily use, but, on passing the accustomed hour, he is immediately seized with pains in the head and a feverish heat, cannot refrain from tears or command himself in any degree. For relief therefore from these painful symptoms, and to regain his wonted health, he has necessarily recourse to the same pernicious substance.

The Canton Hoppo, who as superintendent of the Customs was responsible for enforcing the ban, admitted that opium had been distributed by 'persons without fixed homes or professions who, having prepared an extract from it, opened shops for the support of this branch of trade'; but he was careful to shift the blame on to the Hong merchants. As every ship which traded with China had to have one of them as security, they should have been able to stamp out the traffic. In future, if they failed to do so, they would be severely punished; as would any official who accepted a bribe to allow opium to slip past him. Now that Pekin's attention had been drawn to the imports of the drug, the Supracargoes' Committee feared, there might be a concerted drive against it. The Hong merchants, however, were not inclined to take the Hoppo seriously. He was 'a strict and conscientious mandarin', who had just taken office, and sincerely desired to save his countrymen from what he felt were the baneful consequences of the drug; but they did not think that the drive would amount to anything. To be on the safe side the Council in India renewed its warnings against carrying opium in the Company's ships; but the country ships continued to carry it as before, meeting with no trouble.

Soon, Shore's new system was working smoothly. The Company's agency delivered about four thousand chests (chests of drawers, divided into about twenty compartments, each holding a ball of opium about the size of a grapefruit, wrapped in poppy petals; the opium in the chest weighing about 140 lb.). Of these, half were designated for export to China. From time to time the Canton authorities issued reminders of the ban on opium: in 1807 a new Hoppo repeated the performance of his predecessor, threatening even more savage penalties for those who disobeyed it; but no more was heard from him. Even when a new Viceroy reached Canton four years later with orders from the Emperor that opium smuggling was to be put down, and with special instructions to the Supracargoes' Committee that they must co-operate in enforcing the law, as the opium was known to be produced in British territory, they were not disturbed. 'While we notice the intimation', they reported, 'we are perfectly satisfied that it is merely made *pro forma*, and without the least intention of taking any effectual steps for the suppression of a trade which the officers of the government have so long and so notoriously found it in their interest to connive at.' And so it proved. Although the amount of the Company's opium reaching China remained below 3,000 chests, the price obtained for it rose steadily. The cost per chest to the Company's agency was about $50; but the price rose from little more than $100 in 1796 to $1,400 by 1803. Thereafter the price began to level out; but it provided the Company with a steady revenue of nearly $1,500 a chest, or 2,000 per cent profit, for the next decade.

The Renewal of the Charter

Shore's new policy marked a turning point in the course of events leading to the still distant clash between Britain and China. To revert to the earlier analogy: it was as if the stream had broadened out into a pool, where no flow was perceptible, but when the head of water was all the time building up. In the short term Shore's decision to take opium production into the Company's direct control, and to limit production, was wise and profitable. By restricting the amounts reaching China it reduced the risk of provoking a conflict with the Chinese authorities, and increased the opium's value with beneficial results to the Company's revenue. But the long term consequences were to be serious, because the process distorted the economy of British India, leading the Company to ever greater dependence on opium exports to China, and by extension making the British government more dependent on them too.

In theory, the rapid rise in the price of opium should have provided the opportunity to carry out Cornwallis's intentions, and broaden the base of the Company's fiscal structure by restoring the disposable, and therefore taxable, income of the population. But the need to pay for the campaigns in which Shore's successor, Lord Wellesley, extended the boundaries of British India meant that the Council, endlessly chivvied by the Court of Directors, felt that every available rupee must be extracted; so that little, if any, of the increased profit from opium was retained by the producers. How little, was revealed in Francis Buchanan's survey of the poppy growing regions, in his *Account of the Districts of Bihar and Patna*, published in 1812. A topographer, Buchanan had no social axe to grind; but his description showed that there had been little change in the ryot's circumstances since Colebrooke's study.

The poppy, Buchanan explained, was ordinarily cultivated on garden land, the best land; and the ryot was forbidden to grow anything but poppy, even vegetables for his family, in case in attending to them he took too little care of his poppies. Buchanan provided an estimate he had been given of the finances of what he had been assured was a typical holding (a begah was about a third of an acre).

For the ryots to expect to *lose* the equivalent of a dollar a begah on their opium was not quite so eccentric as it looked. As they lived off the Company's advances, it did not greatly matter to them so long as the Company's agent did not evict them; and he might realise after a bad season that a different tenant would have done no better. Buchanan suspected, too, that the figures were not quite accurate. On average land, he thought, the ryot might hope to make a profit of a rupee or two, from each begah; and a little more on good land. Even assuming Buchanan's estimate was closer to the mark than his informants', though, it showed that the Company, not the poppy cultivators, had been the beneficiary of Shore's reforms. And as Cornwallis's plan for freezing the land tax at a fixed level, in the hope this would encourage higher output, had also failed to work in practice – the new class of settled landowner-cum-tax collector he hoped to establish proved just as rapacious and oppressive as the old tax-farmers had been – the disposable and taxable incomes he had hoped for had failed to materialise.

At the same time, though it had nothing directly to do with the opium trade, another force was at work to make the Council even more dependent upon its opium revenue. Bengal cottons, cheap by comparison with British, had long enjoyed a good sale in Britain, as well as at home. Towards the end of the eighteenth century the Manchester manufacturers had petitioned parliament to ban imports on the ground that the low standard of living of the Indians enabled their employers to undercut British prices. When the growing use of child labour enabled the British manufacturers to reverse the process, they abandoned this line; instead they called for, and obtained, the right to have their goods sold in India duty free, their argument now being that they wanted to provide the mass of the people of India with 'the means of putting on the appearance of respectability by being decently clad at a small cost'. They also secured a ban on the export of any machinery which might enable Indian entrepreneurs to compete. As a result, the trade in Indian cottongoods collapsed, eliminating their competition in Britain, but also eliminating the Bengal incomes which might have been used to buy British manufactured goods.

One further – and, as things turned out, final – opportunity remained for the British government and parliament to reform the system, and give the Indian economy a better balance. Pitt's India Act had awarded the Company its Charter for a limited period of thirty years to 1814; and in 1813 a parliamentary committee was set up to consider whether it should be extended for a further period. A great moral trust reposed on the legislature, Lord Castlereagh reminded its members: 'It was incumbent upon them to weigh all measures in which the interest and the happiness of so large a portion of the human race were involved'.

The proceedings that followed were to be revealing of how such measures were weighed, at Westminster. There was no disposition on the part of the witnesses called by the committee, most of them former servants of the Company, to gloss over the condition of abject poverty to which India had been reduced. Almost without exception, they emphasised it – sometimes unwittingly: as Lord Teignmouth (as Sir John Shore had become) did when he insisted that a native who earned £2 a year could consider he was living in luxury. But this evidence was not produced with a view to persuading Lord Liverpool's Tory government to reform the system by which India was governed. On the contrary, the witnesses' aim was to preserve the Company's Charter intact. The danger, they knew, no longer came from M.P.s who, like Burke, had denounced the Company's wickedness. Its critics, as their questioning showed, were concerned simply to show that its monopoly of trade in the east had held up the sale of British manufacturers there. Among those called to refute them was Warren Hastings, summoned from retirement (such was the change of attitude since his impeachment that he was greeted with an ovation and offered a chair so that he could give evidence seated, an unusual honour). It was not the Company's monopoly which prevented British manufacturers from catering for Indians' wants, he insisted, but the fact that 'the poor of India, who are the people, have no wants; unless the scanty rags of cloth which they wear, their huts and simple food, may be considered as such'. Only Lord Grenville, who had led the short-lived 'All the Talents' government, tried to point the obvious moral. The structure of the Indian administration, he suggested, was at fault: 'the very existence of this blended character of merchant and sovereign, on which our whole Indian system is built, appears to me an anomaly inconsistent with all true principles of government, reprobated by all authority and condemned by all experience'. But the opposition was in disarray; his intervention could safely be ignored. 'The Company', Castlereagh blandly claimed, 'had raised up an Empire unexampled in the world, and the government of that Empire had been administered on principles eminently conducive to the happiness of the numerous individuals living in it. It was a government founded on theory so wise, and brought to such practical perfection, that he did not believe the history of the world could exhibit its equal.'

It was not to be expected, therefore, that the government would make any change in the way India was governed; and in the event, the outcome of parliament's deliberations was from the Indian's point of view the worst possible. Introducing a debate on the subject in the House of Lords, Liverpool unctuously reminded them that what they had to consider 'was not the advantage which England might derive from India – not whether trade could be carried on more beneficially from this country under one system or another – but, circumstanced as we were with respect to fifty million of our fellow-creatures, what system of government would most contribute to their happiness and prosperity'. In fact, profit and revenue decided the issue. By this time critics of the East India Company in parliament were powerful enough to persuade ministers to deprive it of its former trade monopoly (their decisive argument being that if it did not, the Americans would move in and break it anyway). But one segment of its monopoly was to be retained by the Company, in its new Charter: the China trade. On this issue, the Company's spokesmen had been able to argue that as the Chinese authorities insisted upon foreign trade being conducted through a monopoly, the Hong, and expected foreigners to do the same, any attempt to introduce free trade might well jeopardise the trade in tea. This was a risk which ministers, at that crucial stage of the Napoleonic wars, were not prepared to take. As Liverpool admitted, a revenue was 'securely derived from it'; and it was better 'to retain a certain advantageous trade and a certain revenue, than to exchange it for uncertainty'. In order to pay for the tea, it was also considered necessary (though the subject was discreetly not discussed in parliament) to allow the Company to keep its opium monopoly, too. Otherwise there would be no way of ensuring that Indian opium would be channelled into China; and as the increased profits from its sale there had just succeeded in stemming the outflow of bullion, the British government was content to leave that monopoly alone.

So the system by which British India was governed by the Company (nominally at least: Grenville claimed that the British Crown was *de facto* the sovereign, and that the sovereignty 'which we hesitate to assert, necessity compels us to exercise') was to be allowed to continue, for a further period of twenty years; from which it could be inferred that the Company would become even more dependent upon the opium trade with China, deprived as it would henceforth be of its only other source of commercial profit, trade with other countries. And even before the new Charter was safely on the statute book, the Council had felt free to make a change of policy which would enable them to exploit opium's revenue potential even more effectively.

Cornwallis's decision that opium found to be adulterated could be sold locally in Bengal, in order to reduce the risk that it might reach China and spoil the market there, had naturally led the Bengal merchants who dealt in this small but lucrative market to argue that if sales of opium were to be permitted in India at all, there should be quality controls there, too. Why should the opium eater (smoking had hardly caught on in India) be compelled to buy an inferior product? But the Calcutta Board of Trade had objected, ostensibly on moral grounds.

Of all luxuries, opium is said to be the most fascinating. Of course, when people are invited by a 'sign or board' to go into shops to try it, we may naturally suppose many who would otherwise never have thought of using it, may be tempted to do it; and having once enjoyed the delightful intoxication it occasions, will not only persevere in the use of it, but will encourage others to take it, so that in time this pernicious drug may become as generally used in the Company's provinces as in China and the Eastern Islands; and in consequence prove fatal to the morals and health of the inhabitants.

The Board of Trade's real objection, however, was added as an afterthought; licensing would deflect opium from the export market, causing a serious diminution in the revenue. This argument had proved decisive until, ten years later, it became apparent that the policy of limiting the production of opium and channelling it into the export market was creating a black market in Bengal. The high price offered for it was at last encouraging ryots to grow poppy – but not for the Company; for smugglers, and for illicit sales locally. In time, the administration was warned, this would endanger the supply for China. The question of licensing was therefore reconsidered. If opium was being produced and sold illicitly, the Board of Revenue claimed, it was damaging the morals and health of the people anyway; whereas if it were licensed, some control could be exercised over consumption, and smuggling checked. Cole-brooke, by this time a member of the Council, added that even if the sale of illicit opium could be stopped, this would only drive people back on to hemp drugs, which he thought more dangerous. And in 1813, it was decided that retail sales of opium should be licensed in Bengal towns. To save face, the Council gave it out that 'it shall be the duty of the Collectors to discourage, to the utmost extent of their means, the sale and consumption of opium, except for medicinal purposes'; but as the Council had itself been unable to find any way to discourage that sale for purposes other than medicinal, its injunction represented (as H. R. C. Wright remarked, disentangling the story in his *East Indian Economic Problems of the Age of Cornwallis and Raffles*) no more than a pious divesting of responsibility. The Council could continue to pretend that it was discouraging consumption; in fact, it would be using it as an additional source of revenue, and making the government of British India still more dependent upon its production.

The Council, therefore, had manoeuvred itself into a situation where opium was its staple. The East India Company, which required a revenue sufficient to meet the running costs of governing India, as well as profit for its shareholders, relied no less on the sale of the drug. The British government at home, needing tea from China to maintain its revenue, and consequently needing some commodity which would sell in sufficient quantity in China to maintain the balance of trade, was equally involved. As it held the controlling interest parliament, in a sense, had become the chief shareholder in the opium business. And the government had again to consider how best to protect it.

Amherst's Mission

In 1815 an imperial edict from Pekin deplored the way in which opium was 'flowing into the interior of this country, where vagabonds clandestinely purchase and eat it, and continually become sunk into the most stupid and besotted state, so as to cut down the powers of nature, and destroy life'; and the Canton authorities, roused, arrested six of the best-known opium dealers and submitted them to torture. The Company Supracargoes were unimpressed. Although it might mean some delay in completing sales, their Committee reported, and possibly a higher outlay for 'squeeze' owing to 'the greater number of officers and police people being employed', these matters were being taken care of by a levy imposed on all opium consignments through Macao, which would be disbursed where necessary among the mandarins. In any case, experience had shown that where enforcement led to temporary shortage, the price of opium rose, leaving an increased profit out of which to pay the increased squeeze. Yet though the Supracargoes' confidence proved to be justified, the fact that the opium traffic was illegal remained an embarrassment to the British government. And it happened there were other grievances which it could justifiably seek to bring to the attention of the Emperor and which, if he proved amenable, might lead to his legalising opium as well.

The main need was a base. British merchants were still permitted to stay in Canton only during the winter trading season. Lark's Bay was primitive; and though Macao was a pleasant enough retreat, the Portuguese exploited their opportunity to extract all they could from foreign merchants. In 1808 there had been an ingenious attempt to take it over; a force under Admiral William O'Brien Drury occupied the town, on the pretext of protecting

Britain's Portuguese allies from the French. But the Canton authorities had reacted sharply, suspending trade with the British, and withholding provisions from Macao, until Drury had ignominiously to depart. With the defeat of Napoleon, though, it seemed reasonable to assume that the Chinese would hesitate before treating the greatest maritime power the world had ever known with such insolence. Another mission, on the lines of Cathcart's and Macartney's, was despatched to try to persuade the Emperor of the need to come to terms.

The chosen envoy, Lord Amherst, had much the same instructions as his predecessors, except that there was no reference to opium. The reason for the omission can be traced to a message in code sent in 1807 by the Canton Supracargoes' Committee to the Secret Committee of the Company – the three directors whose function was to co-operate with the Secretary of State for India in running the Company's political, as distinct from commercial, affairs. In any negotiations with the Chinese, the Supracargoes pleaded, there should be no direct reference to opium, as it might 'have the effect of causing the restriction against the importation of this drug to be rigorously enforced, and thus counteract the principle object your hon'ble Committee appears to have in view, namely to maintain the favourable sale in China of the produce of Bengal'. There could no longer be any question of offering to stop the export of opium as a bargaining counter. Its sales were of far more value than any which might come as a result of negotiations with the Chinese for free trade.

Whatever chance there might have been of Amherst's persuading the Emperor of the desirability of granting diplomatic recognition, let alone any other concessions, was lost through diplomatic punctilio. Should he – Amherst wondered – perform the kow-tow? Should he prostrate himself three times, each time knocking his head three times on the floor, as was expected of everybody who was received by the Emperor? Macartney had cleverly, and literally, ducked the problem; he had gone down on one knee and bowed the requisite number of times, which had been accepted as displaying due reverence, but enabled him later to deny that he had kow-towed. Henry Ellis, Secretary to the Mission, gave it as his opinion that if Amherst's refusal to kow-tow would mean returning without his having had an audience with the Emperor, he doubted whether the interview would have been too dearly bought 'by sacrificing the distinction between nine prostrations of the head to the ground on two knees, and nine profound bows on one knee'. Sir George Staunton, President of the Canton Supracargoes Committee, disagreed. The audience, he felt, would be too humiliatingly purchased by such a sacrifice. Amherst accepted Staunton's view, refusing to kow-tow; and he had to return with as little accomplished as Macartney.

Of all men, Staunton must have known that his advice could only lead to the failure of the mission. At the age of twelve he had accompanied Macartney on the earlier venture, as a kind of page boy; and he had added Chinese to the other languages in which he was already reputedly fluent, Latin, Greek, German, and French. In 1815 he was, in fact, the only Company man in Canton who knew the language. Why then, did he advise against the kow-tow? It may be that he felt there was no point in the performance; the Emperor would simply take it as a sign of due deference from a tributary power, and refuse any concessions. But as a loyal servant of the Company, he must also have realised that should he be mistaken – should the Emperor prove willing to come to terms – the consequences could hardly be favourable to its interests. The British government was primarily concerned with British, not Indian, prospects; it might allow itself to be deluded into thinking that if trade were opened up, British goods would pour into China, relieving it of the need to depend on Bengal opium to pay for imports of tea. In that case, there would be a temptation for Amherst to promise action against opium smuggling. And by this time, though officially the Supracargoes had nothing to do with it, opium had become the Company's mainstay in Canton. As the Supracargoes explained to Lord Moira, who had come out in 1813 as Governor-General, they were dependent on it for the cash they needed to meet their bills. It was even used as collateral: when the Prussian consul in Macao wanted a loan that year, he designated a consignment of opium as his security. Understandably the Supracargoes did not want to disturb a traffic which, in spite of its illegality, was operating so smoothly.

Competition

But it was about to be disturbed, by the collapse of the Company's monopoly control. The high prices that the Company's opium had been commanding in China had not escaped the attention, and envy, of the country ship owners. Most of them worked on commission, aiming to earn ten to twenty per cent; and they resented the fact that the Company was making ten times as much. But they could not exploit the alternative source of supply, Turkey, because if they were detected by the Supracargoes importing Turkish opium they would lose the Company's licence to trade in Bengal.

This was not a threat, however, to American merchants. They had been late starters in what, like the rest of the mercantile world, they still called the East India Trade, covering the area from India to Japan. Under British rule, the American merchants had been compelled to respect the East India Company's monopoly, the cause of much resentment – the Boston Tea Party had been celebrated at the expense of the Company's product; and when independence had been won, the Napoleonic wars hindered expansion, especially after President Jefferson's embargo on trading in areas where there might be trouble with the belligerents. Still, some owners carried on; to find, as the traders of the West had done, that though the teas and other goods they bought in China could be sold profitably in America, it was much more difficult to sell goods to the Chinese. They had to be paid in silver, usually in Spanish dollars at a premium. So the growing demand for opium of any kind in China, after supplies from Bengal were restricted, encouraged American merchants trading with Europe to pick up Turkish opium in the Mediterranean, and bring it to Macao; a development which had alarmed the Company's Court of Directors, when it was reported to them in 1806. Did it, they had enquired, constitute a threat? The Canton Supracargoes replied that it might, but for the present they were not worried. 'Because of the very inferior estimation in which the Turkey opium is held by the Chinese, comparatively with the produce of Bengal, we do not conceive that speculations of the Americans are likely permanently to interfere with the interests of the hon'ble Company'. Turkish opium was used as an adulterant; so although small quantities might continue to find a ready sale, 'a considerable importation will be unsaleable'. The Supracargoes were more disturbed by the possibility that the American consignment might introduce the plague, then raging in Turkey, to China; but the length of the voyage, they hoped, would diminish the danger of so dreadful a calamity.

The plague did not materialise; nor, for a time, did the competition the directors had feared. But the Americans continued to bring in Turkish opium; and the restricted supply and high price of Bengal consignments made it so profitable that by 1815, even the Supracargoes were growing worried. Although it was not so esteemed as Bengal, they pointed out, 'still, the competition of Turkey opium cannot fail to have material effect on the price'. With the war at an end, that competition was bound to increase.

Malwa

Even more disturbing was the realisation that increasing amounts of Malwa opium, produced in the independent Maratha native states of central and western India, were beginning to reach Macao. The poppy had long been grown in them for local consumption; and from the beginning of the century, perhaps earlier, small amounts had found their way to China through Bombay – the quality, although not regarded as comparable to Bihar or Benares, being good enough for Malwa to be used for smoking in its own right, and not just as an adulterant. By 1803 the quantities reaching China had increased to the point when even Lord Wellesley, ordinarily too occupied in his campaigns to extend the boundaries of British India to concern himself with such matters, suggested that steps should be taken 'for the prevention of further growth of that commerce, and for its ultimate annihilation'. Two years later, the export of Malwa from Bombay was banned; and for a while, it ceased to compete. But gradually the traffic began to build up again, through the Portuguese possessions of Goa, Diu, and Damaun. By 1815 concern about it was being reflected in the correspondence between the Committee in Canton, the Council in Calcutta, and the Court in London; and tentative efforts were made to get the Maratha chiefs to co-operate in closing down the trade. But the Malwa region, as Philip Woodruff was later to describe it, was 'a network, an archipelago, a milky way of small states, each claiming some ill-defined shreds of sovereignty', which the chiefs could not have effectively controlled even if they had wanted to. By 1816 the shipments, which had been desultory, began to be better organised, showing that Malwa could be sold in China for $750 a chest; and the supply was sufficient to pull down the selling price of Bengal from the high point to which it had risen of over $2,000 a chest to $1,000, or even less. The merchants who carried Malwa from Damaun, too, could expect to net 100 per cent profit; far more than they could make from Calcutta, and enough, if the traffic were allowed to continue, to tempt the country ship owners to defy the Company. If it removed their licences to trade, they could simply switch allegiance and carry the opium from Damaun under some other country's flag.

As if this were not bad enough, the Company suddenly found itself assailed on another flank. Although Warren Hastings's description of opium as 'pernicious' had often been echoed, there had been no serious denunciation of the trade until Stamford Raffles' *Java* was published in 1817. Opium, he claimed

has struck deep into the habits and extended its malign influence
to the morals of the people, and is likely to perpetuate its power
in degrading their character and enervating their energies, as long
as the European governments, overlooking every consideration of
policy and humanity, should allow a paltry addition to their finances
to outweigh all regard to the ultimate happiness and prosperity of
the country.

Raffles did not yet have the reputation as an enlightened colonial administrator that he was destined to enjoy, but as a former Governor of Java his words might carry weight. Up to this point the Council had been content to justify its policy of restricting opium production by pointing to the financial benefit from the higher price; but to forestall further criticism, Lord Hastings (as Moira had become, through elevation in the peerage) now took the defence over onto the moral plane. The Company's overriding concern, he claimed, was not to encourage opium consumption but rather to lessen the use or, more properly speaking, the abuse of the drug; and for this end, as well as for the purpose of revenue, to make the price to the public, both in our own and foreign dominions, as high as possible, having due regard to the effects of illicit trade in our own dominions and of competition in foreign places from opium produced in other countries. Were it possible to prevent the use of the drug altogether, except strictly for the purpose of medicine, we would gladly do it in compassion to mankind; but this being absolutely

76

impracticable, we can only endeavour to regulate and palliate an evil which cannot be eradicated.

The same high-minded excuse was also made to justify retrospectively the decision the Council had taken to permit retail shops to be opened for the sale of opium in Bengal. 'The only object is (and it is surely a fair one) to substitute an allowed, instead of an illegal, proceeding, to restrain an evil which cannot be repressed; to place under regulation a habit of indulgence from which the people cannot be wholly weaned, and to employ taxation less as an instrument of raising a revenue than as a preservation of the health and morals of the people.' Yet the embarrassing fact had to be faced by the Council that they would not be able to maintain the high price of Bengal opium if the flow of Malwa were to increase; and they would find it difficult to maintain the high moral tone if, to maintain competitiveness, the price of Bengal opium had to be drastically reduced. Wellesley's proposition was recalled: that the commerce in Malwa should be prevented, and ultimately annihilated.

There is no way of telling how far the need to preserve the Company's opium monopoly, and the government's revenue, was responsible for what came to be known as the Maratha wars, because there were plenty of other nobler-sounding pretexts. They had been provided by, among others, Charles Metcalfe; one of the new generation of administrators, as far removed from William Bolts and his like as it was possible to be. Metcalfe had come out to India from Eton at the beginning of the century, aged fifteen. He had served as Wellesley's secretary, and become imbued with Wellesley's imperialist ideals, which he was able to put into practice when he was appointed British 'Resident' in Delhi at the age of twenty-six. Nominally, the descendants of the Moguls still ruled there; but Metcalfe regarded his function as executive, rather than diplomatic. To restore order and prosperity, he embarked on a campaign to convert swords into ploughshares (almost literally: the peasants were offered agricultural implements in exchange for weapons which they turned in); and so successful were his endeavours that he convinced himself they should be extended to other parts of India not yet under British rule. In 1814 he recommended the occupation of the huge territory of central India, divided up into principalities but dominated by Maratha warlords. They were giving refuge, Metcalfe argued, to ne'er-do-wells, criminals, agitators and rebels, out of reach of British justice, continually seeking to stir up trouble for the British. Occupation of the central region of India, too, would 'improve our frontier – that is, render it more defensible', by linking up all British India from Calcutta to Bombay; and it would assist commerce – which was very necessary, because 'unless we can raise additional resources in our present dominions, it is only by an extension of territory that we can obtain an increase of revenue for the support of our necessary expenses'.

Anxious not to be outdone by Wellesley, Hastings

needed no convincing; but he found the Court of Directors adamant that there must be no more military adventures of the kind that had let them in for so much expense, and George Canning, who became Secretary of State for India in 1816, took their side. Canning, however, felt that the Governor-General must be left with some discretionary powers, to deal with emergencies; and Hastings had no difficulty in convincing himself that a state of emergency existed sufficient to justify a campaign to crush the Maratha chiefs, and incidentally to bring the regions of central India where Malwa opium was produced under British control. This may not have been a prominent consideration in his mind, when he launched his campaigns; or he may not have admitted that it was, even to himself, any more than he would have admitted, even to himself, that he wanted the prestige which victories would provide. Yet it can hardly have escaped him that the 'increase of revenue for the support of our necessary expenses', which Metcalfe had given as one reason for justification for making war on the Marathas, would come chiefly from Malwa opium. The revenue from Bengal opium, in other words, was being used to finance a war to secure the revenue from Malwa opium, by restoring the Company's monopoly of the drug.

The assumption that the Company would be able to restore its former monopoly position, though, was derived from a misunderstanding of the nature of Malwa production. Opium had not been a monopoly there, as it had been under the Moguls in Bengal. The poppy was grown extensively for casual local consumption. Nor was it immediately practicable to restrict production, because so much of the opium was produced in the 'archipelago' of independent states. Many of them had welcomed and helped the British, as deliverers from Maratha exactions. It would be unjust, as well as impolitic, to antagonise them by compelling them to stop opium production. How, in that case, could the smuggling through Damaun be stopped? The only way, the Council decided, would be for the Company's opium agency to buy up all the Malwa which came on the market, depriving the Damaun traffickers of their source of supply; and to sell it in China for whatever price it would fetch there, even if this meant that it would be competing with the opium from Bengal.

If any single policy decision were crucial in determining the course of events leading to the opium war, it was this abandonment by the Company of the policy of restricting output. For form's sake, the Council put it about that no change of principle was involved. The new policy, they insisted, would not tend

> to increase the consumption of the deleterious drug, nor to extend its baneful effects in society. The sole and exclusive object is to secure to ourselves the whole supply by preventing foreigners from participating in a trade of which they at present enjoy no considerable share – for it is evident that the Chinese, as well as the Malays,

cannot live without the use of opium, and if we do not supply
their necessary wants, foreigners will.

But in a letter to the directors on July 30th, 1819, outlining
the new policy, Hastings showed he knew what it would
imply. As the increased supply of Malwa must bring down
the price of opium in China, including the price of Bengal,
it would be necessary to extend the Bengal plantations,
to 'make-up for the depreciation of the article by the
aggregate profit'. Opium production in Bengal, though it
was still to be controlled, was no longer to be restricted
to a fixed amount annually for moral reasons. It would
be regulated to the amount necessary to continue to
provide the revenue it had brought in since the beginning
of the century.

'Solitary Nail'

For a while, the new policy worked satisfactorily. The
Company's sales of Malwa rose to about 1,700 chests in
the 1820-21 trading season, and of Bengal, to about 3,000
chests. In ordinary circumstances, this increase of supply
could have been expected to reduce the selling price. But
the earlier policy of restricting output had led to the
development of a demand in China that had been temporarily filled by the opium from Turkey, brought in by the
Americans; and as Malwa proved more to the Chinese
taste, it took the Turkish opium's place. At the same time,

a way was found to introduce the drug to regions where it had previously been little known, providing new markets.

For this the Portuguese were unwittingly responsible. The bulk of the opium delivered had been brought in through Macao; and the authorities there had been levying a duty of $40 a chest on all consignments. Ostensibly this was to provide the $100,000-a-year needed, they claimed, to sweeten the Chinese mandarins. Doubtless some of it was used for that purpose. Whatever its destination, it operated as an import duty on the Company's product, and led to some speculation by the Council in Calcutta: might it not be wise to try to reach an agreement with the Macao authorities, conceding them their rake-off if they would agree to ban imports of smuggled Malwa? The directors in London felt this project would be unworkable, as it undoubtedly would have been. But in the meantime, the levy had prompted the owners of the country ships to make more use of Lark's Bay, and also of the island of Lintin, 'Solitary Nail', so called because of its single domi-nant peak. Because of its position in mid-estuary, Lintin was particularly convenient for smugglers from both sides; they could carry away their purchases under cover of night. The country ship merchants were able to sell more opium, and so dispose of the increasing amounts reaching China without any serious lowering of prices.

If the mandarins condoned the use of Lintin, the merchants began to ask themselves, why should they not also condone the sale of opium in the port of Canton,

Whampoa? The Supracargoes' Committee would certainly disapprove, for fear of the Company losing its privileges if the Canton authorities objected. But the merchants, knowing how dependent the Company had become on them to sell its opium, were becoming less disposed to accept the Supracargoes' dictation. The rebellion was led by James Matheson, still in his early twenties, who had begun to smuggle Malwa to China under the Danish flag in 1818 and the following year had negotiated a deal with the Portuguese to ship regular consignments of opium from Goa. If he were found out, the worst the East India Company could do would be to deprive him of his licence; and this became an empty threat so long as he could trade in smuggled Malwa.

The merchants decided to experiment by establishing an opium depot ship, *Mentor*, in Whampoa; and the Supracargoes' Committee was powerless to stop them. The procedure for selling the opium remained as before, as Walter Stevenson was to recall in his evidence to the Parliamentary Committee which investigated the affairs of the East India Company in the early 1830s. He had been invited by the Company to act for them in what would ostensibly be a cotton-importing agency; but its real function was to look after the opium arriving in the country ships. Asked how he arranged its sale, he replied:

Nothing was more simple. The ship on board which the opium was, lay generally at Whampoa, at that time: about twelve miles from

Canton. The parties who purchased opium of my house paid the money in Canton, and so soon as it was ascertained that the silver was good, which was done by shroffs I had for the purpose, they received an order from the officer to take the opium out of the ship. The purchasing parties then went down, generally under cover of night, and took the opium out of the ship.

Hearing of the Whampoa depot, the Canton authorities were in a position to increase the amount of 'squeeze' they required of the Hong; which was presumably the reason why they paid no attention to the protests from the Governor of Macao, who had taken care to inform them that British ships were breaking the imperial law by failing to call at Macao, as they were supposed to do to identify themselves before proceeding to the Canton river. Deprived of what had become a substantial revenue, it was now the Governor's turn to try to persuade the Company to reach an agreement profitable to both. A market should be set up in Bombay, he suggested, through which Malwa could legally be exported, Macao being guaranteed a specific amount annually (this would bring the Damaun traffic to an end, but there was more commercial rivalry than sentimental attachment between the Portuguese possessions in the East). Had he put forward the project earlier, it might have had some chance of acceptance; but following the subjugation of the Marathas, the Council felt confident it would gain control of the entire Malwa output and channel it through Calcutta. The offer was ignored.

The new smuggling arrangements worked only for a few months before the kind of situation developed which the Supracargoes had long feared. A new Emperor ascended the Dragon Throne: Tao-Kuang, 'Glorious Rectitude'. He had no outstanding abilities, and was politically naïve; but he had something of the quality which was later to be associated with King George V, an earnest desire to serve his people, and to carry out his duties punctiliously. It would be unwise, the Viceroy and the Hoppo realised, to let news of the drug traffic through Whampoa reach his ears, in case he should inaugurate the new reign by making an example of them. Their feelings were transmitted to the Hong; and the Hong merchant who stood security for *Mentor* warned the country ship merchants that if they continued to use it as a depot ship and, worse, to make no secret of its function, there might be trouble. Assuming that all he wanted was more 'squeeze', they decided to ignore the warning.

Over the years, the Supracargoes' Committee, the Hong merchants and the Hoppo had evolved a kind of diplomatic minuet: a tacitly agreed series of steps, designed to stave off trouble. If there should be an imperial edict, or the threat of one, about contraband, or if a new mandarin was appointed, either unaware of the niceties of the opium situation, or aware of them but anxious to appear to be serving an Emperor energetically, the Hoppo would instruct the Hong in their duties, and the Hong would pass the instruction on to the Committee. The Supracargoes might be well aware that the Hong were not expecting the instructions to be carried out. It was sometimes desirable, though, to save the Hong's 'face', to appear to carry them out; and such an occasion arose when the Viceroy and the Hoppo published a proclamation reminding the Hong of the laws against opium, and warning that as a fresh imperial edict had just been issued on the subject 'our exertions should be more strenuous'. As the proclamation ended not with the customary 'Respect this!' but (according to the translator) 'Feel a cold shiver at this!', it was reasonable to assume that at least a show of compliance with the law was desirable: the withdrawal of *Mentor*, perhaps, or a temporary suspension of opium shipments to Whampoa. But the country ship merchants, still assuming that the proclamations represented no more than a form of official blackmail, refused to co-operate, though advised by the Supracargoes' Committee to do so. Eventually the authorities, putting 'face' before income, or alarmed by information from Pekin, laid charges of smuggling against the owners of four ships at Whampoa, one of them American, three British. The ships were impounded, and the owners told that they could have them back only if they would remove them from Whampoa, giving a pledge that they would not return.

To the Supracargoes' Committee, this was a typical example of the irresponsibility of the merchants. Their tendency, Sir George Staunton wrote, was 'upon almost all occasions, to a state of anarchy and disorder', rendering them odious to the Chinese people and officials alike. As things worked out, however, the expulsion of the ships was to prove an advantage both to the Supracargoes, who no longer had to worry about *Mentor* at Whampoa, and to the Company's future prospects. Two of the expelled ships, *Merope* and *Hooghly*, belonged to James Matheson. He withdrew them to Lintin, setting up an opium depot there; and, realising that it might not be possible to return to Whampoa, he sent *Merope* on an exploratory voyage northwards along the coast to Amoy. It was not profitable; bargaining was difficult in dialects the crew had never heard, reliable charts of the coast were lacking, and there was a danger from sudden typhoons. But enough opium was sold to show that there was a potential demand to be catered for, should it become necessary to find ways of getting rid of mounting stocks.

For a while, too, the strained relations between the Company Supracargoes and the merchants were eased. When in 1822 the Hoppo sent instructions to the Hong that foreign ships must leave Lintin, the Supracargoes feared there might be further trouble. As they explained to the Council, they would plead that what was happening there had nothing to do with them, and hope that the difficulty of driving the ships away would permit 'a relapse into that system of connivance which has hitherto marked the conduct of this extraordinary traffic'. Their hope was fulfilled.

What would have happened if the Canton authorities

had carried out their threat to suspend all trade through Canton until the smugglers left Lintin? The Supracargoes were uneasily aware of the embarrassment that it would cause them, as they revealed in a letter to the Council in Calcutta the following year, after the threat had been repeated. Their instructions, they reminded the Council, had been that they were on no account to let the opium trade interfere with legal commerce. If the worst happened, therefore, they would call upon the opium ships to leave. But it was obvious that they were far from certain their order would be obeyed; perhaps also uncertain whether the Council would want it to be obeyed. And by this time, they no longer enjoyed the sanction they had formerly employed to keep the merchants in order: the regulation that no British subject was permitted to go to Canton without their consent. A merchant, W. S. Davidson, had shown how to circumvent it by obtaining Portuguese nationality. Others found they could acquire consular status at Macao; James Matheson became the Swedish consul; the Magniacs, owners of the firm he was later to take over, consul and vice-consul for Prussia; and the merchant who was to become his chief rival, Thomas Dent, consul for Sardinia. This did not give them diplomatic standing, so far as the Chinese authorities were concerned; but it enabled them to visit Canton without the Supracargoes' permission, ostensibly to look after their country's commercial interests.

The persuaders

The events at Canton had no adverse effect on the sales of the Company's opium; from 1819 to 1822 monopoly control remained apparently secure. The total number of chests exported from Calcutta was held at under 5,000; and although this was about twice as much as had been sent to China before Malwa began to compete, the value also doubled, from about four million dollars in the 1818-19 trading season to well over eight million dollars in 1821-2. At this point, however, the Company's opium agency began to run into difficulties as Sir John Malcolm, the administrator of the territory which came under British control as the result of the Maratha wars, had warned that it would.

Malcolm came from the other end of the social scale to Metcalfe; a Scots boy, brought up in poverty and barely literate. But he had succeeded in impressing the directors of the Company at an interview, so the story ran, by replying, when asked what he would do if he met Hyder Ali – the ogre figure of the time – 'cut off his heid'. Sent out to India, he showed that a lack of formal education was no bar to acquiring a mastery of its languages; he became a respected administrator, received a knighthood, and was asked to undertake the formidable task of bringing tranquillity and prosperity to the conquered regions. He found whole areas devastated, villages abandoned, and fields encroached upon by jungle. The villagers had fled; but he coaxed them back, set agriculture and commerce going again and restored confidence so successfully that when a few years later the hymn-writer Bishop of Calcutta, Reginald Heber, visited the region, he noted that he had heard of no one whom all parties were in such agreement in praising.

One of the immediate consequences of Malcolm's efforts, though, was an upsurge of production, now that the peasants could be sure that their crops would not be carried off, or laid waste. And with the Company and the independent merchants both bidding for their opium, they naturally began to cultivate more poppy. Malcolm became worried. If the Company wanted to control production, it would be tempted to extend its monopoly to Malwa; and that would mean interference with the rights of the local rulers, of a kind he had come to mistrust. But if the Company did not extend the monopoly, then buying up the crop would simply encourage more production. Other British administrators agreed; the Resident in Bombay argued that the plan could work satisfactorily only if the Malwa cultivators were subject to the same regulations as those of Bengal. And in London, the Directors became disturbed by reports that the quality of Malwa was 'approaching and sometimes surpassing the quality of that of Bihar'; how, in that case, could the price of Bihar be maintained? But they could think of no alternative to the new policy. The aim in future, they suggested in January

1822, would have to be an increase in the provision of Company opium of all kinds, of a uniform quality. Then, if confidence could be restored and preserved, 'our resources may still derive considerable benefit from that moderate profit on an enlarged supply to which we must restrict our expectations'. They were therefore prepared to sanction a continuance of the policy of buying up Malwa, provided the Governor-General realised that it was of 'primary importance to obtain the drug of the best possible quality at the smallest possible charge, consistently with the fair remuneration of the cultivator; and to reconcile the security of the present provision with the prevention of the extension of cultivation'.

It was the formula Macaulay described: 'govern leniently, but send more money; practise strict justice and moderation towards neighbouring powers, and send more money.' But in this instance the agreed policy was wildly unrealistic; as, indeed, the directors foresaw. It might work for a time, they hoped, but eventually 'either the competition will not be repressed at all, or it will return with the return of our profit'. The Council made some tentative efforts to persuade local rulers that it was in their interest to put down the contraband traffic, or at least to impose duties on the transit of the drug high enough to discourage the flow to Damaun. But there were too many local rulers; and they had no real incentive to get together to enforce the British government's regulations. The Malwa poppy cultivators, finding that the competition between the

Company and the Damaun smugglers was pushing up the price paid for their opium, stepped up production. In 1821 the Company's agent had considered the purchase of 1,700 chests of Malwa sufficient to deny supplies to the smugglers; in 1822 he had to buy 4,000. Prudently, the quota the Company required from Bihar and Benares was reduced from nearly 3,000 chests to less than 2,000. But to try to maintain the revenue, the price the Company offered for it was lowered. The producers reacted as before by adulterating their opium; poppy petals, traditionally used to form a protective crust around each ball of opium, were found to have been liberally mixed with the contents; and the reputation of Bengal was again damaged. Its price fell; although the total amount of the Company's opium sold in Canton in the 1822-3 trading season was higher than the previous year, the total value was lower, pulling down the revenue derived from its sales.

The next season's figures showed a slight improvement; but the effect of the rise in the price which the opium fetched in Canton was simply to encourage higher production of Malwa. In order to prevent it from falling into the hands of the Damaun smugglers, the Company's agent had to buy an additional 2,000 chests in 1824, making 6,000 in all; and thus, with more than 2,500 chests from Bengal, created a glut which again pulled down prices. Twice as many chests were exported by the Company to China that year as had been sent four years earlier; but their total value was actually lower, and the revenue derived from them consequently lower still – a decline the more worrying because Hastings' successor as Governor-General, Lord Amherst, anxious not to be outshone in the field of battle by his predecessors, had decided in 1824 to subjugate Burma; a campaign which had narrowly escaped ending in humiliation, and which had involved the Company, much to the indignation of the Court of Directors, in considerable and, as they believed, unprofitable expense.

'Friendship or enmity'

Something had to be done. One prescription was available: a project which had been put forward in 1823 by Holt MacKenzie, a young and inexperienced but, as time was to show, shrewd administrator who had been appointed Secretary to the Council. Realising what was going to happen, he had urged a change of policy; instead of encouraging the production of Malwa, as they had done, they must curb it, or 'there is little chance of your being able to prevent such a fall in price, from superabundant supply, as will render the possession of the monopoly in Bihar and Benares of little value'. It would not be enough to enter into mere engagements with the different chiefs for the prevention of the illicit trade. The chiefs must be given some pecuniary interest in making sure that it *was* prevented. This would not be accomplished satisfactorily by giving them a proportion of what the Company received for their opium, because that would simply encourage them to produce more. The Company's interests would be better served 'by purchasing the opium in the first instance at a moderate price, and allowing the chiefs a share in our net receipts'.

In 1825 the Council adopted the plan; except that, reluctant to allow anybody else a share in the profits, they preferred to offer a flat subsidy to the rulers of the states in which Malwa was produced, or through which it could be smuggled to Damaun. In return for an income of £20,000, the pliant Maharajah of Udaipur was willing to pledge himself to put down illicit opium dealing, and ensure that all opium, except the small amounts licensed for local consumption, went to the Company. Mindful of MacKenzie's warning, though, the Council was unwilling to take his word for it, stipulating that supervision would be under the control of a British official, who would have the right to employ agents and informers. They would be paid on a commission basis, receiving half the value of any illicit consignments of opium confiscated as a result of their vigilance.

To Sir John Malcolm this was a deplorable decision. His success as administrator of the Maratha territories had been largely due to the patience with which he had worked to restore the confidence of the rulers of the principalities, through the protection which British suzerainty gave them from the depredations of the Maratha warlords; and so restoring their subjects' confidence in them. If British opium officials were to be put above the law in this way, he had warned, it could only undermine the ruler's authority, and 'give rise to much annoyance, jealousy and bad feeling'. But the need for revenue was paramount. The treaty with the Maharajah of Udaipur was ratified in the spring of 1825, and soon, other native rulers in central India were allowing themselves to be persuaded to follow his example.

It quickly transpired that Malcolm had underestimated the adverse effects the policy would have. Reports began to flow in to the Council from the native states of a kind which had not been heard since before Cornwallis's reforming Governor-Generalship. Cultivators and merchants were being subjected to harassment, intimidation and blackmail. Legitimate commerce was being constantly interfered with through the activities of informers whose livelihood depended upon finding illicit opium; and as their employer, the British opium officer, was above the law, the native officers employed could be as thorough and as leisurely as they wished in their search, or exact a bribe in return for speeding it up. The system, the British agent in Rajputana claimed, was held in universal horror, enforceable 'only by such a mass of evil as must make every good and wise man shudder'.

Sir Charles Metcalfe was shocked by the accounts. He had advocated the occupation of central India to save it from the oppressions of the Maratha chiefs, on the assumption that British rule would restore justice and order there. Instead, it was re-introducing some of the worst features of the bad old days of Company rule half-a-century earlier. He was by this time a member of the Council, and in an impassioned memorandum he denounced the treaties as procured by improper exertion of Britain's irresistible influence, and as detrimental alike to the people, the princes and, in the long run, the Company. 'Rather than forfeit our name and reputation,' he urged, 'the Company should be prepared to resign its pecuniary profits from Malwa opium.' His Council colleagues demurred. They could point to soothing accounts which a few officials were sending in about the popularity of the new system. There had been some demonstrations against it, the Company's Indore agent admitted, but they were simply for the sake of appearances. The Company's price for such opium as was legally produced was regarded as fair, and indeed liberal. As for the stories of vexatious search procedures, they could be discounted; there was no need for them; opium could always easily be detected by its strong odour. Metcalfe, in a minority on the Council, could do nothing; but he refused to give up his campaign. 'I am at war with my colleagues on the opium question, and mean to fight to the last,' he wrote in February 1828; 'they have not a leg to stand on, not one among them all'. And by that time information was coming in which revealed that it was no longer simply a matter of being unfair to the producers of Malwa. The opium smugglers were forming themselves into armed bands capable of fighting off the forces sent to intercept them, and not averse to banditry on their route, so that it was no longer safe for anybody, including British subjects, to travel in those regions. It was essential, Metcalfe argued, to abandon a policy 'so destructive of human life'. Reluctantly, the Council agreed that there should be an enquiry; and British agents and officers in the native states were asked for their views.

The replies provided a devastating indictment of the system. The chief argument used in its favour had been that the native rulers had entered into the treaties voluntarily; but most of the reports confirmed Metcalfe's allegation that this was false. According to Lieutenant Hislop, whose evidence was singled out for special commendation in the report of the enquiry, the rulers of the states with which he had been concerned (there were so many in the 'archipelago' that even such junior officers as Hislop often found themselves in senior executive positions) had 'manifested the utmost aversion to these engagements', and had submitted to them 'only when the question was reduced to a choice between friendship or enmity of the British government'. That 'choice' had become only too familiar to the rulers of native states since Plassey. The enmity of the British government meant the withdrawal not only of its support, political as well as financial, but also of its protection, a term which had acquired something of the connotation which attached itself to it during the bootleg era in America, a century

later. The British Resident or agent would no longer intervene to help the ruler against an enemy, or a pretender.
More probably, the enemy or the pretender would be in
the agent's pay.

Where the ruler had been in favour of the treaty, it was
usually for its financial rewards; as Captain Cobbe, who
had negotiated the first treaty with the Maharajah of
Udaipur, unwittingly disclosed. 'Since the conclusion of
the Treaty,' he explained, 'the enormous sums derived
from the confiscations have unquestionably rendered it a
very profitable engagement both to the Maharajah and to
many of the chiefs and other inhabitants who have been
successful in intercepting the illicit convoys, – the 'other
inhabitants' being the informers. Even the Maharajah,
though, according to the British agent there, had changed
his mind. He had originally taken the money 'caring little
for his people, so long as he derived his profit', but had
come to realise that his authority, and his state's independence, had been weakened. Another of the witnesses, Major
Caulfield, asserted that most rulers had submitted 'only
on a principle of deference to the supreme power of the
British agent They consider them injurious and humiliating
and would gladly be released from them, provided they
are not exposed to the consequences of other and worse
measures adopted in their stead'. Colebrooke agreed; he
doubted whether the acquiescence of the native princes
in the opium treaties 'could in any instance be termed,
properly speaking, voluntary. Malcolm and Metcalfe had

been proved right; the system had brought little but discontent and disorder in the native states, and it was the British who were blamed. The most objectionable feature, Metcalfe felt, was that the blame fell on the army officers who had been employed in enforcement duties. It was disgraceful that men 'who ought to be the instruments of protection, and the representatives of a paternal supremacy, become the mere subaltern agents of an opium monopoly, searchers and confiscators'. In that role, inevitably, they were hated, particularly in regions where opium had long been made and taken as a drink much as beer was in British homes, but where poppy fields had been ploughed up, and opium stocks seized, in case the smugglers might get them.

The most comprehensive onslaught on the system, though, came from an unexpected source: Henry St. George Tucker, a member of the Court of Directors in London. Tucker was the son of a Company agent, and had gone out to India in the 1790s as a youth, attracting the attention of Cornwallis who, on his brief return to office in 1805 (he died soon after arrival) had invited him to take charge of the country's finances. Then, with an assured career ahead of him, Tucker had found himself in the dock in Calcutta, on a charge of common assault with intent to rape. It was customary, owing to the absence of British girls, for the younger members of the Company to take Indian mistresses. In Delhi, Metcalfe lived with an Indian girl for eight years, fathering three children by her, and sending them to English boarding schools. Malcolm, returning in middle age to Hyderabad where he had served his apprenticeship, was touched to find awaiting him a present of fruit and a portrait of 'your old friend Chandah, the celebrated dancing girl'. But Tucker had 'made a pass' – on the evidence, it was little more – at Dorothea Simpson, the highly strung wife of an English merchant; and although character witnesses praised him, and the judge summed-up strongly in his favour, the jury found him guilty, and he was sent to jail for six months. Another man would have regarded himself as ruined, and slunk away to try to start afresh elsewhere. After a holiday in England, where he married, Tucker returned to India, took up his job, and managed the Company's finances so efficiently that when he returned to England he was able to secure election to the Company's Court – no easy matter; and later to become its Chairman.

Tucker's memorandum on the Council's Malwa policy was not published till after his death, nearly a quarter of a century later; but it was circulated at the time, and it remains the most lucid and convincing analysis of the defects of the Malwa system. The opium policy with which he had been identified, Tucker recalled, had been to restrict production, confining poppy cultivation to those regions of Bengal best suited to it; and to prevent its sale and consumption except as a medicine. That policy had been abandoned. Instead, there had been an intensive drive to increase poppy cultivation—

premiums and rewards have been held out – new offices and estab-
lishments have been created – the revenue-officers have been enlisted
in the service – the influence of that department has been brought
into action to promote the production of opium; and what has been
the consequence? By the multiplication of agents, responsibility has
been diminished – their powerful influence has caused the quality
of the drug to be less attended to . . . The Supreme Government
of India, too, have condescended to supply the retail shops with
opium for domestic consumption, and have thus added a new feature
to our fiscal policy.

And now, the system was having disgraceful consequences in central India. Treaties had been entered into with the Native States, Tucker felt, 'such as are not, I believe, to be paralleled in the whole history of diplomacy'. Great sums were being paid out which, though they might ostensibly be for the suppression of poppy cultivation, were based on estimates of the quantity of opium being grown, inevitably operating 'as a direct and powerful stimulant to the production of the article', often to the exclusion of the products which constituted the real riches of the country. The effect on the native ruler, too, was degrading. The presence of British agents with such extensive powers to harass his subjects meant his ministers knew that the ultimate power lay with the agents, which encouraged them to make mischief. Their ruler, his authority weakened, had little to do but fritter away the income the British guaranteed him; 'he engages in low pleasures and puerile amusements; contracts debts; and soon sinks into a state of humiliation and distress'. The British agent, if unscrupulous, would facilitate the process of disintegration. If honest, he would feel compelled to invoke British intervention to avert impending evil. Either way, the principality would eventually collapse, and British suzerainty advance; 'we interpose as umpires, and decide as dictators'.

Metcalfe, Colebrooke and the other administrators who gave evidence were writing as observers, often as eye-witnesses, of the evils of the system. Tucker's criticisms put it into its historical perspective, showing how the Council, in its ignorance, had allowed itself to reintroduce the methods which Cornwallis had outlawed because of their dire consequences. It had brought back informers, 'scarcely a less grievous burden upon the country', in Tucker's experience, 'than the bands of robbers whom they were employed to root out'; and it had given its agents judicial powers, thus restoring the fusion of the administrative and judicial processes which Cornwallis, realising that it led inexorably to injustice and oppression, had ended. So it had come about that the British in India, 'as it were almost by choice and preference' had exhibited themselves to the Marathas and Rajputs, whom they had claimed to be rescuing from oppression, as themselves grasping and selfish. They had even made the people of Britain accessories to corruption, vice and crime.

When the evidence was presented to the new Governor-General, Lord William Bentinck, he had to admit that it led 'irresistibly to the inference that evils of a very serious nature are inflicted by our monopoly system in Central India, on all who fall within its sphere of operations'. The system had been 'vexatious and oppressive'; and there was reason to fear 'that the repeated and desperate efforts made to pass the opium beyond the limits of our restrictions by large armed bands of smugglers, and their open systematic defiance of the local authorities while engaged in the enterprise, are operating to demoralise and disorganise the country, and to revive ferocious and turbulent habits'. The system, he decided, must be abandoned.

Bentinck was a Radical in his political leanings; he could have had little sympathy with the opium monopoly. Nevertheless it must be doubted whether he could have cared to dismantle the system had it been in good working order. He had been sent out by the Company with the specific task of restoring its finances, the intention being to persuade parliament to renew its Charter, due to expire in 1834. If he had found on arrival that the Council had been able to extend its monopoly control to Malwa, thereby ensuring a steady increase in revenue, he would probably have invented suitable excuses to maintain it. But the attempt to restrict production of Malwa had failed. The Company's officials, instructed at all costs to prevent the smugglers from finding opium, were being forced to buy up the increasing amounts which were being produced in spite of their efforts, because officials had found they could make common cause with agents and informers in encouraging illicit production, on the principle that the higher the amounts found and confiscated, the greater the reward. By 1830 the Company was buying over 7,000 chests of Malwa annually; yet so far from putting the smugglers out of business, the amount of Malwa being shipped to China from Damaun had been rapidly increasing – to 10,000 chests a year, the Council estimated. So although the volume of the Company's sales to China had gone up from fewer than 6,000 chests in the 1822-3 trading season, to over 14,000 in 1829-30, their total value had risen only from eight million dollars to twelve and a half million; and the Company's revenue had not risen at all.

A rescue operation was needed, and the Council decided to try the plan which Sir John Malcolm had been advocating: opium merchants would be allowed to bring their Malwa to Bombay, as much as they wished, and to ship it there on payment of a transit duty. The amount of the duty, Bentinck explained to the Court of Directors, would be calculated 'on a consideration equal to the real value of the route to be opened'; in other words, it would be just low enough to make the smugglers' longer Damaun route uneconomic. Later, it could be varied to ensure that it brought in the highest revenue that could be extracted without driving the merchants back to Damaun. The revenue obtained by this means would inevitably be far lower than that which the Company could have hoped for from a monopoly. But a monopoly was clearly unattainable; and at least the new system would remove abuses, allay discontent, and, with luck, dislocate the contraband traffic.

There was, however, a complication. The Company had continued to regulate production in Bengal. If there were to be no restrictions on the export of Malwa, there was no point in restricting the amount of Benares and Bihar. On the contrary, the more opium from Bengal that was sold the better; because as the Company was better able to dictate its price to the Bengal peasants, the profit was higher than it would be from the transit duty on Malwa. It followed that production in Bengal should be encouraged. 'We are taking measures for extending the cultivation of the poppy,' Bentinck wrote to inform the Court of Directors in the autumn of 1830; 'with a view to a large increase in the supply of opium to be offered for sale.'

Even the pretence, therefore, that the Company was keeping its opium monopoly in order to restrict production and keep up prices, 'out of compassion to mankind', was quietly dropped. Production was now to be increased as a deliberate policy, the aim being to sell the maximum possible quantity of opium to the Chinese, even if this meant a drop in price, in the hope that the increased sales would compensate for the lower profit margin. The decision meant that sooner or later a clash with the Chinese was inevitable. The only way by which the merchants could hope to sell the increased supplies reaching Lintin would be by finding fresh markets, not just in Canton but in other provinces; and that must eventually alarm the provincial authorities, fearing the wrath of the Emperor. Bentinck was aware of the dangers, but declined to predict what the ultimate consequences would be: 'the final effect of an increase beyond assignable limit in the quantity of this drug exported to China from both sides of India is a result beyond the power of our foresight, to discover or even to hazard at present any speculation on.' St. George Tucker had not felt similarly inhibited. In his memorandum, he speculated that increasing the exports of opium to China must eventually irritate the imperial government to the point where it would be compelled to 'resort to more peremptory and effectual measures for its suppression'. He was right.

3

SALES DRIVE, 1830-34

Following the *Mentor* episode, the Supracargoes' Committee had managed to keep on good terms with the Canton authorities; so good, in fact, that in 1825 they were actually singled out for praise in an official edict as preserving 'due regard for respectability', unlike the country ship merchants, and some Americans, who were allowing themselves 'to be led away by worthless Chinese'. Not that the Company was innocent: as the American merchant Robert Forbes was to recall in his memoirs, it was still intimately involved in the smuggling operation. The bargains were struck in Canton between the Company's agents and Chinese brokers, of whom there were about fifty, each paying the appropriate mandarin in the Customs his 'squeeze'. The brokers passed the Company's receipt to the buyers, or their agents, who took it to Lintin, to the assigned depot ship, where the amount agreed upon was taken from the Company's chests and transferred to the smugglers' 'fast crabs' or 'scrambling dragons', which raced off for the coast (the multi-oared craft reminded another visitor, Dr. C. Toogood Downing, of centipedes). In theory they should not have been hard to intercept, as Lintin was the centre of the contraband traffic. But the smugglers' boats were manned by men who were well-paid, relative to the mass of the Chinese; and who also, knowing that they would immediately be executed if they were caught, were prepared to fight literally to the death if they were intercepted. The crews of the coastguard craft, on the other hand, were 'persons hired at low wages', as the Supracargoes observed, 'often very ignorant of all seafaring matters'; they had neither the equipment nor the stomach for a fight. The smugglers were rarely interrupted.

So long as the Company's Canton agents could keep up the appearance of having no connection whatsoever with Lintin, the Supracargoes' Committee felt, they would be safe from official reprisals. Their assumption was that the Hong, who made their living (and in a few cases their fortunes) from it, and the authorities, who made much of their living from squeezing the Hong, would have a common interest in maintaining the fiction that the Company had nothing to do with the contraband traffic, at least so long as the agents could preserve that fiction themselves. To this end, the Committee saw to it that strict injunctions were periodically issued banning any communication between the Company's agents and the country ship merchants (which, as they tended to dislike each other, was not great hardship); and the success of the first trading season following Bentinck's decision to expand production seemed to suggest that Tucker's fears had been groundless. The total number of chests of Malwa the Company exported to China almost doubled, from under 7,000 the previous year to over 12,000; but the necessary financial arrangements were made in Canton without a hitch. When in 1831 the Company's agents left Canton for Macao for their usual summer break, they could have nothing to worry about, as they thought, until the opening of the next winter's trading season. Early in May, however, the news reached Macao of the death in a Canton prison of one of the Chinese brokers, who had been arrested and charged with 'traitorous connection with the English'. This was ominous; the authorities were evidently no longer simply pretending to take action against those who were concerned in the smuggling. And a week later, the Supracargoes were told that the British Factory in Canton had been raided in their absence by the Viceroy, accompanied by the Hoppo and an armed escort.

'The Factory', as the Supracargoes ordinarily described it, was one of about a dozen warehouses, partly converted into living quarters, which stood on the four acres which the foreigners were permitted to occupy on the Canton river-front, leaving a space about the size of a football pitch for exercise. As there were still fewer than a hundred Europeans in China, exclusive of the Portuguese, and as some of them like Chinnery the painter lived in Macao, this imposed no great strain. But irritation had been growing in the foreign community that there should be restrictions of any kind; particularly among the country ship merchants. In 1830 they had petitioned parliament, protesting at the humiliating conditions under which they were compelled to do their work, and urging that Britain should insist upon diplomatic recognition. The Supracargoes' Committee might deprecate the merchants' presumption in taking it upon themselves to present such a request; but as individuals, they naturally shared the desire to be free from galling restrictions. That year, in fact, three of them had brought their wives up to Canton, in defiance of the regulations. There had been no immediate repercussions, but the presence of the women had not gone unobserved; and it was made one of the pretexts for the raid on the Factory.

Two of the Company's agents, despatched to Canton to investigate, reported what had happened.

The covering was torn down from His Majesty's picture, which their Excellencies deemed proper to treat with the most marked disrespect. The senior Hong merchant was summoned into the Hall, threatened with immediate imprisonment and death on account of his connection with the English, and compelled to remain for upwards of an hour upon his knees. The senior Chinese linguist for the same alleged cause was thrown into chains and ordered for execution, which was remitted for imprisonment principally on the intercession of the Hoppo. The outer gates of the Factory were pulled down and broken to pieces. The quay on which goods are landed, built by the express sanction of the Governor of Canton, has been completely destroyed, the trees in front of the Factory uprooted; the ground generally laid waste; and the greater part of it dug up and thrown into the river.

The explanation for the Canton authorities' apparent abandonment of connivance was that they had been warned to expect fresh edicts denouncing opium from Pekin, where the Emperor Tao-Kuang was mourning the death of his opium-addicted son and heir. A show of activity was indicated: the foreigners were denounced for breaking the law by bringing women up to Canton, and several brokers were arrested and tortured. 'Considerable alarm prevails in consequence among all the Chinese dealers in the article', the Supracargoes' Committee reported to Bentinck. It might be impossible, they feared, to renew the old amicable connivance.

It did not occur to the Committee that the increasing quantities of contraband opium entering China could be held to justify the Emperor's wrath, and the authorities' intervention. They were 'at a loss', they told the Council, 'to account for these acts'. They were not even prepared to admit that the smuggling from Lintin was in any way the responsibility of the Company. They reacted not as traders, but as British subjects. Emphasising the need to avenge the insult to the Crown – the disrespect shown to the King's portrait – the Committee told Bentinck that as Canton could no longer be considered safe, a force should be sent to occupy an island off the Chinese coast: their belligerence even effecting a reconciliation with the country ship merchants, who met and adopted resolutions approving of the Committee's plan.

Realising that this request was no longer an internal Company affair, Bentinck prudently forwarded it to the Duke of Wellington. But by the time it arrived the Tories, after so many years in office, were in opposition; and neither Lord Grey, involved in the campaign for the Reform Bill, nor his Foreign Secretary Lord Palmerston, wrestling with problems in Europe and the Middle East, wanted Britain to be embroiled in a conflict in the Far East. Britain's only object in China – Sir James Graham, First Lord of the Admiralty, was instructed to reply – was commerce.

Conquest there would be as dangerous as defeat, and commerce never prospers when force is used to sustain it. No glory is to be gained by a victory over the Chinese. Our Factory there can only thrive by a ready compliance with the laws, the prejudices and even the caprices of a nation which we seek to propitiate; and the Supracargoes must not imagine that great national interests are to be sacrificed to their notions of self-importance and to a spirit of haughty defiance, mixed with contempt for the laws and customs of an independent people. Our grand object is to keep the peace, and by the mildest means, by a plastic adaptation of our manners to theirs, to extend our influence in China with the view of extending our commercial relations. It is not a demonstration of force which is required, but proofs of the advantage which China reaps from her peaceful intercourse with our nation.

The Court of Directors sent the Supracargoes Committee a stiff rebuke. 'It is essential', they reminded its members, 'that you should clearly understand that you are not the representatives of the British nation, but of the East India Company, in whom the exclusive trade with China has been invested'. The Committee, too, had failed in its duty by allowing the merchants to petition parliament; 'the freedom with which they comment upon the laws and regulations of an Empire to which they have voluntarily resorted, and that for their own advantage' was, in the directors' view, wholly unwarrantable. Bentinck agreed. The Chinese, he wrote, could not be refused what Britain claimed for herself, 'the right exclusively to negotiate the grounds on which any intercourse would be permitted'.

Charles Gutzlaff

In practice, Bentinck had no intention of permitting the Chinese government to decide whether they wanted the Company's opium. He could not afford to consider their feelings, even had he wished to. His campaign for increased production of Bengal had begun; and Malcolm's scheme for Malwa was proving a success; in its first year it brought in a million dollars in duty, and soon nine-tenths of the exports of Malwa were being channelled through Bombay, only one tenth through Damaun. The production drive, in fact, threatened to be too successful, temporarily glutting the Lintin market; by 1832 the merchants were pleading with the Council to postpone the next Calcutta sales, to enable them to clear their stocks. The Bengal Revenue Board's reply was that as government policy demanded 'the utmost possible extension of the poppy culture, and of the production of opium'; the merchants must do their best to promote sales. They were consequently in a good position to ignore any rebukes they might receive from the Supracargoes' Committee. And as it happened, they were by this time even better placed, relative to the Committee; as a consequence, ironically, of a decision which the Committee itself had taken, in the hope of strengthening its own hand.

Following their requests for a British expeditionary force to occupy an island off the coast of China, the Supracargoes had realised that they had no alternative, pending a reply, but to swallow the Canton Viceroy's insult, and behave as if nothing had happened. As Bentinck refused to act on his own authority, and as it would take about a year before a reply could be expected from London to any request from Canton, the Committee's President Charles Marjoribanks felt justified in doing something which the Committee had always carefully refrained from doing before: seeking ways to open up trade through ports other

114

than Canton. Although voyages undertaken by Matheson's *Merope* and other country ships had shown there was a potential market to the north, the hazards of the coastal waters and the difficulties presented by the multiplicity of dialects had continued to be a deterrent to commercial exploitation. The Committee, too, still had its Canton privileges to worry about. But if those rights were to be withdrawn, Marjoribanks felt, as they presumably would be if the British government sent an expeditionary force, it was desirable to follow Matheson's example, and do some prospecting. A ship would be chartered, he decided, and sent with a cargo of broadcloth, calicoes and cotton 'to ascertain how far the northern ports of the Empire may gradually be opened to British commerce' and to test how the natives and the local mandarins would welcome it. After first trying to use a warship – the captain bluntly refused, on the ground that it was 'at variance with my instructions, and the regulations of the service, and equally illegal in the eye of the Law' – the Committee chartered the *Lord Amherst*, and in February 1832 sent her under a false name, and with false papers, to Amoy, Shanghai, and other ports.

When the Court of Directors heard about the voyage, they roundly condemned it. But this was probably because the wares the ship had to offer attracted few buyers, and the venture lost over $25,000. There was only one commodity which it would have been easy to sell, if it had formed part of her cargo: opium. The news interested

James Matheson and William Jardine – a former ship's surgeon turned merchant, with whom Matheson had gone into partnership in 1828; they were to take over the Magniacs' firm, giving it their joint names (Jardine's first, as the senior of the two: in 1830 he was forty-six, Matheson, thirty-four). Now was the time, they realised, to exploit the knowledge gained from Matheson's earlier prospecting. In the past they had been cautious, carrying opium mainly on commission, rather than speculating in it. But this was too good a chance to miss, particularly as an interpreter was available: Dr. Charles Gutzlaff, who had accompanied the *Lord Amherst*. Gutzlaff, though, had come to China as a medical missionary. It would be unwise, Jardine realised, to try to lure him on board under fake pretences. Although the *Sylph*, as he explained in his letter to Gutzlaff offering him the job, would be carrying a variety of goods.

we have no hesitation in stating to you openly that our principal reliance is on opium. Though it is our earnest wish that you should not in any way injure the grand object you have in view by appearing interested in what by many is considered an immoral traffic, yet such traffic is so absolutely necessary to give any vessel a reasonable chance of defraying her expenses, that we trust you will have no objection to interpret on every occasion when your services may be requested.

The more profitable the expedition, Jardine pointed out, the larger would be the sum by which the Company would be able to devote to furthering Gutzlaff's missionary endeavours, 'for your success in which we feel deeply interested'.

There is nothing to suggest that Jardine was being cynical. He appears genuinely to have believed what the East India Company's directors, from policy, affected to believe: that *caveat emptor* was a maxim which even the most unbending Calvinist could, and indeed must of necessity, adopt in commercial dealings. By all accounts he was an upright man, in private and in public life; 'a most conscientious, honourable and kind-hearted fellow', according to Charles Magniac; and the American merchant William Hunter recalled him as 'a gentleman of great strength of character and of unbounded generosity'. But business affairs, so far as Jardine was concerned, were in a separate living compartment, divorced from the morality of the home. The fact that he was making his fortune by illegally selling a pernicious drug did not disturb him at all. On the contrary, urging a friend to invest in the trade, he called it 'the safest and most gentlemanlike speculation I am aware of'. Those who worked for the firm were expected to accept the owner's principles. 'Employed delivering briskly', James Innes recorded in his diary, 'No time to read my Bible'. Hearing that one of the firm's ships had been delayed because of the captain's unwillingness to load opium on the sabbath, Matheson wrote that though they had every respect for people entertaining strict religious principles, 'we fear that very godly people are not suited to the drug trade. Perhaps it would be better that the captain should resign'.

Gutzlaff – 'a short, square figure', the young Harry Parkes was to describe him, in a letter home, 'with clothes that for shape might have been cut in his native Pomerania ages ago, a broad-brimmed straw hat, his great face beneath with a sinister eye' – had to decide between God and mammon. After what he described as 'much consultation with others, and conflict in my own mind', he settled for both, sailing with the *Sylph*, in October 1832, distributing tracts and pills whenever he had the opportunity. Any fears he might have had of divine wrath were banished when, as he described in his memoirs, a fearful storm threatened the ship with destruction; 'God, who dwelleth on High, did not forsake us; and though often engulfed in the deep, His almighty hand upheld our sinking vessel' – surely a sign that the traffic would 'tend ultimately to the introduction of the gospel, for which many doors are opened'.

The main doors he opened were to the opium traffic. Not only had he managed to acquire familiarity with local dialects; he used his imposing presence to good effect. 'Dressed in his best, which on such occasions is his custom' – Captain McKay of the *John Biggar*, which was following up *Sylph's* voyage, wrote to tell his employers – Gutzlaff was sent to warn off a couple of mandarin junks which had appeared, and which threatened to interrupt business. 'He demanded their instant departure and threatened them

with destruction if they ever again anchored in our neighbourhood. They went away immediately'. His services,
Captain McKay reported, had been of great assistance.
Jardine Matheson could judge that for themselves from
the proceeds; the specie earned was valued at over
$250,000.

Once again, the attempt by the Canton authorities to
exert some control over the opium traffic had not merely
failed; it had resulted in the opening up of fresh markets
for the drug, which Jardine Matheson were quick to consolidate by sending James Innes northwards along the coast
to sell more opium, and to recommend suitable places for
the establishment of opium depot ships. The knowledge
that they could sell their opium along the coast removed
any fears which Jardine Matheson might have had about
trouble in Canton; and the fact that they had chosen to
employ Innes, a notoriously truculent and irresponsible
merchant who had been asked by the Supracargoes'
Committee to leave Canton – a step rarely taken – indicated how little they now worried about keeping on good
terms with the East India Company. Soon, they would
not need to. At Westminster, the future of the Company
was being decided; and with a Whig government in office,
supported and sometimes energetically manipulated by a
fanatically pro-*laissez-faire*, anti-monopoly Radical wing, it
was reasonable to assume that the Company's hold over
the China trade would be finally broken.

'The great anomaly'

The campaign to get rid of the Company's remaining monopolies, and if possible of the Company, had been building up since the early 1820s, when a House of Lords' enquiry into foreign trade had been used by the Company's prospective rivals to draw attention to its shortcomings. They had said little, however, about opium. One witness had pointed out that if British ships were allowed to carry it without having to obtain the Company's licence, British merchants might benefit; but the spokesmen for the British merchants were chiefly concerned to break the Company's China monopoly in order that British ships could take British manufactured goods to China and bring back her tea to Britain. India's trade had not greatly interested them. And when the campaign to terminate the Company's charter re-opened in the late 1820s, although opium was easily the most profitable of the Company's commodity sales, it was still rarely referred to.

The Company, however, was prepared to justify the opium monopoly, should the need arise. In 1829 the Directors had considered a suggestion that it should be defended with the argument that as opium was, or was intended to be, used as a medicine, quality control was needed of a kind that only a monopoly could guarantee. But India opium, though highly prized by smokers, lacked the medicinal properties of the Turkish variety; a fact too widely known for their critics to be fooled by it. When a Commons committee of enquiry began its sittings in 1832 (it had originally been set up under the Wellington government, but the succession of elections which followed caused delays), the Company's witnesses took a different line: they simply denied that it had anything to do with the traffic. The Company produced opium in Bengal and sold it there; and it levied a duty on Malwa passing through Bombay. What happened to the drug later was outside the Company's control and consequently, the members of the committee were left to infer, outside their terms of reference. Questioned about the trade, the former Council member W. B. Bayley blandly replied that as the opium was no longer the Company's when it left India, the Company 'could scarcely be said to trade in it'. And when John Francis Davis, one of the Canton Supracargoes, was asked whether it were not true that the chests of contraband opium reaching China had the Company's trade mark on them, he was able to claim that he had never seen a chest of opium in his life. In all probability, so careful had the Supracargoes been to avoid any contact with the country ships, he never had.

Even Davis, though, when it was put to him that the Supracargoes must surely know the opium had been sold in Calcutta to British subjects trading under the Company's licence, had to admit 'we cannot possibly be ignorant of that'. Other witnesses confirmed that the opium was bought and sold in Calcutta avowedly for the China market.

John Aken, captain of one of the country ships, explained that it had to be carried to China in the Company's chests, so that buyers could see their trade mark; only then was it transferred from the chests to bags for the convenience of 'fast crabs', and to avoid the complications which might have followed for the Company if one of its chests was intercepted. Yet Marjoribanks, seventeen years with the Company, could still in his evidence disavow any connection with opium; he denounced it as 'poison', reiterating that the Company servants 'conceive their connection with it to terminate with the sale in India'.

In different circumstances, members of the Committee would have been tempted to heap ridicule on such a palpable evasion. The Company had a formidable supporter, however, in James Mill. As Ricardo's mentor, one of the founder members of the Political Economy Club and a dedicated believer in *laissez-faire*, Mill could ordinarily have been expected to denounce monopoly whenever and wherever it survived. But he had worked for the Company at Leadenhall Street for fifteen years; and his son, John Stuart Mill, was now also in its employment. He knew that it owed its profitability, and its chances of survival, to opium. When questioned by the Committee on the morality of the traffic, he insisted that it was an economic rather than a moral issue; and in such circumstances, political economy laid down *caveat emptor* as the guiding principle (a few years earlier, Ricardo had argued in the Commons that a publican had a right to sell near-beer to customers who asked for beer, if he could get away with it). But if political economy was to be invoked how, then, could Mill defend the Company's monopoly? Mill was ready for that, too: the Company's opium was being produced not for profit but for revenue: and of all species of tax it was the least undesirable, because 'it falls on the greatest part not on the subjects of the government, but on foreigners'. There appeared to be two great questions, Mill said: 'one is as to the possibility of maintaining file monopoly profit which the Company at present obtain from it; the other is as to the mode in which file profit or duty should be realised'. If the rate of profit was reduced, he went on to explain, as if lecturing a group of first-year students (which was probably how he regarded the Committee), 'a larger quantity must be sold'. And when a questioner tried to pin him down by suggesting that there might be better ways to obtain the required revenue than by maintaining the monopoly, such as an export duty (as with Malwa) or a special land tax, he stuck to his point that 'the only question as to the mode of raising the revenue from opium is how it can be done cheapest'.

It did not require any intimate knowledge of Indian finances to realise why monopoly was the cheapest mode. All that was needed was a comparison of the cost of Bengal opium, over which the Company still exerted its monopoly control, with the cost of Malwa opium, which was determined by market forces: Malwa, the Committee were told, cost twice as much. Only by holding down the price paid to the Bengal producers could the Company continue to secure such a profit as, in Holt MacKenzie's opinion, it would be 'hopeless to get from any other device'. Commercially speaking, he conceded, there were strong objections to the system; 'yet we must set that against the necessity of the revenue, and my belief is, that the revenue cannot be otherwise got'. It was an argument which would appeal to members of both political parties; for the Tories could expect to return to office eventually (even if at the time they can hardly have expected to return quite as quickly as they did, little more than a year later). Whoever was in office, the administration of British India would have to be paid for; there was no mind to allow it to become a charge on the British taxpayer. As for the Chinese, it would be unfair to them, one witness suggested, to deprive them of the drug; 'once a person has become accustomed to the use of it, it cannot easily be dispensed with without danger to his health and perhaps his life'. Another pointed out that this addiction might later be put to diplomatic use; as those who took opium soon could not do without it, all that Britain would have to do to get her own way in negotiations would be to threaten to cut off the supply. Only Marjoribanks expressed concern about the increasing amounts of opium being smuggled into China, but not because it was poison (though that was his description); only because, being contraband, it was free of import duty, and consequently enjoyed an unfair advantage; 'articles smuggled into the country which evade duty can be sold at a profit, when articles which pay government duties cannot'.

That the Company would be stripped of its only external trade monopoly, with China, was a foregone conclusion; *laissez-faire* was now firmly established in the minds of the leaders and most of the followers of all the parties. The Company, the Committee in fact recommended, should cease to trade at all. But it must, they argued in their report, be allowed to retain such internal monopolies as were required for purposes of revenue; opium chief among them. They had looked at four other possible sources of revenue: a special tax on the land used for poppy cultivation; an *ad valorem* duty on the value of the crop; an excise duty on the product; or a customs duty on exports. All four had to be rejected, as impracticable or unenforceable. So the Committee had elected to follow James Mill's advice, even to copying some of the wording of his memorandum. 'In the present state of the revenue of India', they explained, 'it does not appear advisable to abandon so important a source of revenue'; and as it represented 'a tax which falls principally upon the foreign consumer', it was 'upon the whole less objectionable than any other which could be substituted'.

As there was no party capital to be made out of the opium issue, there were few references to it in the parliamentary debates on the future of the East India Company which followed the enquiry. Other aspects were vigorously argued, from the duration of its new Charter to the number of bishops who ought to be appointed; but on opium the tone was set by Charles Grant, introducing the government's resolutions on the Charter in June 1833, when he managed to use the success of the merchants' trade with China as justification for the government's policy of terminating the Company's Canton monopoly without actually mentioning that they were dealing in opium, except by implication. Whereas the value of the Company's trade with China had fallen since the end of the war in Europe, he was able to show, the value of the merchants' trade had more than trebled; 'a complete and perfect system had been established under which the private trader was enabled to evade the jealous laws of the country, and carry on the traffic with security', providing a clear indication that free trade must always prevail.

Only one M.P. refused to permit opium to be discreetly kept out of sight: James Silk Buckingham, a crusading journalist who had been expelled from India and come back to England carrying several scores to settle with the Company. He was himself a free trader; but in this case, he reminded the House, the trade was not free. It was built on the Company's opium monopoly; a monopoly so productive that in consequence

the article was often sold at the Company's sales at Calcutta at an advance of 1000 per cent above the actual price at which it might be produced. So much importance, indeed, was attached to this traffic that the superintendent of the cultivation of opium, residing at Patna, was paid by the Company a larger salary than that given to the Chief Justice of the King's Bench, the representative of His Majesty, and the head of the judicial establishment in India. And yet, while the Company claimed to themselves the high prerogative of being the guardian of the laws, and the preserver of the morals of the people over whom they ruled, and punished with extreme severity any infraction of their own regulations, they cultivated the opium for no other purpose than for smuggling it into China, against the laws and edicts of the Empire; and, as had been truly said, of poisoning the health, and destroying the morals of the people of that country.

It was painful, Buckingham felt, to think of the damage which had been done to the Chinese. But thought should also be given to the damage which was being done to Britain, because Indian opium stood in the way of expanding her legal trade. 'If the traders of China could be supplied with British manufactures in payment for their goods, instead of this deleterious drug, a wholesome and reciprocally beneficial commerce would be created, instead of the mischievous and demoralising traffic which now did injury to both'.

Buckingham, however, was less concerned with the opium issue than with a 'monstrous proposition', as he described it when he opened the debate on the second reading of the Bill to renew the Company's Charter. The Bill was designed to prohibit the Company, which had originally been established and run as a commercial enterprise, from trading; 'Yet in the same breath, it erected the members of this joint stock association – who were deemed unworthy of any exclusive privileges of a commercial nature being continued to them – into a governing body, to whose wisdom and to whose care was to be consigned the welfare and happiness of a population four times as large as that of all Great Britain, and living at a distance of at least 10,000 miles.' This gave Macaulay his opportunity. In a speech which Grant described as never having been excelled in the House 'for the development of statesman-like policy and practical good sense', and which certainly is one of the great masterpieces of the art of rationalisation in the English language, Macaulay agreed with Buckingham that the Company was an anomaly; 'but it is part of a system where everything is anomaly. It is the strangest of all governments, but it is designed for the strangest of all Empires'. The ruse worked; Buckingham received so little support that he did not even demand a vote. On the Bill's second reading, opium was mentioned only once; by Daniel O'Connell – an ally of the Radicals in his devotion to political economy – protesting against the retention of any monopolies, and urging that they should be dealt with by an amendment in Committee. They were; but the clause was opposed by Grant. He was careful to reassure the Radicals; the government, he explained, was as anxious as anybody to get rid of the monopoly as soon as possible. But for the time being, the needs of the revenue were paramount, and prudence dictated that there should be no change. The amendment was not pressed; and the Bill passed without further difficulty.

The opium traffic, therefore, would continue as before. What this was likely to mean for the opium producers had just been illustrated in two detailed surveys of the Indian scene; one of them, by Robert Rickards, being quoted by Buckingham in the debate at such length that the editors of *Hansard* decided simply to say he *had* quoted from it, without reproducing the passages or even indicating which they were. Rickards' thesis was that British rule, so far from benefiting the Indian peasants, had disgracefully oppressed them; the administration's juggernaut being the land tax. The Moguls and the lesser princes had traditionally exacted in tribute only one half of the peasant's disposable income. By their land tax, 'this detestable exaction', the British were taking the lot, leaving him with no more than subsistence for himself and his family. According to an official report, which Rickards cited, the system was being conducted by the Company's agents with 'habitual extortion and injustice'; and it was leaving the peasant 'little more than what he was enabled to secure by evasion and concealment'.

The Bengal poppy growers were already effectively controlled by the existence of the opium monopoly, which kept them at subsistence level by ruthlessly keeping down the price paid for their opium. In Malwa,the land tax was now being used to perform the same function; for although the peasant could hope to earn more for his produce, it could still be stripped from him in tax. In his book on central India, published in 1832, Sir John Malcolm provided figures which showed that the expense incurred in cultivating a begah of poppy (including the tax) amounted to about thirty rupees. As the return varied according to the state of the crop and of the market, it could not be precisely estimated; but on the available evidence the cultivator, though in a good season he could earn a profit of twelve rupees, in a poor one would lose nine. Over a span of years, he could just about break even, making a profit of one rupee per begah. The land tax, in other words, was precisely calculated, at its rate of six rupees a begah, to leave the peasant with his keep: nothing more.

Rickards and Malcolm were both respected members of the Company; unlike Buckingham, they did not have a personal grudge. But their evidence confirmed Buckingham's (and, looking back, Colebrooke's) diagnosis; that the opium traffic, lucrative though it was to the administration, brought no benefit to the producers. All it did was provide the means by which the British could extend their hold, and pay for the administrative and judicial services which they established. Without opium, in fact, it is difficult to see how the control could have been maintained, let alone extended through the whole of the sub-continent. By allowing the monopoly to continue, the British government had now guaranteed the colony a further lease of financially precarious life.

The new Charter, though, contained one change from the old which was to have serious consequences. Tenuous though the authority of the Supracargoes' Committee had been, it had at least provided a recognised channel of communication, through the Hong, with the Canton authorities. When the Viceroy heard that the Company was to lose its monopoly of the China trade, he had pointed out that as this would entail the dissolution of the Committee, because there would no longer be Company Supracargoes, something else would have to be put in its place, to keep the channel open, and to maintain discipline. But the British government neglected to make the necessary arrangements. When the Committee was wound up in 1834, there was nothing to replace it with, and no means to keep the merchants under any form of control.

4

THE SUPERINTENDENCE
OF TRADE, 1834-39

Rockets and Blue Lights

Even before the future status of the East India Company had been settled, the merchants and the Company Supracargoes had reverted to their traditional hostility; and when James Innes came back from his exploratory voyage for Jardine Matheson in the spring of 1833 he had taken advantage of his new employment to return to Canton, and to show his contempt for the Supracargoes, and for the Chinese. A Chinese customs officer had promised to stop his servants from piling up wood on the pavement outside Innes's house; but they had continued to do so, and Innes went with Jardine and another merchant to lodge a formal protest. As they were returning, a coolie struck him, wounding him in the arm. Innes' reply was to tell the chief Hong merchant that if the culprit were not arrested before sundown, he would set fire to the customs officer's house. Finding his threat was not taken seriously, Innes fired off what he described as 'rockets and blue lights', and by eight p.m. the house was ablaze. When the Supracargoes' Committee protested, Innes mocked them. Why, he wanted to know, should he have to ask them to act on his behalf? 'It would have been the deepest satire to ask the Hon'ble East India Company to remedy the grievances of others, when they themselves have submitted unredressed to the *grossest public insult and injustice* ever offered in any country' – the raid on the Factory. But after what he had done, 'the coolie was publicly punished next day, being exposed all over Canton wearing the wooden collar with his offence prescribed upon it' – because the authorities were prepared to 'yield to violence, and from fear, what was refused to reason and justice'.

It was typical of Innes that he should not have grasped the real reason why the Canton authorities had taken the action they did. To react by expelling him, or threatening reprisals, would have been to lose 'face'. That a foreigner had behaved in that way, should a report of it reach Pekin, would have been enough to call down an imperial rebuke, or worse. It had to be hushed up. But Innes had never attempted to understand the Chinese mentality; and this was true of the merchants in general.

To some extent the responsibility lay with the system which had evolved to keep the Company men and the merchants apart; the merchants, being chiefly engaged in smuggling, rarely had official dealings with the Chinese. There was also the language barrier; strengthened, if anything, by the prevailing medium of communication, pidgin English. Pidgin consisted of a limited range of English and Portuguese terms, or syllables from them, further corrupted by the fact that the Chinese found it hard to pronounce a number of consonants, b, d, v, r, and st. It was easy to learn and speak, but as the American merchant William Hunter recalled, it had one grave disadvantage; to English ears it sounded comical. Some of the Hong were men of culture and refinement; but it was hard to take seriously men who spoke in such a language, especially as it involved calling themselves by such absurd names, 'Howqua' and 'Mowqua'. These were, in fact, English corruptions of the Chinese; the 'qua' being the equivalent of Mr., and the 'How' of Wu. But as John Francis Davis complained in his book on the Chinese, they became invested with an air of 'silly levity', though in reality they were 'the most steady, considerate and matter-of-fact people in the world'.

The opium merchants, therefore, tended to regard the Chinese as, at home, the English regarded the Irish, a standing joke; and to be all the more furious (as also with the Irish) at being compelled to take them seriously. And not being dependent on the continuing goodwill of the Chinese authorities, the merchants had no incentive to listen to the pleas of the Supracargoes' Committee unless they had to. They no longer had to, as the Calcutta Council had revealed its dependence upon them to get rid of the mounting stocks of the drug. Incidents began to multiply in which the Supracargoes' authority was deliberately flouted. In the summer of 1833 one of Jardine Matheson's captains, hearing that a bag of mail addressed to the Company in Canton had been put ashore in Macao, collected it and tipped its contents out onto a tavern table, to find if there were any letters for him; and the Committee could do no more than register an ineffectual protest. Nor could they intervene when Jardine Matheson, deciding that the Lintin anchorage was not sufficiently well protected from the prevailing winds during the summer, moved their depot ships to Kumsingmoon, on the coast near Macao, beached one of them for caulking, and erected sheds around it, firing on some Chinese who approached, and driving them away. 'It is impossible,' the Supracargoes' Committee observed, 'not to perceive a systematic and factious opposition to the Company's authority, which we feel it our imperative duty to resist by every means in our power, both with the view of holding that authority, and of properly maintaining the general interests of commerce'.

That the opposition was indeed systematic, part of a deliberate design, was to be revealed in a contribution by 'A British Merchant' in the December 1833 issue of the *Chinese Repository*. The *Repository* had been founded the year before by Elijah Bridgman, the first missionary from the United States to come to China, and Robert Morrison, the Company's translator; and because of their knowledge of the language they were able to reproduce proclamations, edicts and sundry news items from Chinese sources, thereby keeping the English-speaking community considerably better informed of what was happening around them than they had been before. Editorially the *Repository* was liberal (except about the Chinese religion: Protestant missionaries tended to be even more intolerant of other brands of deism, such as the Chinese practised, than of outright paganism) and conciliatory. But the journal owed its existence and its circulation to the local traders, and it was prepared to include letters giving their point of view. 'A British Merchant' set out the policies which the country ship owners wished to see adopted, now that the Company's authority in Canton was about to end. It was no use expecting some other body to take over the functions of the Supracargoes' Committee, and carry on as before; the attack on the Factory had demonstrated that the Company's policy of conciliating the Chinese authorities had failed. It had failed because it was interpreted by the Chinese as a symptom of weakness, as it had always been; for example, in the *Lady* Hughes' episode half-a-century before, when the unfortunate gunner who had been handed over on the assumption he would not be punished for the accidental death of a Chinese had been executed. That death, 'A British Merchant' felt, should be on the conscience of the British community; 'there is the smell of blood still'. Now was the time to avenge it.

There had in fact been cases since when British subjects had killed Chinese, without serious repercussions, because the Supracargoes had been careful to see that the 'face' of the Canton authorities was saved by an appropriate gesture. On one occasion the concurrent suicide of a British subject had been accepted, on the eye-for-an-eye principle, though it had in no way been related. And when in the 1820s the American merchants in Canton had allowed the Chinese to bully them into handing over an Italian sailor on one of their ships on a homicide charge, and he had been executed, the British attitude had been that the Americans were being silly; they could easily have found a way to soothe the authorities. But it was not in the interest of 'A British Merchant' to emphasise how conciliatory the authorities invariably were, when properly handled. He was recalling the case of the *Lady Hughes'* gunner to prove they could not be trusted to behave in a civilised fashion until they were compelled to. In place of the Supracargoes, the British government must send a Commissioner to Canton whose social and diplomatic status would enable him to negotiate with the Viceroy on equal terms; and, in case the Viceroy should refuse to meet him, he must be 'vested with powers of no ordinary nature, as being placed in a position that may force him into a state of war in spite of his best endeavours to the contrary'. The meeting arranged, the Commissioner should present Britain's terms: free trade with China, and the concession of an island off the coast for a base.

There was only one small indication, in the article, that 'A British Merchant' was in any way concerned with opium; but it was significant. Ten or twelve years ago, he remarked, 6,000 chests supplied the market; 'now, 22,000 is about the amount annually consumed'. But this was not because the traders were forcing a drug which was deleterious (as he admitted it was) on the people of China. The people of China were only too willing to receive it. Surely, therefore, 'no *morale* will be urged against it'. In any case, 'this illicit commerce is so interwoven with our financial system in India, as well as with our commerce, that it is not inferior in importance to revenue obtained from tea at home'.

In *Foreign Mud*, Maurice Collis suggested that 'A British Merchant' might well have been Jardine. More probably it was Matheson, who in 1827 had founded the first British language newspaper in Canton (which included, among other commodity reports, not merely the latest prices for opium, but also the prevailing rates for smuggling craft), and who soon afterwards was to write a treatise on the China trade. Whoever the writer was, it did not need his pseudonym to reveal that he must have been one of the handful of country ship owners (there were only half-a-dozen of them, of any importance) whose fortunes were, and would continue to be, derived from opium. They badly needed an island as a base, for their smuggling operations, opening up the coast of the north. Opium being contraband, they could not avow that aim. Nor would assistance to the opium traffic be calculated to arouse any enthusiasm at Westminster. Opium was therefore kept in the background, except for the discreet reminder that in any agreement imposing free trade on the Chinese, care would have to be taken not to tamper with a traffic so essential to the Treasury's peace of mind.

In view of Graham's reply to the Supracargoes, it was obvious that the British government was not yet prepared to take up a belligerent stance. But the British manufacturers, anxious to take advantage of the ending of the East India Company's monopoly, could be expected to begin to put pressure on the government to secure freer trade with China; and the government had no reason to refuse at least to try. What was essential, 'A British Merchant' had realised, was that whoever was sent out should be provided with sufficient force to take whatever action he might think fit when the Viceroy declined to receive him – as on past form the Viceroy certainly would. It seems likely, in fact, that the audience the writer had in mind was not the handful of readers of the *Repository* in China, but Palmerston, with whom Jardine Matheson were shortly to establish a link through their London agent, John Abel Smith. But if this was their intention, they were too late. In December, the month the article appeared, Palmerston made his dispositions; and as events were to show, in making them he had been, from the merchants' point of view, not quite well-briefed enough.

Admiral Napier

Palmerston owed his elevation to the Foreign Office not
to any long-standing interest in foreign affairs, but to his
ministerial experience (he had been in a government as
far back as 1809), and his influence over the followers of
Canning, needed to hold the Whig Party together. He
knew nothing of China. He was required, he found, to
decide on a replacement for the Supracargoes' Committee;
and he decided in December 1833 to send out three
Superintendents of Trade, as they were to be called. They
would be salaried officials, not permitted to engage in
commerce. They would not, however, be given diplomatic
status, as the Chinese authorities would refuse to recognise
them. The pretence was to be maintained that they were
merchants, two of them in fact being former Supracargoes,
men of long experience in Canton; John Francis Davis,
who had taken over the Presidency of the Committee
from Marjoribanks, and William Plowden. Their functions,
too – 'to watch over and protect the interests of our
subjects' and 'to adjust by arbitration, or persuasion, all
disputes in which any of our subjects may be there engaged
with each other, or with the subjects or citizens of any
foreign state' – were in theory to be much the same as
those which the Committee had exercised informally
before. In their dealings with the Chinese, Palmerston
emphasised, they must 'observe all possible moderation,

and cautiously abstain from all unnecessary use of menacing language; or from making any appeal for protection to our military or naval forces unless, in any extreme cases, the most evident necessity shall require it': an indication that there was to be no change in policy unless the Chinese themselves made it unworkable.

Over Davis and Plowden, however, Palmerston appointed as Chief Superintendent a man who had never been to China, and had never been in trade: Lord Napier. His personal instructions were rather different, and convoluted. In addition to fostering the established trade through Canton, he was to find whether it might be practicable to extend it to other parts of China. This might require a survey; if so, he was to ascertain the best means of carrying it out, and the likely expense involved. But he was not actually to make it before receiving Palmerston's authorisation. If he found that merchants were independently attempting to explore the coast, 'it is not desirable that you should encourage such adventures; but you must never lose sight of the fact that you have no authority to interfere with, or to prevent them'. Palmerston, evidently, was not unaware of the importance of the opium traffic. Napier was also to seek to persuade the Chinese government to accept and introduce free trade—

it is obvious that, with a view to the attainment of this object, the establishment of direct communications with the Imperial Court at Pekin would be desirable; and you will accordingly direct your attention to discover the best means of preparing the way for such communications; bearing in mind, however, that particular caution and circumspection will be indispensable on this point, lest you should awaken the fears, or offend the prejudices, of the Chinese government; and thus put to hazard the existing opportunities of intercourse, by a precipitate attempt to extend them.

Napier's qualifications for undertaking these tasks remain elusive. In his 'teens he had served under Nelson at Trafalgar; but his naval service had ended in 1815, and apart from a brief spell in command of a frigate on the South American station, his chief occupation had been sheep farming. Presumably the job was reward for the support which he had given Grey in the Lords, including his vote for the Reform Bill. Or perhaps he had made an impression with one of his infrequent contributions to debates, in the spring of 1832. When Lord Ellenborough, proposing reforms in the navy's civil departments, suggested that naval officers did not necessarily make good accountants, Napier had wrathfully protested that they were 'as capable of conducting the country as any members of their Lordships' House', and in fact that they could do more in ten minutes 'than any noble Lord who has been brought up in the public offices would do in as many hours'. Whatever Grey's reasons may have been for giving Napier the chance to prove his contention, it proved to be a singularly inept choice. If he had been ordered to offend the susceptibilities and awaken the fears of the

Chinese authorities, he could hardly have done so more effectively from the start; for on reaching Macao in the frigate *Andromache*, on July 15th, 1834, he announced that he did not propose to await the Viceroy's permission, as all foreigners were expected to do, before proceeding to Canton.

The fact that Napier was an official, rather than a merchant, and that he had arrived in a warship, was immediately reported to the Viceroy, Lu K'un. Instructions went out to the Hong merchants that they had better warn him to await the Emperor's pleasure in Macao. Again, 'face' was involved; Lu would appear to have failed in his duty if Napier presented himself in Canton. And Napier did. The Hong emissaries, hurrying down to Macao by a short cut, missed him as he was on his way up the main river. It did not matter, he explained when he reached Canton on July 25th, that the Hong merchants had not reached Macao in time, as he would in any case have refused to receive them. They were merchants; he was in China on affairs of state. His powers had been given to him by the King of England. He would treat only with the Viceroy.

'Laboriously Vile'

At this point, it had to be explained to Napier that there was no way in which he could formally communicate his decision to the Viceroy except through the Hong. There was, however, one informal course which had sometimes been productive of results in the past. It involved taking a letter to the Petition Gate, in the hope that some passing mandarin would condescend to accept and forward it. The procedure might be humiliating, if a mob collected to jeer; Jardine had actually been rapped on the head, on one such occasion (the way he had behaved, as if nothing had happened, had earned him the not entirely disparaging nickname of 'the iron-headed old rat'). But Napier, having committed himself to rejection of the authorised channel, was left with no other alternative. On July 27th, the Secretary to the Superintendent was sent to the Gate, to try to effect delivery. The mandarins, though curious, would not take the missive – because, they explained, it was in the form of a letter; not, as protocol prescribed, of a petition. Recalling that he had been warned not to demean himself in such ways, Napier felt he could not make the required change.

It was an unsatisfactory issue on which to take a stand. In principle, there was little difference between the Viceroy insisting that he, as the representative of the Emperor, must be addressed only by petition, and the British Houses of Parliament imposing a similar convention. Nor was the fact that this would entail describing himself as the Viceroy's 'slave' different, in principle, from British practice. Members of the East India Company traditionally called themselves its 'servants'; and in correspondence Napier himself must frequently have called himself the 'most obedient and humble servant' of men to whom he would not have deigned to lift his hat if he met them in the street. But he was adamant. And soon, he was presented with evidence which confirmed him in his opinion that he had been right. In the edict which the Viceroy put out, instructing the foreigners that they must obey the laws of the Empire or risk all trade being stopped, Napier was described as 'the Barbarian Eye', in his official capacity; and the character used to describe him designated him as 'laboriously vile'.

It was unfortunate, for Napier, that the only translator employed by the Company should have been the Rev. Dr. Robert Morrison. He was a man of great singleness of purpose, as his earlier career had shown. Refused permission to go to China as a missionary in any of the Company's ships, he had travelled to the United States and there managed to get a letter of recommendation from the Secretary of State – James Madison, the future President – to the American acting-consul in Canton with whom Morrison worked until he could persuade the Supracargoes to accept his presence. He was alarmingly conscientious, and devoted much of his off-duty time to such enterprises as an Anglo-Chinese dictionary. But he was a pedant. Although he knew that literal translations did not necessarily convey the true sense of the Chinese he felt compelled, in dealing with official documents, to use them.

'Eye', with its rather sinister connotation of espionage, was commonly used to describe any official; and 'laboriously vile', though deliberately offensive, was in the literary convention that mandarins used, a kind of 'in' joke. Napier regarded them as an insult not just to him, but to his country. He also, which was just as misguided, came to the conclusion that the fact the Viceroy used such inflammatory language, rather than simply ordering his expulsion, could only mean that he was bluffing. 'I have been ordered off', he wrote to tell Palmerston, 'and entreated to depart; and yet with all this, and the forty thousand men, and the flaming bright laws' (Morrison's literal translation of one of the Viceroy's flowery denunciatory phrases) 'and the terrible thunderbolts, they have not yet taken me and sent me down the river'. Napier therefore proposed to set aside Palmerston's instructions not to 'put to hazard the existing opportunities for intercourse, by a precipitate attempt to extend them'; and instead, to take advantage of the instruction that he was not to undertake new negotiations with the Chinese authorities 'except under very urgent and unforeseen circumstances'. The circumstances, he claimed, were unforeseen, and very urgent.

The Viceroy has committed an outrage against the British Crown, which should be equally chastised. The whole system of government here is that of subterfuge, and shifting the blame from the shoulders of the one to the other. Act with firmness and spirit, and the Emperor will punish the Viceroy – as the mandarin did the woodcutter for Mr. Innes.

The last sentence in his despatch was revealing. When Napier had disembarked at Macao, he had declined the accommodation offered to him in the mansion traditionally used for the purpose of entertaining distinguished guests of the East India Company, saying that he would prefer to stay in a house which had been offered to him by Jardine Matheson, as he felt it would mark his recognition of the new order. In Canton, he showed himself increasingly impatient of the advice of his deputy Superintendent of Trade, Davis (Plowden had declined the appointment, and had gone home); and more disposed to listen to Jardine, who had encouraged him to believe that the Viceroy was bluffing, no doubt citing the example of his employee Innes, and the 'rockets and blue lights'. When, on August 17th Napier heard that the Hong were suspending dealings with British merchants because he had disobeyed the Viceroy's edicts, he still allowed himself to be persuaded that the bluff could be called. 'The merchants are of opinion,' he wrote in a despatch on the 21st, 'that it cannot last' And he was encouraged in his optimism by the report that *Andromache*, which had been on a cruise, had returned to the Canton estuary, along with the frigate which had come to relieve her; which was immediately followed by the news that three important mandarins who had arrived from Pekin were anxious to call on him.

Assuming that the appearance of the frigates must have been responsible, Napier determined to follow up his advantage. Before the meeting, on August 23rd, he re-arranged the chairs in defiance of Chinese protocol, in a manner calculated to upset the mandarins. When they arrived late (as Chinese protocol also dictated), he lectured them on their unpunctuality. And when they offered politely to transmit the contents of his letter to the Viceroy, he refused. 'The act of sending three great men to confer with an outside barbarian, contrary to all custom,' he boasted in his next despatch to Palmerston, 'is a strong instance of their vacillation'; so he was now preparing to take advantage of their weakness with a proclamation which would appeal direct to the merchants and shop-keepers of Canton who, he was assured, 'would be happy to trade with us on any terms'.

The Cantonese, Napier's proclamation was designed to explain, were allowing themselves to be deluded by the sinister machinations of the Hong, and the shifty evasions of the Viceroy. Although Napier had come to Canton for the most laudable purposes, the Hong had refused to convey his letters to the authorities. They had even stopped trading, which the Viceroy had only threatened to do.

The consequence is that thousands of industrious Chinese, who live by the European trade, must suffer ruin and discomfort through the perversity of their government. The merchants of Britain wish to trade with all China, on principles of mutual benefit. They will never relax their exertions till they gain a point of equal importance to both countries, and the Viceroy will find it as easy to stop the current of the Canton river, as to carry into effect the insane determination of the Hong.

On August 26th the proclamation, translated into Chinese by Morrison, was lithographed and pinned up at the street corners where the Viceroy's edicts were ordinarily to be found. And when, two days later, Napier heard that four mandarins wanted to call on him, he added a complacent footnote to his despatch in which he described the course he had taken forecasting that their negotiations would soon lead 'to an amicable adjustment of our difficulties'.

It was to be the last despatch he ever wrote. Napier, and his advisers, had utterly misjudged the Canton situation. The Pekin mandarins had come to Canton with instructions from the Emperor to investigate the situation there, but their arrival while Napier was at the Factory was coincidental, and their decision to call on him had nothing to do with the arrival of the frigates. It was to gratify a natural curiosity about the Barbarian Eye, a species not ordinarily encountered in Canton, let alone in Pekin (he happened also to be a striking example of the species; 'a tall, raw Scotsman', as Jardine Matheson's representative at Macao described him), who was behaving just as the Chinese history books taught that the barbarians traditionally behaved. The fact that the Viceroy had refrained from taking more energetic steps against Napier and the British community was a sign of weakness only in the sense that it revealed how anxious he was not to lose 'face' with the Emperor; if he could get Napier out of Canton without Draconian measures, he would be better placed to pass the whole affair off as trivial, the mistake of a silly and ignorant barbarian, but he was not bluffing. He was an administrator of long and varied experience, and it had included managing the administrative side of two campaigns against rebels, which meant he had some knowledge of both the effectiveness and the limitations of his forces, relative to those at the disposal of the British. There would be no difficulty, he realised, in bringing the British to terms, if he had to. And Napier's proclamation forced his hand; if he did not act, 'face' would be irretrievably lost. A retaliatory notice was affixed to the notice boards, denouncing the 'lawless foreign slave', Napier ('according to the laws of the nation, the Royal Warrant should be respectfully requested to behead you'). Orders were given on September 2nd that all trade with the British should cease; men employed by them were not to turn up for work; and the Factory was to be blockaded.

In one of his earlier and more conciliatory instructions to the Hong merchants, designed to be passed on to Napier, Lu had said that he heard he was a man of 'solid and expansive mind' doubtless capable of distinguishing right from wrong; 'let him, on no account, be deluded by men around him' – the Jardine faction. With the stoppage of trade, the fears of those merchants who were primarily concerned with tea, rather than with opium, were confirmed. One of them, Sir George Robinson, was later to recall how 'bitter party feeling' had then reigned, at the very time when unanimity was most needed. As Napier's second-in-command, Davis ought to have been his chief

adviser; but Napier, rejecting Davis's counsel of moderation, had despatched him before the end of August to
Macao, where he could exert no further influence on the
course of events. Instead, Napier continued to rely on
Jardine; and Jardine's advice, still consistent with the views
expressed by 'A British Merchant', was to call Lu's bluff
by ordering up the frigates. Napier agreed. On September
7th they sailed up from the estuary through 'the Bogue'
into the Canton river, exchanging some gunfire with the
forts on the banks, and losing two men killed.

Napier, by this time, had fallen ill. It was described as
'summer fever', and to judge from a letter he wrote the
following day, ostensibly to the Secretary of the Canton
Chamber of Commerce, but designed to reach the Viceroy,
it had made him light in the head. After a rambling historical survey designed to show that Viceroys in the past had
made personal contact with foreigners, and a denunciation
of Lu, Napier announced that he proposed to appeal direct
to the Emperor over the heads of Lu and his colleagues.
'His Imperial Majesty will not permit such folly, wickedness
and cruelty as they have been guilty of, since my arrival
here, to go unpunished.' And in what was intended to be
a mocking parody of the Viceroy's warnings to the Hong,
Napier could not resist adding 'Therefore tremble,
Governor Lu, intensely tremble!'

Lu would not have needed to be a psychologist to
realise, when the contents of the letter were transmitted
to him, that Napier must be growing desperate; and he

knew why. From his experience of his military campaigns Lu had learned enough to realise that the imperial forces at his command would be little use in battle. The way to deal with the frigates was simply to isolate them, where they were powerless to intervene. When they reached Whampoa, on the 11th, they heard that the river above was blocked; and that the river below was also being blocked, to confine them to a stretch where their cannon would be useless. So strong was Lu's position that he could now afford to be conciliatory; or, more probably, he felt conciliation would be the best way to get Napier out quietly, so that the line being taken in despatches to the Emperor, that it had all been a fuss about nothing, could be maintained. 'If the Barbarian Eye will speedily repent of his errors, withdraw the ships of war, and remain obedient to the old rules,' Lu promised, 'I will yet give him some indulgence.' The indulgence, the merchants who opposed the Jardine policy were told, would be that as soon as Napier left for Macao, trade would be resumed. The fever provided the necessary excuse for him to leave without undue humiliation; and his doctor took the opportunity to tell him he must. On September 19th Napier left on a Chinese boat which Lu, as an additional indulgence, had placed at his disposal.

His doctor had asked that, in view of his illness, the voyage should not be made the occasion for any public demonstrations; and the Viceroy agreed. But there was no way in which the Chinese along the banks of the river could be prevented from flocking to see the boat on its way downstream, beating their gongs and letting off their fire crackers; and the formalities of the passage, some British observers felt, were deliberately protracted to give the Chinese the opportunity, as the official report put it, of 'prolonging their insulting cruelties'. It was not until the 26th that, Napier, his fever aggravated, reached Macao; and there, a fortnight later, he died.

The triumph of Lu

Napier had managed to make almost every mistake he could have made. Yet he must be accounted trebly unlucky: in the Foreign Secretary who chose and briefed him; in the adviser, Jardine, upon whom he chose to rely in Canton; and in the adversary, Lu, he encountered there.

The chief responsibility for the debacle lay with Palmerston, for appointing the inexperienced Napier and for giving him the illusion that he was going in a diplomatic capacity. As the historian James Eames, not himself inclined to be tolerant of the Chinese, put it in *The English in China*, 'no attempt was made to understand the Chinese point of view, or to secure that the changes introduced were such as would be acceptable to the Chinese authorities'. Not that such an attempt would have had much chance of success, Eames thought; but at least the policy ought to have been tried.

That Napier should have come under Jardine's influence

revealed how unwise the government's choice had been. Napier's despatches might have been dictated by Jardine, so closely did they follow and reflect the policies set out in the merchants' petition to parliament. Justifying his resolute line in a despatch on August 21st, Napier even argued that it would not matter if the Chinese did stop trade; 'the greater part of trade is already carried on by smuggling; and I think that which remains, and cannot also be smuggled, may be allowed to rest without any loss or hardship'. But Jardine was not really his ally. As 'A British Merchant' had broadly hinted, the merchants were convinced that sooner or later there must be a confrontation with the Chinese. It consequently did not greatly matter to Jardine whether the policy he recommended succeeded or failed. If it succeeded, his advice would have been shown to be sound. If it ended in humiliation, the home government would surely feel compelled to avenge it. In Jardine's mind, Napier was expendable.

Owing to the contempt in which he and his fellow-merchants held the Chinese, however, Jardine had not foreseen that Lu would be able to outmanoeuvre them. Instead of giving way, or of taking some rash step which would have provoked a punitive expedition, Lu had behaved with exemplary patience, doing nothing which could compel the British government to intervene. Had Napier decided to make a final show of force, sacrificing the frigates in the process, there might have been a different outcome. But Napier's illness, his decision to return to Macao, and his acceptance of Chinese hospitality on his last voyage, removed any excuse there might have been for retaliation.

Napier's death spared him the final indignity of hearing what the government thought of his actions. By the time his despatches began to reach the Foreign Office, the Whigs had resigned; Peel had formed his first ministry; and Wellington was Foreign Secretary. Wellington's reply was characteristically succinct. Napier's attention was drawn to the instructions he had received from Palmerston before he sailed, 'and most particularly the 18th and 19th articles'. In the 18th, Palmerston had warned Napier to avoid conduct, language or demeanour 'which might unnecessarily irritate the feelings or revolt the opinions or prejudices of the Chinese people or government'. The 19th had impressed upon Napier the duty of conforming to the laws and usages of the Chinese empire. 'It is not by force and violence', Wellington curtly concluded, 'that His Majesty intends to establish a commercial intercourse between his subjects and China; but by the other conciliatory measures so strongly inculcated in all the instructions which you have received'.

John Francis Davis

Napier's death left Davis as Acting Chief Superintendent. By experience, he was well qualified for the post; not only had he worked for the Company in Canton for many years, but he had been given time off to learn Chinese at their expense, the first Company servant to be given that opportunity. As he showed in his book *The Chinese*, published in 1836, he had a considerable, if grudging, admiration for their civilisation; and although he felt just as strongly as the merchants that China ought to be opened up to foreign commerce, he regarded the merchants as relatively uncouth, and their tactics as execrable. As the sour comments in their Canton news sheet showed, they resented him; but after the Napier fiasco, they were in no position to dispute his contention that until further instructions were received from Palmerston, 'absolute silence and quiescence on our part seems to be the most eligible course'.

Wellington was still Foreign Secretary when Davis's first despatch arrived; and it prompted him to produce one of his characteristically terse memoranda, as a guide to future policy. What had irritated the Chinese authorities, he thought, was that Napier had gone to Canton without their permission, and had tried to get into direct communication with the Viceroy. Such a mistake must not be made again. But it did not really matter to the Chinese 'what we call our officer', or who the officer might be. He should therefore be a man of reputation, Wellington felt, with military rank, and powers to keep British subjects in order. And there should always be, within reach, 'a stout frigate and a smaller vessel of war.' This would do for the present. The government could decide at its leisure what should be done to improve commercial and political relations with the Chinese; but 'that which we require now is, not to lose the enjoyment of what we have got'.

Wellington's assumption that the Chinese would not care who was sent as Chief Superintendent, so long as he was guided by the appropriate etiquette in his dealings with them, was incorrect. Lu had done his best to disguise the fact that his authority had been flouted; but when the news reached Pekin that a British official had defied the law, and proceeded to Canton without awaiting his permission, the Emperor had stripped him of his honours and degraded him from his rank as Viceroy, though instructing him to continue to act in that capacity. By the time the Emperor's instructions reached Canton, however, Napier had been disposed of. It was safe, Lu felt, to behave as if nothing untoward had happened; and in the course of a lecture to the Hong on their duties, he reminded them that no British official would be recognised in China. The next Superintendent of Trade must be a trader.

Lu's assumption was that when the Emperor found how expeditiously he had dealt with Napier, he would be forgiven (as he was; his honours, though not his rank, were restored), and to that end he wrote a masterly apologia. Because its main aim was to set Lu's decisions and actions in the most favourable light, it was often misleading about the reasons for British decisions and actions; and it showed that for all his shrewdness, he had not realised the full significance of Jardine's intervention. The British, Lu claimed, were avaricious; they lived by and for commerce.

That was why he had known he would be able to reduce them to obedience simply by closing down their trade, rather than by resorting to force, which the Emperor himself had wisely advised against. Force would have been costly. As it was, the imperial revenue had not been reduced by 'the value of a hair, or a feather's down!' The British, Lu felt sure, had learned their lesson. They had, but not the one he assumed he had taught them. Merchants involved only in the legal trade through Canton could have eventually been reduced to submission by stopping it; but the stoppage made no great difference to the opium traffic. Bentinck's production drive had pushed up the number of chests exported to China from an average of less than 9,000 in the 1820s to 24,000 in the 1833-4 trading season; and the slight falling-off the following winter, to 21,000, could be attributed to the vagaries of the market, rather than to the Napier affair. Although Jardine Matheson enjoyed easily the biggest share in the traffic, the profits from it were naturally attracting rivals; and with the winding up of the East India Company's agency in Canton, there was nothing to stop any British subject from becoming involved as a dealer or an agent.

So far from being reduced to obedience by Lu's strategy, too, the merchants realised that they had gained one vital point. The Chinese shore defences had been tested, and found wanting. While they were sailing up through the Bogue, the British frigates had been left by a capricious breeze in the direct line of fire from the cannon in the formidable-looking forts guarding the entrance. The Chinese bombardment, though, had caused negligible damage, and had easily been silenced by the frigates' broadsides. As Maurice Collis was to observe, this was really the first clash in the first war between China and the West, but it was so one-sided that its implications were not grasped, except by the merchants. So long as British warships did not allow themselves to get trapped, their fire power would enable them to enjoy an overwhelming superiority over anything the Chinese could pit against them; for the naval junks were a joke, and the soldiers, with their antiquated muskets, hardly more formidable.

The merchants, therefore, prompted by Jardine, composed another petition to the King only two months after Napier's death, calling for the despatch of an expeditionary force to demand reparation for the insults offered to the Crown by the Viceroy, and for the insult offered to the flag by the Bogue forts firing on it; as well as compensation to the merchants for any losses they had sustained owing to the suspension of trade. The plenipotentiary who would accompany the expedition should be further authorised to blockade certain Chinese ports until the Emperor agreed to open them up to foreign traders. The first essential, therefore, was that he should be accompanied by 'a sufficient maritime force, which we are of opinion need not consist of more than two frigates and three or four armed vessels of light draft, together with a steam vessel, all fully manned'. Wellington's reply would have made interesting reading.

While the petition was on its way, however, Peel had resigned, Melbourne had formed his second administration, and Palmerston was back as Foreign Secretary in time to receive it, along with a covering letter from Davis, saying he thought the petition crude and ill-digested, and pointing out that some of the representatives of the most respectable firms had refused to sign it. Palmerston's sympathies, as he was soon to demonstrate, were with those who had signed, and he was understandably irritated at the fate of Napier's mission. But Wellington still wielded great authority. To have repudiated his policy would have been politically unwise. It would be better, Palmerston decided, to let the Napier fiasco be buried in silence – as Matheson, who was in England, for health reasons, sadly reported to Jardine. When he arrived he found Wellington, 'a cold-blooded fellow', and 'a strenuous advocate of submissiveness and servility', at the Foreign Office. The fall of Peel's government raised his hopes; but not for long. The British people were so comfortable, Matheson complained, 'so entirely satisfied in all their desires, that so long as domestic affairs, including markets, go right, they cannot really be brought to think of us outlanders'. Even Palmerston would do nothing.

Sir George Best Robinson, Bart

If Lu had been goaded into reprisals against the British merchants, Palmerston might have been more disposed to heed the outlanders. But with the resumption of trade, it quickly became clear that Davis's policy of silence and quiescence, however galling to the merchants' pride, was very satisfactory in terms of profit. Davis, though, was not there to witness the results. Rather than remain only in nominal control, without any authority to discipline the merchants, he had decided to resign; and his second-in-command, Sir George Robinson, took his place.

Robinson had been with the East India Company for many years, though not because his work had given his employers satisfaction. In 1828 he had twice earned rebukes from the Supracargoes' Committee: for failing to exercise more care in the supervision of the Company's accounts; and for applying to take home leave again only nine months after he had returned from England. He had survived, perhaps, because socially he was a cut above most of his colleagues; and he owed his elevation to the Superintendency solely to the fact that the seven members of the Company who were senior to him at the time it was wound up had all since left Canton. His only fixed determination, as his correspondence with Palmerston reveals, was to carry on Davis's policy. 'My anxious endeavours,' he wrote in the autumn of 1835, 'will be used for the maintenance of tranquillity and the prevention of disorders and difficulties of any kind'. The simplest way to effect this would be to live and work on His Majesty's cutter *Louisa*, an eighty-ton vessel, which lay in the anchorage off Lintin. He would be best placed there, he felt, to avoid trouble with the mandarins arising out of 'the insecure and doubtful position wherein we find ourselves at Canton', and also to control the activities of British subjects.

This was not a policy which commended itself to Jardine Matheson; or to Captain Charles Elliot, who had come out with Napier, and stayed on to become one of the Junior Superintendents of Trade. After peacetime service in the navy, Elliot had been appointed in 1830 as 'Protector of Slaves to British Guiana'; only to find that the post was, as he described it in a despatch, 'a delusion'. In view of the problems he was to encounter later in China, his attitude to his work was illuminating. His function, he felt, was to carry out the duties laid down in his briefing. But the system frustrated him; and when he wrote back to Whitehall, all he had in return was 'despatches full of hopes and exhortations', without any authority to deal with the problems that confronted him. As a result, he warned, the slave in British Guiana had been brought to a certain point of civilisation where 'he perceives the utter insufficiency of your System either for his further advancement or for his control. What should be given to slaves is *such a state of freedom as they are now fit for.*' Otherwise, he warned, the slaves would 'very shortly take the matter into their own hands'. It was to remain characteristic of him to foresee that the consequence of employers thinking only in terms of their property rights might be the ultimate destruction of the property.

As a nephew of a former Governor General, Lord

Minto, and a close friend of the Under Secretary for the Colonies, Lord Howick, Elliot – still in his early thirties – was able to secure permission to communicate informally from China with a friend, Lennox Conyngham, in the Foreign Office, enabling him to describe to Conyngham what was happening in Canton, Macao and Lintin without having to reveal the contents of his letters to Robinson. As it happened, however, Robinson's decision to stay in Lintin, with only occasional visits to Macao and none to Canton, gave Elliot a pretext to write despatches describing at first hand what Robinson could only hear about at second hand; and at the same time, to upbraid Robinson for a decision that was 'not only unlawful and disobedient on your part, but entirely suspends the action of the King's authority in China for all purposes of controlling the trade'.

Robinson forwarded this rebuke, written in November 1835, to the Foreign Office; along with the first of a number of despatches seeking to justify his decision, and to discredit Elliot. Elliot was insubordinate: 'in a conversation he informed me that although he appreciated my amiable disposition, he was bound to say he considered me utterly incompetent to fill the duties of my present office, and did me the honour to add, that it could hardly be expected from a person who had been all his life "measuring tea".' Elliot had also, Robinson complained, boasted about having friends in high places; and to prove it 'has now in his writing desk a copious expression of their sentiments, views, decisions and plans for the future' which he was not at liberty to disclose. But behind the mutual antipathy between the first and second Superintendents, as both realised, there was a conflict of opinion on a point of principle which only Palmerston could settle. Were the Superintendents to conceive their function as simply to facilitate trade, legal or illegal, to the best of their ability? Or were they to regard themselves as emissaries of the Crown, charged with establishing better diplomatic relations, formal or informal, with the Chinese authorities?

Robinson's defence of his policy was that it worked. Not merely did the 1835-6 trading season go by without serious interruption to the legal trade; that winter, imports of the Company's opium rose to over 26,000 chests, nearly three times as many as in 1825-6. Their value, admittedly, had only doubled in that period, from seven and a half to fifteen million dollars; but at least the aim of making up for the lower profit margin by increased output was paying off. The Company's profit from opium exports that year reached its highest level, well over seven million dollars.

Elliot, for his part, did not dispute the need to be cautious and conciliatory with the Chinese. Nevertheless he felt certain that the aim must be to secure direct communication between the Superintendents and the Canton authorities; and that could not be accomplished from Lintin. The need was to impress upon them that the British were as anxious as they were to maintain an efficient, quiet trading system: 'as soon as the Viceroy found out that we were sincere allies with them in that object, he would sedulously cultivate our friendliness'. The majority of the Canton merchants, he had to admit, disagreed with him. 'One set of gentlemen,' he wrote to tell Conyngham, 'are absolutely in a passion with the whole Chinese government and people because they are very ill-inclined to another set of gentlemen who, they imagine, are willing to conciliate the Chinese and go on smuggling quietly. I wish I could add that the moderate party were the stronger, but that is not at all the case. The ardent gentlemen have it hollow in point of numbers'. Palmerston's sympathies, as he was soon to show, lay with the ardent gentlemen. For the time being, though, Elliot's cautious but forward-looking approach appealed to him more than Robinson's. In June 1836 he decided to get rid of the Chief Superintendent by the simple and economical device of abolishing both the office and the salary attached to it. Five months later, Robinson had just settled down in the expectation of presiding over another untroubled trading season when he read in some English papers brought to Lintin that his post was rumoured to be no more; news which 'had the natural effect', he complained in a despatch, 'of paralysing my best efforts'. What he felt when, a fortnight later, it was officially intimated to him not merely that he had been dismissed, but that Elliot was to take over the superintendence of trade (without promotion or more pay), is not recorded.

Even before Robinson's departure, though, there had been the first indication that neither his policy nor Elliot's could hope to achieve their aims, because of the stresses that were building up as a result of the huge increase in the amount of opium reaching Lintin. Jardine Matheson had been quietly consolidating the coast trade they had developed to the north; but now other firms were finding themselves compelled to follow them, in the search for new markets – much to Jardine's irritation. He had even been driven to enlist his old adversaries the mandarins, with whom his agents had since managed to establish cordial relations, as allies. 'If you could manage matters so as to make the mandarins attack everyone but your own party', he instructed Captain Rees in March 1835, 'it would have a good effect'; and that winter he told Rees that he had found a mandarin who claimed he would negotiate with the Chinese Admiral in charge of the Amoy area, 'for the easy carrying on of the coast trade', so that the market would be left exclusively to Jardine Matheson's ships. Though sceptical, Jardine felt it would be worth Rees's while to encourage the scheme, if anything should come of it. The mandarins, however, were not always willing to differentiate between his ships and his competitors'. He was hurt to find that the *Lord Amherst*, chartered by a rival firm to smuggle opium, had been deliberately undercutting his prices; 'mean acts', he complained, 'for the petty consideration of selling a few additional chests'. Rees must be ready to retaliate: 'as you have more vessels than your opponents, how would it answer to place one of them alongside the *Amherst*, and run prices down as low as they may think fit to go; while you keep prices up in distant bays?'

The spread of the traffic had led to an outbreak of what Robinson described as 'scuffles,' between smugglers and mandarins; and though British subjects were not directly involved, he felt that the incidents provided him with further self-justification. 'Whenever his Majesty's government direct us to prevent British vessels engaging in the traffic', he wrote to tell Palmerston, 'we can enforce any order to that effect'. A more certain method, he suggested, would be 'to prohibit the growth of the poppy and manufacture of opium in British India'; but, in the meantime, 'if British ships are in the habit of committing irregularities and crimes, it seems doubly necessary to exercise a salutary control over them by the presence of an authority at Lintin'. As it happened, his despatch did not reach London until after his dismissal; but it was to be a source of some embarrassment to Palmerston later, when he was trying to persuade the Commons that the British government could not, even if it had wished, have controlled the opium traffic. It did not wish to, for a reason the next trade figures disclosed; exports of opium to China that year were valued at over seventeen million dollars, one million more than the value of the tea and silk purchased at Canton. The last thing Palmerston could have wanted to hear was that even the indolent Robinson felt he could cut off the traffic, if he were authorised to do so.

Captain Charles Elliot

It was essential, Palmerston had realised, to deter Robinson's successor from interfering with the country ships – the opium clippers, as they were now coming to be called, the newest of them having been custom-built: and he took the opportunity which Elliot had presented by one of his actions while he was second-in-command at Macao, to lecture him on the subject. In December 1835 Jardine Matheson had taken delivery of a paddle-steamer, the first to appear in Chinese waters: and Jardine decided that the boat, which was named after him, could best be used as a ferry between Whampoa and Canton. The Chinese authorities objected; and Elliot, hearing that the Captain had instructions to proceed to Canton anyway, issued a public letter to him enjoining him not to take it up river, for fear it should be made the pretext for a stoppage of trade: 'no government can afford, if I may so express it, to be reduced to utter contempt in the sight of its own people by a handful of heedless foreigners'. But hardly had he succeeded Robinson in the new year of 1837, than a curt note arrived from Palmerston rebuking him:

I think it necessary to recommend to you great caution in interfering in such a manner with the undertakings of British merchants. In the present state of our relations with China, it is especially incumbent

upon you, while you do all that lies in your power to avoid giving just
cause of offence to the Chinese authorities, to be at the same time very
careful not to assume a greater degree of authority over British subjects
than in fact you possess.

'Avoid giving just cause for offence', Palmerston was in effect saying 'but you may not do anything to stop the merchants giving it'. And in a later despatch, he reminded Elliot that he no longer possessed even the sanction the Company Supracargoes had formerly wielded, of refusing permission to British subjects to come up to Canton, which had amounted to the right to keep out of Canton any merchant whose conduct they disapproved of. The last time they had invoked it was to try to get rid of Innes; now, Innes had again been making mischief, threatening further reprisals for the loss of some of his merchandise, which he claimed had been stolen. Palmerston had put the case to the Crown law officers, whose advice was that though his threatened action would amount to piracy, there was nothing Elliot could do but leave him to the fate 'which such a course will bring upon him', at the hands of the Chinese; unless the commander of one of His Majesty's ships might 'fall in with him', in which case, naval law would apply. As His Majesty's ships were not permitted to proceed to Canton, where Innes's piracy was in contemplation, the contingency was remote.

In another despatch, Palmerston told Elliot it was considered inexpedient that he should either try to resume communication with the Viceroy through the Hong merchants, or couch his communications in the form of a petition. It was too late. Realising that only by observing protocol, at least in the early stages, could permission be obtained to go to Canton, Elliot had already adopted the prescribed forms. He could therefore expect to be reprimanded. Still, it would take the best part of a year before the reprimand would reach him; and in the meantime, he hoped, he would have been able to put relations between himself and the Viceroy on a more regular basis.

Even the instruction not to interfere with the merchants was not so depressing to him as it might have been; by the time it reached him there had been a development which, he hoped, would transform the trading situation. 'I have now the honour to transmit to your Lordship', he wrote in a despatch in February 1837, 'as remarkable a series of papers as has ever yet emanated from the government of this country in respect to the foreign trade'. The papers consisted of memorials which the Emperor had asked for concerning the possibility of legalising the opium traffic, and admitting the drug on payment of a duty; a case formally presented by Hsü Nai-chi, a member of the royal court who had formerly lived in Canton. The law as it stood, Hsü argued, had demonstrably failed. It was no good saying that this was because it was unenforceable. As the ban had failed to prevent the drug from entering the country, it could not be said to do any good; but demonstrably it did immense harm, breeding crime, banditry, extortion and blackmail. If opium exports were legalised, the only sufferers would be the addicts; and the community could well afford them to smoke themselves to death, as the country was already over-populated.

Elliot persuaded himself that such a view would not have been allowed expression unless there was a powerful party in Pekin favourable to the idea; and this led him to hope that legislation would shortly follow. What he had not realised (nor, presumably, had Hsü) was the effect that the revelations about the failure of the ban, and the consequent great increase in opium smoking, would have in Pekin. To those in favour of legalising the drug, it seemed reasonable to emphasise that opium was 'to smokers, their very life; and when they are seized and brought before magistrates, they will sooner suffer a severe chastisement than inform against those who sell it', because this explained why enforcement had proved impracticable. But to memorialists from the provinces, who had not experienced the problem at first hand, Hsü's arguments appeared subversive. The fact that laws did not always prevent crime, Chu Tsun – Vice President of the Board of Ceremonies – observed, was not an argument for legalising crime.

While the stream of importation of opium is not turned aside, it is impossible to attain any certainty that none within the camp do ever secretly inhale the drug. And if the camp be once contaminated by it, the harmful influence will work its way, and the habit will be contracted beyond the power of reform. When the periodical times of desire for it come around, how can the victims – their legs tottering, their hands trembling, their eyes flowing with child-like tears – be able in any way to attend to their proper exercises? How can such men form strong and powerful legions?

Already, Chu Tsun reminded the Emperor, an army sent against some rebels in 1832 had been found to contain so many opium smokers that though it was great in numbers, it was feeble in the field. The Emperor made up his mind that prohibition should continue: Hsü was degraded; and orders were issued for an intensification of the campaign to stamp out the traffic in the drug. The possibility of legalisation had sent up the price of opium; but by the spring of 1837, Jardine was reporting that all hope had vanished, and the market as a consequence was very dull.

It was very dull because measures taken by the Canton authorities to put down smuggling were at last beginning to bite. The first warning that under a determined Viceroy the law could be enforced had been given shortly before Napier's arrival, when the Canton correspondent of the *Calcutta Courier* reported that a 'smug boat' had been captured with 100 chests 'and, what is worse, many orders in Chinese for sycee and opium'. In the past such seizures had caused only momentary interruption of the traffic; but this, he warned, looking serious, whether it was caused by a genuine policy of increasing severity, or because the Viceroy 'aims at extorting a higher pecuniary compromise for the offence'. There is nothing to suggest, in Lu's case, that venality had anything to do with it: three weeks after Napier's death he issued an edict foreshadowing a renewed campaign against the smugglers, and though he died early in 1835 his successor, Teng T'ing-chen, carried on his policy, regardless of the prospect of legalisation. Elliot realised what the effect was going to be when the opium from the next lot of opium sales in Calcutta began to arrive. 'From a traffic prohibited in point of form', he wrote to warn Palmerston in February 1837:

> *but essentially countenanced, and carried on entirely by natives in native boats, it will come to be a complete smuggling trade. The opium will be conveyed to parts of the coast previously concerted in Canton, in British boats, and thence be run by the natives; thus throwing our people into immediate contact with the inhabitants on shore . . . vastly enhancing the chances of serious disputes and collision with the government officers.*

Elliot's fears were realised. That summer the campaign against the Chinese smugglers led to what he described as a vast increase in the traffic to the north-east. Where previously only two or three opium ships had been operating, 'there have not been less than twenty sail'; and he was sorry to have to add that there was every reason 'to believe blood has been spilt in the interchange of shot which has ever and anon taken place between them and the mandarin boats'. The gravest consequence, though, was in the Canton estuary and river. As the native boats had been burned, and the native smugglers scattered—

a complete and very hazardous change has been worked in the whole manner of conducting the Canton portion of the trade. The opium is now carried on (and a great of it inwards to Whampoa) in European passage boats belonging to British owners, slenderly manned with Lascar seamen, and furnished with a scanty armament, which may rather be said to provoke or to justify search, accompanied by violence, than to furnish the means of effectual defence.

For some reason, Elliot went on, the Canton officials had not yet intervened to stop this new traffic; but the continuance of their inertness could not be depended upon. 'In fact, my Lord, looking around me, and weighing the whole body of circumstances as carefully as I can, it seems to me that the moment has arrived for such active interposition on the part of H.M. government as can be properly afforded; and that it cannot be deferred without great hazard to the safety of the whole trade'.

In his despatch the previous February, though Elliot had warned what was likely to happen, he had also held out hopes that the effect might be to improve the chances of opium imports being legalised. Palmerston, therefore, had been given an excuse for inaction. He no longer had it now that the news of the 'complete and very hazardous change' had reached him, coupled with Elliot's plea for more authority. Yet a month elapsed before he replied, and then it was simply to remind Elliot that H.M. government 'cannot interfere for the purpose of enabling British subjects to violate the laws of the country to which they trade'. Elliot had not, in fact, asked him for intervention with that object. What Elliot wanted was the power to prevent the opium merchants from goading the Chinese authorities to the point where they would stop the legal trade; and this, Palmerston was not disposed to grant. He did bring in a Bill in 1838 to set up courts in China; but as it was not introduced until a few days before the end of the session, the opposition was able to take the safe line that too short a time had been left for adequate debate; and when the government's Radical allies came out against the proposal, on behalf of the merchants, Palmerston lamely withdrew it, before parliament went into recess for the rest of the year.

The Bill would have come too late to help Elliot, even if it had gone through. By that time, events had swept past the stage where courts could have achieved anything. He had continued to sound warnings; the number of British ships engaged in bringing opium from Lintin to Whampoa had greatly increased, he told Palmerston in a despatch in the spring of 1838, and their deliveries had 'frequently been accompanied by conflict of fire-arms between these vessels and government preventive craft'. The consequence had been an intensification of Teng's measures against those Chinese caught dealing in the drug; one had been publicly strangled outside the walls of Macao, as a warning. 'With the prisons full of persons charged with similar offences, and with public executions for them, it is not to be supposed that the provincial government can venture much longer to permit the delivery of opium out of British armed boats, almost under the walls of the Governor's palace at Canton'. That it was lucrative to the merchants immediately concerned there could be no doubt; 'but it is at the same time a state of circumstances which must necessarily, sooner or later, force itself under the active treatment of the Chinese government. And whenever that result does take place, it cannot fail to be extensively mischievous'.

And extensively mischievous it was. Appropriately, James Innes gave the final provocation. Early in December, on receipt of a consignment of opium, he insisted on having it unloaded openly at the wharf beside the Factory. The Viceroy had the Chinese dockers arrested, and having extracted the name of the culprit by torture, ordered Innes and the ship which he reported as having brought the opium (an American merchantman, the *Thomas Perkins*) to depart from Canton. He also suspended trade until they should leave. To show he was serious, he further ordered that a Chinese opium dealer who had been sentenced to death should be publicly executed in the square in front of the Factories. Some British sailors, objecting, broke up the proceedings; laying about them (according to the American William Hunter (who was there) with the executioner's implements. That afternoon, a Chinese mob retaliated, attacking the Factories with clubs and stones.

177

Elliot was in Macao at the time. It was futile, he had realised, to stay in Canton, where the authorities would not recognise his existence unless he accepted protocol which Palmerston was constantly reminding him to reject. But as he explained to Palmerston, in this emergency he felt that 'difficulties in points of form' ought not to deter him, and he went up to Canton to see what could be done. The Hong merchants, when he met them, 'complained in bitter terms that they should be exposed to the cruel and ruinous consequences which were arising out of this forced trade, not merely at Whampoa, but at the Factories'; as they were technically the owners, they could be held responsible for the opium which had been smuggled in to them, and could expect to suffer the punishment – the cangue – which had already been inflicted on the man who had given security for the *Thomas Perkins*. Elliot had every sympathy with them – particularly with the cangue wearer, as Innes now admitted he had lied; the opium had been smuggled not in the *Thomas Perkins* but in his own ship. The time had come, Elliot decided, with or without formal authority, to bring the traffic to an end. Calling the merchants together, he told them that all British boats engaged in smuggling must leave the river within three days; or if they refused, he would have no alternative but to put himself in communication with the Chinese authorities, 'and frankly and fully express his own views upon the necessary and perfectly admissible treatment of so serious an evil'. It would be an open invitation to the

Viceroy to use the powers which Palmerston had conceded that the Chinese enjoyed, in his despatch saying the British government would not interfere in such circumstances; a despatch which must have reached Elliot only a few days earlier. A public notice was displayed, setting out Elliot's instructions; Innes agreed to depart from Canton; and the Viceroy, mollified, allowed the legal trade to be resumed.

It had become clear earlier, Elliot explained in his despatch informing Palmerston of the action he had taken,

> *from the origin of this peculiar branch of the opium traffic, that it must grow to be more and more mischievous to every branch of the trade, and certainly to none more than to that of opium itself. As the danger and the shame of its pursuit increased, it was obvious that it would fall by rapid degrees into the hands of more and more desperate men; that it would stain the foreign character with constantly aggravating disgrace, in the sight of the whole of the better portion of this people; and lastly that it would connect itself more and more intimately with our lawful commercial intercourse, to the great peril of vast public and private interests.*

This last was precisely the trouble. It was all very well for Elliot to order out boats connected with the opium traffic; but hardly a British firm or boat had not been connected with it, and there was no certainty that all concerned would obey his injunction. If the established trade were not to be sacrificed to some chance event which would goad the Chinese government 'into some sudden and violent assertion of its own authority', Elliot pleaded, 'there is certainly no time to be lost in providing for the defined and reasonable control of Her Majesty's subjects in China'. Again, his instinct was sound. But it was already too late. His despatch was sent off on January 2nd, 1839. Two days earlier the Emperor had made up his mind that it was time to assert his authority in Canton, suddenly and if necessary violently; and he had made the necessary arrangements.

Commissioner Lin

Following his decision to maintain the ban on imports of opium, the Emperor had decided to repeat the procedure he had adopted in the debate over legislation: he invited his officials to send him memorials suggesting ways by which the ban could be more effectively enforced. Among the usual run of ideas – including harsher penalties, and a naval expedition to clear the ships from Lintin – was an unusual proposal put forward by a provincial Viceroy, calling for a more punitive policy, but insisting that it must be linked to a preventive system designed to give addicts the chance to break the habit.

Lin Tse-hsü, then in his early fifties, had already made a reputation as an energetic and incorruptible provincial Viceroy. He had also some experience of the traffic. When the *Lord Amherst* had been forced to take shelter from a typhoon on her prospecting voyage, Gutzlaff explained to the local mandarins that she was on her way from

Calcutta to Japan; but tracts which he distributed, printed in Chinese, had revealed to Lin the intention behind the voyage, leaving him sceptical of foreigners' veracity. Later, when opium began to come in from the country ships, he had carried out what he claimed was a successful purge. As he explained in his memorial, it was based on the simple principle that although involvement with opium, whether as a smuggler, or a dealer, or a consumer, merited punishment – imprisonment, flogging, and even, in certain cases, the death penalty – experience had shown that it was not the severity of the penalties which was the most effective deterrent, but the likelihood of being caught. If addicts were given no chance to reform, the traffic would continue through underground channels. If they could be persuaded to try to give up the drug they might be cured; and even if they were not, they would have been identified, so that if they relapsed they could easily be picked up. The Emperor, impressed, called Lin to Pekin for consultations; and on New Year's Eve he was appointed Imperial Commissioner for Canton, with full authority over the officials there, and with a mandate to introduce and enforce whatever regulations he might think necessary to bring the smuggling, the selling, and the smoking of opium to an end.

William Hunter went with some friends to watch Lin's arrival down the Canton river; 'a large, corpulent man, with heavy black moustache and long beard', a dignified air, and a 'rather harsh or firm expression'. Little sign of a tyrant, however, emerges from the extracts from his journal which Arthur Waley translated and quoted in *The Opium War through Chinese Eyes*. They show that Lin's outlook was humane, though of the efficient and rather calculating type expressed in the tag about its being necessary, on occasion, to be cruel to be kind.

As he had intimated in his memorials, Lin began with an appeal to the people of Canton to support him in certain preventive measures, which he had obviously worked out with considerable care. To facilitate detection of opium-smoking among the young, who were most in need of protection, schoolmasters were to report any student who to their knowledge took the drug; and also to form the students into groups of five, each being responsible for the good behaviour of the other four (Lin's reasoning being that as no group would wittingly include anybody known to smoke, it would be easier to discover who the smokers were). Members of the public who in their own interest admitted their addiction would be helped to give up the drug. This, Lin promised, they would find they could do; he had known a man in his last province who had smoked an ounce a day, for thirty years, but had managed to stop, 'and immediately his cheeks began to fill out and the strength came back to his limbs. I saw the same thing happen in case after case'. And if the people of Canton would voluntarily co-operate, Lin for his part would see that any official found using bribery, extortion or blackmail would be severely punished.

Lin also addressed the British, by way of an appeal to Queen Victoria, who had succeeded to the throne. This 'poisonous article', he reminded her, was made 'by certain devilish persons in places subject to your rule' – though not, he felt sure, with her sanction.

I am told that in your own country opium-smoking is forbidden under severe penalties. This means you are aware how harmful it is. But better than to forbid the smoking of it would be to forbid the sale of it and, better still, to forbid the production of it, which is the only way of cleansing the contamination of its source. So long as you do not take it yourselves, but continue to make it and tempt the people of China to buy it, you will be showing yourselves careful of your own lives, but careless of the lives of other people, indifferent in your greed for gain to the harm you do to others. Such conduct is repugnant to human feeling, and at variance with the Way of Heaven.

'That this is a noble letter,' Arthur Waley commented, 'no one will deny'. But it did not reach Queen Victoria (perhaps lost, he surmised, in transit overland at Suez – a method which was being used to speed up important deliveries; in which case it may yet 'one day be rescued, like so many interesting documents, from the sands of Egypt'). In any case, Lin did not propose to await an answer. On February 26th another show execution was staged in front of the factories, this time with an armed force sufficient to deter the foreigners from intervention. And three weeks later, his preparations complete, Lin informed the foreign merchants in Canton through the Hong that all stocks of opium in Chinese ports and Chinese waters must be handed over, and that they must all sign an undertaking never to trade in opium again.

I have heard that you foreigners are used to attach great importance to the word 'good faith'. If then you will really do as I, the High Commissioner, have commanded – will deliver up every particle of the opium that is already here, and will stay altogether its future introduction – as this will prove also that you are capable of feeling contrition for your offences, and of entertaining a salutary dread of punishment, the past may be left unnoticed . . . You will continue to enjoy the advantages of commercial intercourse; and as you will not lose the character of being 'good foreigners', and will be enabled to acquire profits and gain wealth by an honest trade, will you not, indeed, stand in a most honourable position?

If they refused, the legal trade would be brought to an end. Jardine had returned to England; and his firm, in any case, were less immediately involved in the Canton trade than the others, including that of his chief rival, Launcelot Dent. The Hong, Dent decided, must be angling for more 'squeeze'; he advised playing for time; and they were told that Lin would get his reply the following week. Lin's reaction was to order the closing of the custom house, bringing trade to a stand-still. If the opium were not handed over immediately, he warned the Hong, some of them would suffer with their lives. More to relieve their fears than placate Lin, the merchants decided to offer a thousand chests. Dent's firm alone, Lin claimed, had six thousand chests in store in Canton; and the Hong, presenting Dent with the information, told him they had orders to bring him to Lin. Should he refuse to come, he would be arrested. Dent was willing to go; but his fellow-merchants refused to allow him. The next day, March 24th, happened to be a Sunday; and Lin, himself punctilious in his religious observances, decided to permit the foreigners to observe it without molestation. That afternoon Elliot, on his way up from Macao in his accustomed role as conciliator, found when he reached Whampoa that all communication with Canton had been cut off. The time was past, he decided, for protocol play-acting. Providentially the sloop H.M.S. *Larne* had just reached Macao; he had come up in its gig. He put on his naval uniform, hoisted the ensign, and set off for the wharves of Canton:

> *with all possible celerity, pulling and sailing. At my nearer approach to the factories, armed boats pushed out from every side, but the admirable steadiness of the four people from the* Larne, *and a commanding favourable breeze, enabled me to baffle the attempts to obstruct me; and at about 6 p.m. I pushed into those stairs, to the great relief of my distressed countrymen, many of whom had watched the latter part of my approach with feelings of the keenest solicitude. The topmast of the flagstaff had been struck since the*

execution; but I immediately desired that the boat's ensign should be taken up and made fast to the lower mast-head, for I well knew, my Lord, that there is a sense of support in the sight of that honoured flag, fly where it will, that none can feel but men who look upon it in some such dismal strait as ours.

Elliot's gesture might not amount to a declaration of war, but it was certainly a calculated defiance of imperial commands; and Lin's immediate reaction was to impose a blockade of the Factories. The Chinese who ordinarily worked in them were ordered to stay away; the entrances were blocked with barricades guarded by armed men; and a fleet of miscellaneous craft patrolled the river to ensure that nobody entered or left without permission. If any attempt were made to evade his restrictions, Lin announced, he would obtain Pekin's permission to close the harbour to foreign trade for ever; and he reminded them that as under Chinese law they were subject to the same penalties as Chinese lawbreakers, foreigners who had sold opium were liable to suffer the death penalty.

Lin clearly was not bluffing. On March 27th Elliot told the merchants they must arrange to give up all their opium; a decision made necessary, he explained in a despatch to Palmerston, to secure the safety of the whole foreign community in the Factories. Although he had no formal authority to issue the order, British merchants were not disposed to quarrel with it, because in spite of his instructions from Palmerston that any losses incurred through violation of the Chinese laws must be borne by the violaters, he had assured them that they would receive compensation. His excuse was that Lin, not the merchants, had been to blame; for 'the first time, in our intercourse with this Empire, its government has taken the unprovoked initiative in aggressive measures against British life, liberty, and property, and against the dignity of the Crown'. With the promise of compensation, and in the knowledge that there was no prospect of selling their opium, the merchants – even those who, like Jardine Matheson, had been little concerned in the Canton smuggling – agreed with alacrity to hand over all their stocks. The arrangements were quickly made, and 20,000 chests, close on 2,500,000 lb. of opium, were duly delivered; Jardine Matheson's being by far the largest consignment, more than 7,000 chests. The opium was taken to an enclosure at Chuenpi, near the mouth of the Canton river, where Lin supervised the mixing of the drug with salt, lime and water; then, after a sacrifice to the Spirit of the Sea to warn him of the impending pollution, the mixture was flushed down into the estuary, an operation lasting several days. When it was complete, Lin magnanimously promised, the blockade of the Factories would be lifted, and trade could be resumed.

So could the literary pursuits which were Lin's delight. On May 16th, when the last load of opium was awaited, he had received a present of lychees from the Viceroy, Teng, with whom he had struck up a close friendship;

and he sent back his thanks in an impromptu verse, which
Waley translated.

> *The mists and rains of foreign seas darken Lintin*
> *Suddenly I was handed on a carven platter 'a sky of populous stars'*
> *Eighteen young damsels, each with the same smile*
> *Your kindness indeed is ever fresh as the green of the lychees*

Two days later Lin heard he had been promoted to be
Viceroy of the province which headed the imperial list in
terms of prestige; the post would be his as soon as the
opium traffic and traffickers had been disposed of.
Believing as he did that the foreigners would never dare
to risk the stoppage of trade again, he could confidently
assume that later in the summer he would be on his way
to his new provincial capital, secure in the Emperor's
favour.

5

SHAREHOLDERS' MEETING, 1839-40

Until the news reached England of the blockade of the Factories, Palmerston had shown little concern about the course events were taking in China. His only reaction to Elliot's report of the December riot, and the resulting stoppage of trade by Teng, had been to ask whether the foreigners who had intervened to try to prevent the execution were British subjects and if so, 'upon what alleged ground of right these persons considered themselves entitled to interfere with the arrangements made by the Chinese officers of justice for carrying into effect, in a Chinese town, the orders of their superior authorities'. When Elliot's despatch giving the full story of how and why he had tried to stop the smuggling through Whampoa and Canton, and adding his plea for legal powers, reached the Foreign Office in May 1839, Palmerston did not reply until a month later; and then, though he signified the government's approval of the steps Elliot was taking, said nothing about providing him with the power to enforce them. He merely reminded Elliot that he should press for an alteration in the form of petition used in his communications with the authorities, which Palmerston still objected to as humiliating.

By a wry coincidence, however, on the same day that Elliot had set out from Macao to the rescue of the Canton merchants – March 23rd, 1839 – Palmerston had sent him a despatch saying that although Her Majesty's government had felt disposed to take steps to secure redress of grievances from the Chinese government, 'it was thought expedient to abstain from doing anything with that in view, until the necessity for the interference of British government shall have become more manifest'. It began to become more manifest when, that July, reports began to appear in the London newspapers about the Chinese authorities' campaign against the opium traffic, following the appointment of Commissioner Lin. On August 1st, Lord Ellenborough, remarking that it would be 'very difficult for any man to say one word against the grounds on which the Chinese government insist on its discontinuance', asked Melbourne for further information on the subject; but Melbourne was able to side-step the question by saying that no official despatch had been received. Five days later, the 1839 parliamentary session ended, a piece of singular good fortune for the government; the first of many. Elliot's despatches describing his experiences on the way to Canton, the blockade of the Factories, the negotiations with Lin, and the decision to give up the opium reached Whitehall later in August, a time of the year when political activity was apt to be muted; and the government was given time to decide what course of action to pursue.

Melbourne and Palmerston were confronted with what amounted to a broad choice between two possible courses. They could take the line that Elliot had already prompted, and was passionately to urge in subsequent despatches, that the Chinese had to be taught a lesson; or they could repudiate him, and disown the opium merchants. But it was not simply a matter of impartially weighing whether the provocation the Chinese had received could be held to justify what Lin had done. On the side of belligerence, to which Palmerston by temperament was naturally inclined, there were also powerful commercial and fiscal pressures, which became manifest that autumn in the form of requests for his intervention to save the Indian economy from bankruptcy.

When the news of Lin's measures had reached Calcutta in April 1839, the opium merchants there, realising that huge stocks which had already reached China were unlikely to be sold, requested that the next season's sales of the Company's opium should be postponed. The Company's Council, determined as always not to sacrifice its revenue, refused. In May the Bengal Chamber of Commerce pleaded that the least the Council could do, in the circumstances, was take steps to protect the Canton merchants, who by this time were known to be blockaded in the Factories. The Council blandly replied that it had no authority to intervene. The Calcutta merchants thereupon switched their pleas to the Privy Council in London, taking care to make the point that the opium trade had been 'encouraged and promoted by the Indian government', and that this had been almost sufficient to pay the entire dividends of the Company's shareholders and the Council's expenses – a broad hint that if the opium merchants were to be let down, revenue and dividends would have to be provided by the taxpayer. In the enfeebled condition of the Indian economy, that could only mean the British taxpayer. Nor was this all. Everyone engaged in trade in India, the opium merchants pointed out, was 'more or less mixed up with the opium business, from the magnitude of the capital required in it'. If the opium shippers failed, such was the dependence of the Indian economy on their efforts that commerce in general would come tumbling down in ruins with them. And this, in turn, could have a catastrophic effect on firms in Britain which had trading interests in the east.

Jardine and Palmerston

When Jardine reached England in September 1839, around the time these communications were reaching the Foreign Office, he brought with him a letter of introduction to Palmerston from Elliot; 'this gentleman has for several years stood at the head of our commercial community and he carries with him the esteem and kind wishes of the whole foreign society, honourably acquired by a long career of private charity and public spirit'. Jardine could furnish the Foreign Office, Elliot felt, 'with much useful information'. Jardine thought so, too; and he was gratified to find that his agent John Abel Smith, who was a member of parliament, could claim to be on intimate terms with the Foreign Secretary. To judge by the cursory replies Palmerston had been making to Abel Smith's communications, this was an exaggeration; and when on September 16th Abel Smith took Jardine to keep an appointment which had been arranged at the Foreign Office, Palmerston failed to show up. But the information which arrived in the next few days from Elliot, along with a petition from the British merchants in Canton warning that Lin's new trade regulations there offered no security for life or property, led to a new appointment being made for September 27th; and this time it was kept. Although Palmerston made no direct avowal of his intentions, it was immediately clear to Jardine that he had an expeditionary force in mind, and needed the help of the firm's maps and charts to form some idea of what would be involved. 'The extent of armament, number of shipping etc', Jardine wrote to tell Matheson 'were all discussed'.

Reluctant though Melbourne notoriously was to go into such details, Palmerston realised that he must be consulted. The correspondence and memoranda relating to the opium traffic through Canton were collected and sent to him; they might seem long, Palmerston observed, 'but they are not so long as they look, and they require to be read'. Certain practical questions needed to be answered.

1. *Will the government adopt or reject the responsibility undertaken by Captain Elliot in the name of the government for the 20,000 chests of opium?*

2. *If the government rejects that responsibility, will it leave the suffering parties to their fate?*

3. *If the government adopts the responsibility, will it simply propose to parliament to make good the amount, or will the government consider the engagement taken in its name by Captain Elliot as an engagement to compel the Chinese government to make good to the parties the losses which they have sustained; founding the demand against the Chinese government upon the outrageous nature of the proceedings resorted to by the High Commissioner Lin?*

4. *Will the government, when it makes its demand for compensation to the persons whose property has been thus forcibly seized, accompany that demand by a further demand of a treaty placing the intercourse of British subjects with China on a footing of security for the future; and also by a demand of apology or reparation of some kind for the gross indignity put upon the officer of the British Crown by the whole tenor and character of these proceedings?*

5. *If such should be the determination of the government, what are the coercive measures which can most easily and effectually be put into force to compel acquiescence on the part of the Chinese?*

The way the questions were put shows that Palmerston had already pre-judged the issue. The confiscated opium was not contraband; it was 'property'. The merchants from whom it was taken were not smugglers; they were 'suffering parties'. If Melbourne agreed, Palmerston explained, preparations would be made to send an expeditionary force to China. Melbourne agreed; and on October 18th Palmerston wrote to Elliot, telling him in confidence what was in contemplation. It was impossible, the government had decided, for Britain not to resent the outrages which had been committed by the Chinese; so a naval and probably a small military force was to be despatched to deal with them. The conduct of the operations would be left to the Governor-General of India, Lord Auckland, in consultation with the appointed admiral and Elliot himself; but the general idea was to blockade the Pei-ho river (to cut off Pekin) and any other rivers thought worthy of such attention; and to occupy one of the Chusan islands, with a view to taking permanent possession of it later.

Palmerston made no secret of the fact that he had been guided by the merchants. They had made two requests, he explained; 'first, that vigorous measures shall be postponed until the commercial transactions of the present season shall be complete; that is to say, until March next' – when the weather conditions, too, could be expected to be favourable. In a memorandum on October 26th Jardine gave his opinion that two men of war, two frigates, two river steamers, and troopships to carry 7,000 soldiers, would suffice; two days later Palmerston's instructions to the Admiralty, worked out 'by persons possessed of much local knowledge', followed this recommendation. In the memorandum, Jardine suggested that the Emperor should be compelled to allow free trade through Amoy, Fuchow, Ningpo and Shanghai as well as Canton, and to insist on compensation for the merchants; proposals which Palmerston also accepted. Jardine was even able to persuade Palmerston that any debts which might be incurred by bankruptcies among the Hong merchants should be included in the compensation.

The price of blood

By the middle of November the plans for the expedition were laid; and though it was by this time too late for it to be ready for action in China the following March, there was no reason to fear that a delayed start would seriously jeopardise its prospects of success. The government, though, had still to worry about possible hostile reactions in Britain. Palmerston's intention was to present Lin's actions to the British as Elliot had presented them to him: as unprovoked aggression against British life, liberty and property, and against the dignity of the Crown. But would it be accepted that the actions were unprovoked? Already, by that winter, there were indications of a campaign to rouse public opinion against the opium traders, much as they had been aroused against the slave traders not long before.

Until reports began to appear in the London newspapers of the December events in Canton, people in Britain had scarcely been aware of the existence of the opium traffic, let alone its scale. The Chinese had made no attempt to publicise their objections to it, outside their own territories; and the East India Company had done its best to ensure that it received as little publicity as possible. As for the merchants, so anxious were they to avoid being criticised for their part in it that in his treatise *British Trade with China*, published in 1836, James Matheson had made no mention of opium, either in the text or in the detailed trade statistics which he presented in tabular form. Even in India, opium production had aroused little criticism. 'I was glad to see that the people were at work in their poppy grounds', Reginald Heber noted benevolently in his journal, while he was Bishop of Calcutta in the 1820s; 'and that the frost, to all appearance, had not extended far in this direction'. Its baneful effects on some of those who became addicted had occasionally excited concern, as when Raffles denounced it for its effects in Java; but the fact that exports were channelled to China meant that most of the product from India disappeared without trace. When in 1836 Archdeacon Dealtry of Calcutta was sent a commentary on the effects of Indian opium on the Chinese, he was wholly unaware – as he ruefully admitted in a foreword when it was published as a pamphlet – that the traffic existed.

Opium, the writer (he did not disclose his identity)

pointed out, was capable of enslaving addicts even more completely than alcohol, creating intense agonies of mind – 'fiction can paint nothing of horror half so horrible'. This had never been denied by its manufacturers, the East India Company. All that the Company had done was plead justification on the grounds of financial necessity. But since 1834 the Company could no longer be regarded as just the Company. It was also the government of India, responsible to the British people. 'How long', the writer asked, *is a British government to be seen drawing revenue from this source,* admitting the misery and excusing itself for abetting it by a fallacy the most contemptible and insulting even to commonsense? *How long is a whole community of British merchants to be content with* earning the price of blood, because if they do not, others will in their stead?

A copy of the pamphlet found its way to Canton, where it was reprinted in the November issue of the *Chinese Repository*. The *Repository* had already included, the previous month, a letter from 'A Resident in China', observing that those who clamoured for free trade should realise it was the opium smugglers who gave the Chinese government the strongest justification for rejecting it, and for restricting foreigners to Canton. 'It is this trade which throws such deep discredit on our character, and such suspicion on our intercourse.' The reprinting of the Calcutta pamphlet confirmed that the missionaries in China were at last becoming seriously alarmed. The editors of the *Repository*, though, were in a difficult situation. It was the British and American merchants, most of them by this time dealers in opium, who subsidised the magazine, and constituted its main body of subscribers. The following month they resorted to the tactic editors commonly employed in such circumstances; space was given for a reply. Addiction, 'A Reader' argued, could not present a very serious problem, in view of the fact that the opium, distributed among the entire population of China, could at the very most enslave only one in every three hundred Chinese – and that was making no allowance for casual smokers, or people who needed the drug medicinally. If the traffic in opium were to be stopped, why not also the traffic in alcohol? In any case, it could not be stopped. If the merchants were prevented from carrying opium, this would simply mean 'throwing its supply into the hands of desperadoes, pirates and marauders, instead of a body of capitalists, not participating, certainly, in what they carry, but in fact supplying an important branch of the Indian revenue safely and peaceably'.

This attempted justification of the traffic, the first of many, was to provide the *Repository* with a running controversy for months. 'A Reader' was challenged on various grounds. Opium smoking, it was pointed out to him, was largely confined to the coastal provinces, so that the proportion of addicts in them was much higher. In any case, if the traffic was ethically wrong, it was ethically wrong whatever the proportion of addicts might be. The alcohol parallel was dismissed as irrelevant; the missionaries had found, as Wells Williams was later to recall in his *The Middle Kingdom*, that drink was not a Chinese problem, consumption being small and usually confined to ceremonial occasions. It was the third contention, though, which chiefly infuriated the critics of 'A Reader', perhaps because it was at first sight so plausible. The hypocrisy of claiming that the merchants were 'not participating' in what they carried excited less anger than his 'if we don't, others will' attitude; it was likened by 'Another Reader', in the next *Repository*, to a hired bravo saying, 'I do not see that I am doing any harm; if I did not take the profit someone else, not so thin-skinned, would'. This, 'Another Reader' felt, might be pronounced 'the most mischievous, false and dangerous principle to morality that has ever been invented'. Did 'A Reader' really believe that the Chinese would care 'whether they were poisoned by desperadoes or genteel capitalists'? And what would the ordinary Englishman think—

if it became fashionable to consume some poison – arsenic, say – in England; and when it was prohibited, Chinese ships were stationed in St. George's Channel, with occasional trips to the Isle of Wight or the Thames, with mandarins saying 'Hai yu, my friend . . . do you not see that the barbarians are passionately fond of arsenic, and that they will have it – that they go so far as to pay for it; and can you for a moment doubt that it would not be much worse for them if, instead of my bringing it, it were left to the uncertain supply which low 'men of no capital' could afford to bring?

The protests in the *Repository*, cogent though they might be, could not be expected to make converts in Canton; nor were they likely to be read in those circles in Britain where they might have been influential in awakening public opinion. There had been occasional intimation of uneasiness about the growth of the traffic: in the summer of 1836 John Barrow had noted in the *Quarterly* magazine that the value of tea exported from China, and of opium imported into it, appeared to be linked, commenting, 'it is a curious circumstance that we grow poppy in our Indian territories to poison the people of China, in return for a wholesome beverage which they prepare almost exclusively for us'; and the following year a former missionary, George Tradescant Lay, had denounced the sale of a commodity which 'as merchandise, blasts and withers every kind of dealing that is mixed up with it'; but such criticisms had attracted little notice. Eventually, however, the traffic came to the attention of a clergyman in London, the Rev. A. S. Thelwall, Secretary to the Trinitarian Bible Society. Thelwall had never been to the East and, like Archdeacon Dealtry, he had had no idea what had been happening there. The British public, he decided, must be aroused to the enormity of the crime being committed in their name; and in *The Iniquities of the Opium Trade with China*, published in 1839, he set out to bring their responsibility home to them.

It was not in dispute, Thelwall argued, that opium was a deleterious drug. Yet it was being manufactured in India for the express purpose of inflicting it upon the Chinese.

'The great object of the Bengal opium agencies', (he quoted what D. Butter, who combined the jobs of surgeon and opium examiner to the Benares agency of the Company, had written in the *Journal of the Bengal Asiatic Society*) 'is to furnish an article suitable to the peculiar tastes of the peoples of China'. To swell the Company's profits there had been a huge increase in production for that purpose; and vast sums had been expended to expedite its transit by corrupting Chinese officials. What was happening, Thelwall felt, could only be described as murder; and 'he who stands unconcerned when murder is committed, and (still more) he who shelters the murderer, and facilitates his escape, according to all law, divine and human, is justly deemed an accomplice in the crime'.

Thelwall's arguments were reinforced in another treatise published in the same year, *Report on the Tea Plantations of Assam*, written by a former plantation superintendent, C. A. Bruce, and describing how opium was also having a devastating effect in a territory for which Britain was responsible. When it had been found that the climate of Assam was suitable for tea plantations, cheap labour had been brought in to work on them; the coolies had introduced the drug; and the result had been the spread of opium mania: 'that dreadful plague', Bruce described it, 'which has depopulated this beautiful country, turned it into a land of wild beasts, with which it is overrun, and has degenerated the Assamese from a fine race of people to the most abject, servile, crafty and demoralised race in

India'. Once in opium's grip, there was nothing the native would not do to secure supplies; 'he will steal, sell his property, his children, the mother of his children; and finally, even commit murder'.

Laissez-faire

In ordinary circumstances such revelations should have provided the Tory opposition under Peel with just the opportunity they were looking for to attract waverers from the Whig benches, and finally to push Melbourne out of office. His government had often seemed to be tottering, since he had returned to power; and only the Queen's aversion to Peel had saved it at the time of the Bedchamber Crisis, a few months before. Palmerston's rashness at the Foreign Office had contributed to its chronic instability; and his China policy had brought little but humiliation. First he had sent out Napier with insufficient support to carry out his instructions; now, he had left Elliot in the same predicament. When parliament reassembled in 1840, it would be possible to attack him both for his failure to provide adequate protection for British subjects, and for his refusal to recognise that his government and his country were compromised by their identification with the contraband traffic in a dangerous drug.

The Tories, though, had to be mindful of the fact that the majority of the potential waverers on the government benches were Radicals. This presented a problem, as in the political spectrum they lay on the opposite wing; it had been largely due to their tireless propaganda that the Tories had been defeated over the Reform Bill. Yet though they had secured increased representation in the Commons (the diarist Charles Greville estimated that there were over sixty of them) they had not been able to use their strength effectively to dictate to their Whig allies; and from time to time enough of them had defected, in disgust at Melbourne's trimming, to bring about government defeats. Another such defeat on a major issue would surely mean Melbourne's resignation. The Tories' first need, if they were to make an issue of China, would be to make it in such a way that the Radicals would not be offended.

In practice, this meant that the Tories would have to be wary about criticising the Canton merchants. On economic issues, the Radicals' gospel was free trade, as advocated in the *The Wealth of Nations* and Ricardo's *Principles of Political Economy*; a point which had not escaped James Matheson when he was in England trying to get support for the British opium merchants in Canton. In his *British Trade with China*, Matheson had ingeniously contrived to prove that they were asking for no more than the chance to introduce commercial practices based on the teachings of Adam Smith and Ricardo; accepted in all other parts of the civilised world, but rejected by the Chinese. Matheson's thesis was simple. Britain had an abundance of goods for sale (over-production had just resulted in another slump). The Chinese people needed them. But the Chinese, as he had found in seventeen years' experience, were 'characterised by a marvellous degree of imbecility, avarice, conceit and obstinacy'. Their government did not realise what was good for them; it had rejected free trade. And it was not enough, Matheson claimed, to say they had a right to reject it, if they wanted to; as Emerich de Vattel had said, a government had no right to stop its subjects enjoying free trade's benefits.

The name of Vattel, a Swiss writer on international law, is not now familiar. Nor, in all probability, would his seventy-year-old work have come to Matheson's notice then, had not some English admirer published a new translation in 1834. All men, Vattel had argued, have a right to provide for their needs on earth. But all men do not have equal opportunities to make such provision, because some countries are supplied with some of the necessities of life; others, with different necessities. Free trade is consequently essential, to secure a fair distribution.

> Men, therefore, are under an obligation to carry on that commerce with each other, if they wish not to depart from the views of nature. And this obligation extends also to whole nations, or states . . . If trade and barter take place, every nation, on the certainty of procuring what it wants, will employ its land and its industry in the most advantageous manner, and mankind in general prove gainers by it. Such are the foundations of the general obligation incumbent on nations reciprocally to cultivate commerce.

Even Vattel had not gone so far as to suggest that a state had no right to refuse the goods of other nations. Matheson, however, insisted that as China had accepted British goods through Canton, she had forfeited the right to refuse them through other ports. It would therefore be legitimate for the British government to use force to compel China to open up other ports to foreign merchants; and also to compel her to cede an island (he suggested Chusan, as being strategically placed to gain the maximum benefits from the new markets).

Jardine took up the cause on his return to England, with the help of a fund of $20,000 (one dollar for each confiscated chest of opium) which the Canton merchants voted to put at his disposal. More would be available if he needed it, Matheson wrote from China to assure him in the spring of 1839; 'you may find it expedient to secure, at a high price, the services of some leading newspaper to advocate the cause. The best legal advice will of course be engaged at the outset to make the most of the strong points of our case, and we are told there are literary men whom it is usual to employ for drawing up the requisite memorials in the most concise and clear shape'. The literary and legal side would take a little time to arrange, but petitions to parliament could quickly be presented; they began pouring in that autumn from Manchester, Leeds and the other industrial towns of the north; from the ports concerned in the legal trade with the East, Liverpool, and Bristol; and from London. Though the petitions varied, the gist of them was that the Canton merchants must be compensated for their loss, and the Chinese authorities compelled to allow foreign trade on a secure, sound and permanent basis.

Early in the new year of 1840 what appears to have been the first product of Matheson's literary and legal enterprise appeared in the form of a treatise, *The Opium Question*, by Samuel Warren; a shrewd choice, as Warren combined legal training with a considerable literary talent that was soon to make him a reputation as a popular writer. He did not waste time trying to defend the morality of the opium traffic. Regardless of the rights and wrongs of dealing in a drug, he argued, the merchants could not be held accountable. The responsibility lay exclusively with the British government. The evidence provided by the enquiry into the East India Company's affairs, and the decisions based on it, showed that the government knew and approved of the Company's decision to abandon restrictions on opium production, and go all out for maximum sales in China. The pretence that when the opium left India, the Company was no longer concerned what happened to it, was belied in the Company's own books; they showed that of the chests leaving Calcutta in the 1830s, over 80 per cent received clearances expressly for China. This had been deliberate government, as well as Company policy, because of the need to pay for Britain's tea. It was therefore absurd, Warren went on, to blame the merchants for what had happened. 'Do we venture to call them smugglers?', he asked. 'Are they not some of our most eminent British merchants – men whose names would command respect and confidence in Great Britain and in India – in short, in every quarter of the world where commercial enterprise, honour, and good faith are known?' Were these the men who were to be branded with so ignominious a name? No! They were in precisely the same position as the Elizabethans who had been sent out to trade with South America, at the time when the Spaniards and the Portuguese were trying to keep trade there to themselves. 'In the name of the dear glory and honour of old England'; Warren concluded in an impassioned postscript, 'where are the counsels which will hesitate for a moment in cleansing them, even if it be in blood, from the stains with which barbarian insolence has so deeply tarnished them? Why are not thousands of our bayonets bristling at this moment, on the shores of China?'

Warren's tract came in for ridicule from the small but vociferous group of pamphleteers who were keeping up the campaign begun by Thelwall the year before. Sydney S. Bell, for one, observed that the quality of an act cannot be altered by the station of the person who perpetrates it; 'if Mr. Warren's clients, though eminent British merchants, will stoop for profit to do what they are afraid to be detected in doing, they can be eminent only for their wealth'. But the humanitarians were not Warren's real concern. His aim, it quickly became clear, was to exert pressure on the government. When the news of Elliot's

208

compensation pledge had reached London, the Treasury's instinctive reaction had been to repudiate it, and Palmerston's reply to the requests for it which came in that autumn was that the government had no funds at its disposal out of which compensation could be paid, and no intention of asking parliament to provide them. Privately, Palmerston assured Abel Smith that the Chinese would be compelled to pay. But this was not something which the government could afford to disclose, or it would give the humanitarians additional ammunition: and the floating humanitarian vote in the Commons had to be taken into consideration, too. In all likelihood, therefore, the government would have to put up with denunciations by Radicals, quoting Warren, without being able to pacify them by agreeing to honour Elliot's pledge.

To the Tories, the prospect of the government in trouble with its Radical allies was a good excuse to lie low. In the Queen's Speech at the opening of parliament, the line taken on China in any case offered them little scope: 'I have given, and shall continue to give, the most serious consideration to a matter so deeply affecting the interests of my subjects and the dignity of my Crown'. They allowed a month to go by before Sir James Graham, who had left Grey's government to become a back-bencher, and then crossed the floor of the House to become Peel's right-hand man, asked Palmerston for information. The relevant papers, Palmerston replied, were being collected and would be laid before the House; an assured way of putting off a debate, at least for a few days. And by a further stroke of good luck for the government, by the time the papers were ready the news from China had relieved ministers of any uncertainty they might still have felt about the wisdom of despatching the expedition. British lives and property had again been menaced; and the navy had had to go into action to protect them.

The Battle of Chuenpi

With the handing over of the opium, Lin had been able to savour the satisfaction of having successfully carried out a project which he had outlined in his memorials to the Emperor. Not merely had the foreigners been compelled to give way; the Cantonese smokers had been responsive to his offer of an amnesty. In the first four months of the campaign, 70,000 opium pipes were handed in and destroyed. In the circumstances, Lin felt, he could afford to be on more friendly terms with the foreigners, at least with those who had not been connected with the traffic. Earlier, he had refused to make any distinction; but when the opium was handed over, the blockade was lifted, and he invited two Americans, the missionary Elijah Bridgman and a young merchant, Charles King, to be eye-witnesses of the destruction of the confiscated stocks. They found him 'bland and vivacious, without a trace of the fanatic's sternness'. It was not enough, he urged them, simply to refrain from engaging in smuggling; they must

210

'persuade the foreigners of every country to devote themselves from now onward to legitimate trade' – a homily
to which they listened, he reported to the Emperor on
July 5th, 1839, 'attentively and respectfully'. It was the last
attention and respect that Lin was to secure from the
foreigners. A week later, he noted casually in his diary
some sailors from a foreign ship had 'beaten up some
Chinese peasants and killed one of them'. His reference
to the weather that day, 'sudden changes from fine to rain',
might have been a portent; what happened as a consequence was to precipitate the collapse of his authority.

The chief mischief of Lin's proceedings, Elliot had
warned Palmerston in a despatch on April 9th, 'is the evil
feeling of revenge they will unquestionably produce in the
minds of the class of men otherwise disposed to engage
in the traffic for the mere love of gain; they will seem to
justify, in the consciences of such persons, every species
of retaliation'. As soon as the blockade had been lifted,
Elliot had ordered all British ships and merchants to leave
Canton and Whampoa, the ships to put themselves under
the protection of the *Larne* in the Hong Kong anchorage:
depriving Lin of the hostages he would otherwise have
held, in the event of hostilities, and also, Elliot hoped,
keeping the British crews out of mischief. But it had not
been long before the captain of one of the English
merchant ships, who had been celebrating the Queen's
birthday, decided it would be amusing to open fire on a
Chinese vessel moored nearby; his aim, however, was

erratic and only one of nine cannon balls hit the target, doing no damage, and provoking no reprisals. The affray which Lin had been told about had arisen when some drunken sailors from two of the ships lying off Kowloon (one Jardine Matheson's; the other, Dent's) went ashore and threw stones at a temple; in a scuffle, one of the locals who tried to intervene was killed. Lavish compensation was promised, in return for an admission that the death had been accidental; but when the episode was reported to Lin, he decided it was time the British were punished. If they would not hand over the murderer, he decided, they must be starved out; cut off from all supplies of food and of water, if necessary by poisoning all the wells. 'No doubt they have on their ships a certain stock of dried provisions', he remarked complacently in a letter to the Emperor early in September; 'but they will very soon find themselves without the heavy greasy meat dishes for which they have such a passion. Moreover the mere fact that they will be prevented from going ashore and getting fresh water is enough by itself to give power of life and death over them'.

Whatever justification there might be for Lin's plans, they could work only if he did have power of life and death over the British; and he had it no longer. Well-read and intelligent though he was, he shared the complacent ignorance of his class about the West. He was under the impression that the British would be unable to fight on land as 'they do not know how to use fists and swords.

Also, their legs are firmly bound with cloth and in consequence it is very inconvenient for them to stretch'; and he believed that British warships, though effective in the open sea, would be useless in coastal waters. Here, it was not just ignorance that was the problem; 'face' was involved. The inability of the Chinese naval junks to deal with the opium clippers, and the ease with which the British frigates had disposed of the forts at the mouth of the Bogue when they went to rescue Napier, ought to have given warning how little protection could be expected from the available defences. But successive Viceroys, in self-protection, had learned how to convert defeats into victories, and Lin did not realise the weakness of the Chinese naval force. On the day he had written to the Emperor boasting about the prospects of starving out the British, H.M.S. *Volage*, a twenty-eight-gun frigate, had reached the Kowloon anchorage, sent from India in response to Elliot's appeal, and bringing the news that another frigate, *Hyacinth*, was on its way. It was now Elliot who held the power of life and death. On September 4th, hearing that the mandarins were refusing to sell provisions (in spite of impassioned appeals by Gutzlaff, in employment again as interpreter) Elliot gave the order for an attack on the war junks which Lin had ordered to Kowloon to enforce his blockade; and the junks were easily routed.

Until this point, Lin had appeared to be in entire command of the situation. Suddenly it was lost to him. The success of his strategy had concealed the fact that he had made a succession of tactical errors, not noticeable at the time, but storing up trouble: beginning with the demand that Dent should appear before him. Legally Lin had been entirely within his rights; but recollection of the fate of the *Lady Hughes'* gunner had frightened the British merchants, enabling Elliot, on his arrival, immediately to impose his authority over them.

Lin's second mistake, ironically, had been the destruction of the opium. He could have made no move better calculated to serve the opium smugglers' interests. If the opium had remained in their depots, they would have had to face the daunting prospect of the product of the next season's harvest arriving with their old stock still unsold. By Elliot's computation, as well as the 20,000 chests delivered up to Lin there had been almost as many awaiting export in Calcutta, and nearly 12,000 in Bombay; double the number which had ever been sold in a year through the normal channels. The merchants were in no doubt that they faced catastrophe. So glad were they to get rid of their opium, in fact, with the promise of compensation, that some of them had actually declared opium which had not reached them, but which was due to arrive at Lintin. The merchants' chief worry was that Lin, or his subordinates, attracted by the profit that could be made from the confiscated opium, might only pretend to destroy it; in which case its sale would ruin the prospects for the new Indian poppy crop. But by inviting Bridgman and King, whose accounts of the disposal of the opium were published in the merchants' papers, Lin did much to banish these fears.

It would have been difficult for Lin to find any other way of getting rid of the opium; but his next tactical error was one which he could easily have averted. His assumption had been that the British merchants, grateful for his decision to allow a resumption of trade, would return to Canton and take care not to offend again. He shared the prevailing mandarin belief that the British could not do without their imports from China, for health reasons. As Viceroy Teng had observed in one of his warning edicts, if the decision was taken to stop trade 'it will no longer be a question whether opium is bought or sold, but even the teas and the rhubarb of the inner land will be withheld from exportation. Thus are the lives of all you foreigners held within our grasp'. Holding this belief, Lin and Teng had unwisely allowed the 1838-9 trading season to be all but completed before imposing the blockade (Elliot had noted with relief that it was near completion even before the Chinese New Year; the celebrations every February were apt to be protracted). But it was to prove far more unwise of Lin to let all the British merchants and their ships depart from the Canton river, on the assumption they would soon be forced to return. Realising that their compensation might depend on their obedience to Elliot's orders, even though he had no authority to make them, they were prepared to obey him except, predictably, James Innes. In Macao, Innes had embarrassed the Portuguese authorities, by this time terrified of Lin, by allowing himself to be caught with a consignment of opium. When Elliot told him to leave he flatly refused: 'I give you distinctly to understand', he replied to Elliot, 'that looking on your Order as illegal, I shall land and stay in China whenever I consider it prudent to do so, without any reference to you'.

In August, however, Innes and all the other British subjects in Macao, including such political innocents as Chinnery, were told by the Portuguese Governor they must leave immediately. Incensed by Elliot's refusal to hand over the culprits responsible for the Kowloon murder, Lin was about to descend on the town; and the Governor did not feel that he could guarantee the safety of any Britons who might still be there. It proved to be a wise precaution; the correspondence between Elliot and Lin, which was maintained throughout that summer, reveals an almost paranoid determination on Lin's part to obtain retribution. And it was to prove fatal to his prospects of persuading the British merchants engaged in the legal trade to defy Elliot, and return to Canton.

By a curious twist, it was these legitimate traders, rather than the opium ship owners, who were threatening to undermine Elliot's authority. If Lin was prepared to allow them to resume trade, they argued, who was Elliot to interfere? After taking legal advice Marjoribanks, who had so often had trouble with merchants refusing to accept his authority when he was President of the Supracargoes'

Committee, now refused to accept Elliot's; the captain of his ship the *Thomas Coutts* was ordered to take it up to Canton. If other captains took it into their heads similarly to defy his authority, Elliot realised, Lin would again have the chance to take British ships and British subjects as hostages; and he instructed Captain Smith of the *Volage* to prevent British ships from entering the Bogue. It was an order which Palmerston was to repudiate. A blockade of this kind, he reminded Elliot, was a measure of war, which could be resorted to only by a belligerent. But long before Palmerston had even heard about Elliot's order, it had been carried out. Sailing up to the mouth of the Canton river to attempt to enforce Elliot's instructions, Captain Smith found a fleet of war junks Lin had assembled (by one of those casual ironies with which the story is littered, they were off Chuenpi, where the opium had been destroyed) to try to compel the British to hand over the Kowloon murderer. It was just the excuse needed for a pre-emptive strike; and on November 3rd *Volage* and *Hyacinth* went into action with their greatly superior fire power, destroying many of the junks and scattering the remainder.

The Kowloon action could be put down to desperation; the Battle of Chuenpi was a full-scale, though small, naval action, meticulously executed. In effect, it was a declaration of war. Irrespective of what had already been decided in London, it would certainly be regarded there as establishing that a state of conflict existed. By the time the news reached England, the following March, the expeditionary force was already on its way; but the news of the battle of Chuenpi would make it easier for ministers to defend their decision to despatch it.

'They will go!'

The papers relating to the trade with China were tabled on March 5th 1840, in the form of a Blue Book. It contained the despatches, letters, enclosures and memoranda which had passed between the Superintendents of Trade and the Foreign Office, from Napier's appointment to the first of the naval actions, off Kowloon; and it is difficult to escape the conclusion that a great deal of the material in the 455 closely packed foolscap-size pages was included chiefly because it would help to confuse the government's critics, a process made simpler by the admitted difficulty of keeping the material in its chronological order. For a question from Canton to receive an answer from London still took anything up to a year, during which time a mass of other material had been accumulated, so it was not easy to impose continuity. Nevertheless some attempt could have been made to provide either an index, or indications of the 'See page 20' variety, when one letter referred to another. Palmerston, as usual, had a ready explanation. It had been the Tories' fault, he explained, for demanding to have the papers ready so quickly. Simply to get them printed had been a

formidable task, necessitating such a mountain of type
that one of the Foreign Office floors had collapsed under
its weight.

On March 18th opposition leaders met in Peel's London
home to decide what line they should take in the debate
on China. There was no doubt what line they would have
liked to take: most of them despised the merchant class,
and particularly the *nouveaux riches* 'Nabobs' (an attitude
reflected in Disraeli's *Sybil*, published in 1837: Lord
Egremont derided 'a dreadful man, richer than Croesus,
one McDrug, fresh from Canton with a million of opium
in each pocket, denouncing corruption and bellowing free
trade' – a barely disguised reference to Matheson). But if
there was to be any hope of persuading the Radicals to
vote against the government, it was essential not to let
this prejudice show. And things had gone too far,
Wellington argued, for any peaceful solution. Some military
and naval demonstration there would have to be, to rees-
tablish Britain's authority. The only issue on which it would
be safe to attack the government was the government's
earlier mishandling of the situation, which had placed
British lives in jeopardy, and British property at forfeit.
This, they could easily show, was because Palmerston had
failed to define Elliot's functions and powers. They could
hardly complain that Elliot had not been given greater
powers, because Palmerston would then remind him that
they had shown no great enthusiasm for his proposal to
invest the Superintendents with some modest judicial

authority. But they could show that Palmerston's instructions had been inadequate, confused, and even contradictory. As much of the Radicals' irritation with the Melbourne government had been about its indecisiveness, this line of attack should provide the best, and safest, material for a motion of censure. The prospect looked promising; the young William Ewart Gladstone, who was present, noted in his diary that the optimism bred by Wellington's plan infected even Wellington himself. 'God!' he exclaimed, 'if it is carried, they will go!'

The following day, in reply to a question in the Commons from Abel Smith about the warlike preparations which had been observed in India, Lord John Russell made the first public announcement that a punitive expedition was on its way to China; and indemnification for loss of property, he admitted, was one of its objects. This might have satisfied Abel Smith, as he was now in Palmerston's confidence; but it was not enough for Sir George Staunton, who the following week demanded that in advance of whatever happened as a consequence of the expedition, the government should agree to pay the merchants full compensation. He himself detested the opium traffic, he explained, and hoped that it would be stopped; but it had been 'sanctioned and protected and authorised by the representatives of the British nation. There was at least so much of sanction, that it could not be regarded as a smuggling transaction'. And when Palmerston replied that the British government had no legal power to stop it, Staunton was able to quote Elliot's pledge to Lin, which the merchants themselves had accepted, that it would be stopped; 'if he had power to prohibit it then, he might have prohibited it before'.

Staunton was by this time a notorious bore, but he was the doyen of the old China hands at Westminster, and the government could not afford to alienate him. Nor, though, could Palmerston afford to accept government responsibility, which the Treasury would condemn as too dangerous a precedent. The simplest way out was one which the Whigs had frequently used during their period in office in the 1830s: a select committee of enquiry to examine the merchants' grievances. As it would not meet until after the Commons debate on China, any M.P. who brought up the subject of compensation could be told to await the Committee's findings. But to reassure the mercantile interest and the Radicals, when its composition was announced fifteen of the twenty-one members were found to be government supporters, and the chairman was to be Abel Smith.

Facts and Evidence

By this time members of parliament could not complain, as they might have done a few weeks earlier, that they were insufficiently briefed. Apart from the Blue Book, pamphlets and tracts had been appearing, two of them obviously the product of the Canton merchants' lobby fund; one published in London, by H. Hamilton Lindsay, a former Chairman of the Canton Chamber of Commerce; another, by Alexander Graham, published in Glasgow. Both followed up and elaborated the arguments put forward earlier by Matheson and Warren. And at the end of March the case against the opium traffic was also put, for the first time in detail, in *Facts and Evidence Relating to the Opium Trade with China*, written by the respected Quaker, William Storrs Fry, and containing a mass of evidence from sources in India as well as China.

Fry asked his readers to imagine what would happen if French wines were banned in Britain and the French government, holding a wine monopoly, had proceeded deliberately to make wines suited to the British taste; established depot ships off the English coast; corrupted the English customs service by bribery; when warned, taken no notice; and when intercepted, employed armed craft to fight their way through with the contraband wine. Would this not inevitably have led to war? Yet wine was considered harmless, even wholesome; while 'the opium which is introduced by English merchants, under the sanction of the British Indian government – yes, and for the emolument of that government which monopolises the preparation and sale of it – IS A POISONOUS DRUG'.

The opium traffic was not coming to an end, Fry insisted, even though all the Canton merchants had signed papers pledging themselves that they would bring in no more. He had heard from a correspondent in Macao that in spite of this promise, 'vessels armed to the teeth are employed along the coast, and actually forcing it into the country'. The smugglers had even acquired a new base, the island of Hong Kong, which they were using as their depot. They were not hesitating to attack junks sent against them; another correspondent had described to him how the *Sir Edward Ryan*, 'fully armed and manned by a set of desperate fellows' had been despatched to 'burn and destroy everything that comes in the way of disposing of their opium'.

Fry also took up the line of criticism which Buckingham had put forward in the Commons in the debates on the Company's Charter, and which had been the theme of a tract *Appeal from the Inhabitants of India to the Justice of the People of England* written by one of the Company's ablest servants, John Crawfurd, and published in 1839. The Indian government, Crawfurd claimed, 'under colour of law, is at present engaged in carrying into effect a more comprehensive system of disturbance and real spoliation than there is any example of in our history since we became civilised people', the poppy cultivators being the hardest hit, because, as the holders of the best land, they could have profited most if the government had permitted them to enjoy anything more than subsistence. The need for more opium to send to China, too, had led to the development of ingenious new devices to persuade the peasant to cultivate poppy. If one of them refused a proffered advance to pay for seed and labour (a writer in the *Chinese*

Repository had alleged) 'the simplest plan of throwing the rupees into his house is adopted; should he attempt to abscond, the peons seize him, tie the advance up in his clothes, and push him into his house. The business now being settled, and there being no remedy, he applies himself as he may to the fulfilment of his contract'. The peasants had no protection, Fry explained, because the government allowed its opium agents a free hand. They could enter property at any time, ostensibly to look for contraband opium, but often for purposes of harassment and extortion. The agents were also able to use their powers to interrupt legal trade, as Andrew Sym, a former opium agent employed by the Company had complained. In order to ensure that opium was sold only to the Company, he had told Fry, search procedures had been adopted which led to:

> *grievous delay; the insolent exercise of low, ill-paid authority; the interruptions of communication by shutting up ferries, roads, and routes; the distress and ruin resulting from false seizures and confiscations (got up by the Custom House people to blind the government); the diversion of trade into channels less impeded; the advancement of the price of all goods, by reason of these checks and annoyances; and, first of all, the demoralisation of the habits of all parties connected with, or exposed to the influence of, these oppressive and unjust measures.*

The China Debate

Powerful though Fry's case was, it was little use to the Tories. Not merely were they anxious not to offend the Radicals; they were also aware that if they succeeded in toppling the government, they would be compelled to clear up the mess without funds to do it, unless the Chinese paid the required compensation. Opening the debate for the opposition on April 7th, Sir James Graham hit out hard where he felt safe to do so, notably at the Blue Book, 'a labyrinth of inextricable confusion'; but he was careful to reassure the House that the Tories had no intention of saying or doing anything which might jeopardise British commercial interests or India's future. One sixth of the whole united revenue of Great Britain and India, he remarked, depended on continued commercial relations with China; the Tories were not proposing to throw it away. On the contrary, they proposed to show how close the Whig government had been to throwing it away. Its spokesmen had been trying to pretend that they had been caught out by a sudden shift in Chinese policy. The correspondence which they had laid before the House revealed that the shift had not been sudden; the Chinese had given warning after warning of their determination to stamp out smuggling. Any inconsistency had been on the British government's side. The instructions given to Napier and Elliot had been contradictory, urging them both to respect and to defy protocol, so that whatever they did could only land them in trouble. Again and again, Elliot had warned that if the contraband traffic were not brought under control, legitimate trade would be endangered. What had Palmerston done? He had replied that he would not countenance any violation of Chinese law; but he had also said, in effect, that he would not do that which would amount to an absolute discountenance of it. Elliot had been left helpless. This was why the British merchants had been compelled to make their withdrawal from Canton. It was not the fault of the Chinese, but of the British government's lack of foresight, 'especially their neglect to furnish the Superintendent at Canton with powers and instructions calculated to provide against the growing evils connected with the contraband traffic'.

The government's case was put by Macaulay, who had just been made Secretary of War after some years as chief administrator of the emerging Indian civil service. He knew a great deal more about the East and the opium traffic than Graham; but he did not try to exploit his advantage. Graham had concentrated his attention on the government's relations with Elliot: so would he. Was it not significant, he asked, that the last example Graham had been able to find to prove that the government's instructions had been imprecise had been taken from a year before? It was indeed significant, because this had been the only instruction Elliot had received that year; but the opposition did not seize the chance to make the point, before Macauley went on to argue that the government had deliberately avoided giving Elliot precise instructions for the very good reason that they knew they would take so long to reach him that the situation might by then have entirely changed. Ministers, Macaulay explained, had been led to expect that it would change. On the basis of the information they had received down to the spring of 1838, they could reasonably have hoped that the Chinese were going to legalise the opium traffic. That was why the Foreign Secretary had hesitated, before giving orders.

As if aware that this was not a very convincing line to take – Palmerston could easily have given Elliot alternative courses to pursue, according to whether or not opium was legalised; and the case against him was not simply that his instructions had been imprecise, but that Elliot had not been given the authority to act as circumstances dictated – Macaulay switched to safer ground. What would the opposition do, if the responsibility were theirs? Was Graham saying that the opium traffic should be stopped? 'Did the Rt. Hon. Baronet mean, that the country should pay the expenses of a preventive service for the whole coast of China?' The Chinese had a right to impose a ban on opium, if they chose. But they did not have a right, Macaulay insisted, to use the means they had chosen. They had 'confined our innocent countrymen, and insulted the Sovereign in the presence of her representatives'. Then, just as they had given themselves up for lost, the 'innocent countrymen' had seen the British flag, flying on Elliot's orders from a Factory balcony.

> *It reminded them that they belonged to a country unaccustomed to defeat, to submission or to shame; to a country which had exacted such reparation for the wrongs of her children as had made the ears of all who hear it to tingle; to a country which had made the Dey of Algiers humble himself in the dust before her insulted consul; to a country which had avenged the Black Hole on the field of Plassey.*

Surrounded though they were by enemies, and separated by the oceans from help, they had known that 'not a hair of their heads would be harmed with impunity'.

So carried away had Macaulay been by his own rhetoric – Sir William Follett, who followed for the opposition, observed – that his speech, whatever its oratorical merits, had had nothing to do with the motion of censure. The motion was not about the government's handling of the unfortunate situation which had arisen; it was about its responsibility for the preceding events. The responsibility, Follett had no difficulty in showing, was Palmerston's, for his refusal to give Elliot any positive instructions. But Macaulay's debating trick had worked. Speaker after speaker dealt with the more immediate issue of what ought to be done. Sir George Staunton insisted that what was past was past; all that mattered now was that the insults offered by the Chinese had become too great to be borne.

The Radicals, too, showed that the opportunity which these insults had provided to impose a new trading agreement was too good to be missed. Either the very lucrative China trade must be lost, Charles Buller argued, or the interruption that had taken place must be turned 'to such account as to enable them to place that trade on an entirely new, secure and progressive footing'. Nor should they think of this in terms of trade alone, Benjamin Hawes unctuously added. 'All history proved that the success of any nation was proportioned to the physical powers with which she supported her negotiations'; and it was particularly necessary that they should now be supported, so that China could be given the benefits of Christianity, which had not yet dawned there, and which could be introduced there 'solely through the medium of commercial agency'.

Of the M.P.S who raised the moral issue as an argument against any punitive campaign, two were on the threshold of their political careers. Unless blinded by party feelings, Sidney Herbert felt, nobody could shut his eyes to the fact 'that we were endeavouring to maintain a treaty resting upon unsound principles, and to justify proceedings which were a disgrace to the British flag'. Gladstone was even more vehement. He had an intimate acquaintance with the effects of opium: his sister Helen had become an addict. His diaries show that he had read Bruce's 'appalling account' – as he described it – of the opium plague in Assam; and that he had talked to Thelwall a few days before the debate. So far from being the aggressors, he argued, the Chinese authorities had shown 'unwearied and exemplary patience', under continued provocation. Again and again they had asked for the removal of the opium depot ships, and as both Robinson and Elliot had agreed, this would have been easy to do, and at least would have kept the British government out of the business. But the government had refused its sanction even for that move. In the circumstances, 'was it not mere mockery to affect – to pretend – indignation as to the pernicious consequences of the opium trade, and yet exhaust all the armoury of ingenuity and eloquence to prove that the Chinese government were not justified in taking effectual means for crushing the trade?' A more unjust war in its origin, Gladstone claimed, he had never heard of. Macaulay had spoken of the British flag waving in glory in Canton:

The flag is hoisted to protect an infamous contraband traffic; and if it were never hoisted except as it is now hoisted on the coast of China, we could recoil from its sight with horror. Although the Chinese were undoubtedly guilty of much absurd phraseology, of no little ostentatious pride, and of some excess, justice in my opinion is with them; and whilst they, the pagans, the semi-civilised barbarians, have it on their side, we, the enlighted and civilised Christians, are pursuing objects at variance with justice and with religion.

Gladstone, however, made a small but damaging slip, which was to give government supporters the chance to reply to him with ribaldry. Recounting the course of events, he described how the Chinese had announced they would refuse the British food, 'and then, of course, they poisoned the wells'. The reference was greeted by ironic cheers; and Gladstone, trying to extricate himself, said he meant it was alleged they had poisoned the wells, which hardly helped matters. It was to be used against him, then and later, that he had appeared to condone so inhumane a proceeding.

Summing up for the opposition, in a speech chiefly designed to clarify the issues which Macaulay had deliberately confused, Peel admitted that force was now necessary; but only because of Palmerston's gross negligence. For the government, Palmerston had no difficulty in confusing the issues again. He had been accused, he said, of not giving sufficiently clear instructions. 'Gentlemen who make long speeches' (Graham's had lasted two hours) 'think, I suppose, that I should write long letters'. There had not, in fact, been any complaint of the brevity of his instructions; only of their imprecision and inadequacies. But as the last speaker in the debate Palmerston did not need to fear being taken up on that, or the other schoolboy debating points he was to make. His aim, it soon became clear, was to win back any waverers who might have been swayed by the moral arguments of Gladstone and Herbert. It had been implied, he complained, that he had encouraged the opium traffic.

Now, those who held that opinion could not have read the papers which had been laid upon the table. Had they done so, they could have seen, that from the first to the last he had endeavoured to discountenance the traffic to the utmost in his power. It would be seen by the papers that he himself had lost much social enjoyment by his persevering opposition to the traffic.

Palmerston's political opponents might have pointed out that he had been even more persevering in his opposition to Elliot's efforts to bring the traffic under control; and even his admirers must have found it a little hard to believe that he had sacrificed any social pleasures worrying over the fate of Chinese opium addicts. But with considerable subtlety, among the oratorical flourishes, he also contrived to give reassurances to the M.P.s on whose votes he might have to rely. The Chinese authorities, he insisted (for the benefit of the humanitarians) were not really worried about opium. What they were worried about was the outflow of silver, to pay for it, and the prosperity of Chinese poppy farmers who wanted protection. There was consequently no need for anybody in Britain to feel he was responsible for the miseries of the opium addict in Canton. And in his closing argument, Palmerston hardly attempted to hide that he was angling for Radical support. Suppose the Chinese were to suppress home production and the British to suppress production in India: what then? The opium would be produced elsewhere: in Turkey, Persia, and other countries. If merchants were forbidden to carry it in British ships, they would transfer their allegiance to the Stars and Stripes; 'under that flag, they would snap their fingers at our cruisers; and thus, the trade in opium would not be put down' – the Chinese would gain no benefit. With a quiet but effective gesture, he produced corroborative evidence; a memorial from the American merchants in Canton to their government, calling for the same concessions from the Chinese that the British merchants there had been demanding.

Palmerston had shifted the debate even further from the motion than Macaulay; but in view of the line the Radicals had taken in their speeches, he could afford the liberty. Gladstone's slip, in particular, gave him his chance. As Palmerston pronounced them, Gladstone's words, 'of course they poisoned the wells', appeared to carry the message that it was only natural and right for the Chinese to wish to poison British subjects. Palmerston 'did not argue much', John Cam Hobhouse noted in his diary; 'he was so gallant and confident, and claimed the support of all on our side with so much gay assurance, that he completely succeeded in his appeal, and sat down amid thunders of applause, which lasted some time'. Graham tried to get a further hearing; but M.P.s, weary after three nights of speeches, were in no humour for more. He was overridden by cries of 'Divide!', and the motion went to a vote. With Radical support, the Tories would have won; as it was, the government's majority was only nine.

The government still had to face a debate in the Lords, on May 12th; but their task was simplified by the nature of the motion, and the reputation of the peer who proposed it. Lord Stanhope was President of the Medico-Botanical Society, and a Fellow of the Royal Society; but he was best known as the eccentric philanthropist who in 1832 had adopted Kaspar Hauser, the 'wild boy of Bavaria'. He was also a dedicated teetotaller, hostile to any form of drug taking; and his aim, expressed in a petition which had been decided on at a public meeting in London, was to bring the opium traffic to an end, if necessary by obtaining additional legislative powers for that purpose. Dissociating the Tories from the proposal, Wellington took the chance to clarify his own position. For his part, he would not take upon himself the responsibility of advising Her Majesty 'to submit to an insult and injuries such as he believed had never been before inflicted on this country'. So little support did Stanhope attract that at the end of the debate he did not even press his motion to a vote.

Feeling that through Wellington's attitude an opportunity had been wasted, some Tories were inclined to be angry with him. 'I know that well enough and I don't care *one damn*,' he replied, when Greville mentioned their displeasure: 'I was afraid Lord Stanhope would have a majority, and *I have not time not to do what is right*'.

6

SETTLEMENT OF
ACCOUNTS, 1840-42

Still assuming that the British would be forced to capitu-
late at some time during the 1839-40 trading season, Lin
had made no attempt to change his policy; but in order
to reassure the Emperor, he had to pretend that the naval
engagements off Hong Kong and Chuenpi were Chinese
victories, adding another, the product of his own fantasy.
The Emperor enthusiastically doubled the number; 'the
Six Smashing Blows', Waley found, still featured in some
history books at the time he was writing his *Opium War
through Chinese Eyes*. It was a disappointment to Lin that
as he could not yet boast that the British had given in,
the move to his new post had to be delayed. But he still
had no reason to doubt he would be taking it up some
time in the new year; and in February 1840 the Emperor
confirmed him in the appointment, though again reminding
him that the opium traffic must be finally put down, first.

The Queen's Americans

By this time, however, another flaw in Lin's reasoning was becoming apparent. He had allowed merchants of any nationality to stay on in Canton and continue to trade, provided that they signed the pledge not to trade again in opium. The American merchants had accepted his offer. Most of them, apart from King's firm, Olyphant and Co., had been involved in the smuggling, because the amount of opium being produced in India had begun to outstrip the resources of the British merchants, leaving a small surplus which the Americans were able to carry; 1,500 of the chests which Lin confiscated had been from American ships. But their legal trade had also grown to the point where it was worth too much to sacrifice for opium; and Elliot's decision to withdraw all British ships and citizens gave them the opportunity to expand it still further, by taking over the British share. When Elliot pleaded with them to leave Canton the manager of one of the American firms, Robert Forbes, bluntly replied, 'we Yankees have no queen to guarantee our losses'; he had not come to China for his health, and proposed to stay as long as he could 'sell a yard of goods or buy a pound of tea'.

Yet although commercial rivalry was keen, there was no disposition on the Americans' part to take Lin's side against the British. On the contrary, in many ways they were dependent upon British co-operation. They had a currency problem, an adverse balance of payments; and they had been circumventing it by using British credit, based on opium. They had also had trouble with the Chinese authorities, such as the occasion where a sailor on one of their ships had been handed over in a homicide case, and executed. And their growing involvement in the smuggling had given them a measure of solidarity with the British. Called upon to defend himself for his part in it Forbes was later to insist that he felt no need for justification: 'I considered it right to follow the example of England, the East India Company, the countries that cleared it for China, and the merchants, to whom I always have been accustomed to look up to as exponents of all that was honorable in trade.'

The friendly relations which existed between the British and American merchants would not ordinarily have prevented the Americans from appropriating all they could of the British Canton trade, as Elliot feared (he had earlier warned Palmerston they would, if they got the chance). But without the revenue from opium, they would not have been able to pay for the goods they ordered in Canton. It was more profitable, they quickly realised, to load the tea that would have been carried by British ships and bring it to Hong Kong, where it could be transferred to waiting British ships and taken to England, while the Americans went back for more, along with some British merchantmen sailing under the American flag. According to Forbes, an American ship could actually earn more on this short ferry run than it later expected to earn from taking a cargo from China to the United States; and although the British protested at the charges, they cannot have been too extortionate, as when the figures for 1839-40 were published they showed that it had been the most profitable trading season for British firms since the end of the East India Company's monopoly. Elliot, who had threatened he would make Canton too hot for the Americans, now handsomely apologised to them: 'the Queen owes you many thanks', he told Forbes, 'for not taking my advice as to leaving Canton'. Forbes' account, admittedly, appeared in his *Reminiscences* half-a-century later, and he had probably dined out on it too frequently for its accuracy to be accepted uncritically; but there is no reason to doubt that this was Elliot's opinion.

Had Lin's campaign against opium been as successful as he boasted in his accounts to the Emperor, this Anglo-American venture would soon have run into currency difficulties; for as Russell and Co. told their customers in America in February 1839, in a circular announcing they would have nothing further to do with the opium traffic, new sources would have to be found to pay for China tea. But the traffic quickly built up again. Elliot was not to blame: having given his pledge to Lin that British ships would cease to bring opium to China, he did his best to keep it. 'No man', he wrote to Palmerston on November 16th, 1839, 'entertains a deeper detestation of the disgrace and sin of this forced traffic on the coast of China than the humble individual who signs this despatch. I see little to choose between it and piracy'. In his communications to Lin, too, which continued up to the time of the arrival of the expeditionary force, he showed that he was doing his best to prevent the merchants under his charge from having any dealings in contraband. He even published an order that no ships having opium on board would be allowed to remain in the Hong Kong anchorage; nor would they be given any protection by the navy while they were engaged in the traffic (Palmerston, when he heard, wrote to remind Elliot that although it was entirely contrary to the wishes of the government that any countenance or protection should be given to opium smugglers, he had no authority to make the order). But the opium clippers by this time needed neither the anchorage nor the protection. Lin could exercise little control outside Canton and its neighbourhood, and none at all along the coast; and in so far as his campaign had been locally successful, it had merely created a scarcity which led to a substantial increase in the price of the drug.

Jardine Matheson were the first to seize the opportunity, with a coup which excited William Hunter's admiration. Hearing that opium was piling up at Singapore after Lin's confiscation, owing to doubts whether it could be sold, Matheson despatched twenty chests back there from Hong Kong ostensibly for sale. Their arrival caused consternation. If Jardine Matheson could no longer sell opium in China, who could? Along with the chests, though, the clipper's captain carried a secret letter to Jardine Matheson's Singapore agent, who took advantage of the resulting fall in price to buy 700 chests (through brokers, to avoid disclosing his identity) at $250 a chest. Along with the original twenty, which nobody would buy, these were shipped back to China where according to Hunter they were 'readily disposed of at an average of $2,500 a chest'. Hunter may have exaggerated the profit in recollection; but the traffic that winter certainly flourished, with prices running at over $1,500 a chest, three times what they had been during the mid-1830s. Other merchants joined in. Elliot had warned Palmerston in one of his despatches from Canton during the blockade that Lin's action could only throw the coast trade 'into desperate hands; with this long line of unprotected coast, abounding in safe anchorages, and covered with defenceless cities, I foresee a state of things terrible to reflect on'. That winter his prediction was fulfilled. The *Chinese Repository* confirmed that British smugglers were not hesitating to land their valuable consignments with the help of armed force. In the towns, Lin told the Emperor, the drug was generally under control; but in the country, enforcement faced insuperable difficulties. Smuggled opium was being hidden in places his officers did not care to go: in women's rooms; in temples; even in tombs. And it was no longer possible to recruit spies, because the smugglers could afford to pay them more than the authorities. By the time the expeditionary force reached Macao in the summer of 1840, Lin knew that his project had been a failure.

240

War

The campaign was to have two stages. In the first, the aim was to compel the Emperor to accept the British terms, as interpreted by Elliot. The second, under Elliot's successor, was to compel the Emperor to accept the settlement which Palmerston claimed Elliot ought to have imposed, as soon as he had realised the full measure of Chinese military weakness. Both contests were too one-sided to be more than curiosities, in terms of military history: particularly the first.

The expeditionary force was under the command of Admiral George Elliot, Charles's cousin, the two of them sharing plenipotentiary powers. At their disposal they had sixteen warships, four armed paddle steamers ('Cartwheel ships', Lin described them, 'that put the axles in motion by means of fire, and can move rather fast'). It was not their speed which was decisive; in a breeze, the faster opium clippers could outpace them; it was their shallow draught, and their ability to move and to tow other ships, in a calm, or up wind, or up tide. When the fleet sailed away, Lin was unwise enough to boast to the Emperor that it had been driven off. In fact, it had sailed north to take its first objective; Tinghai, on the island of Chusan. Although there was still no declaration of war, the Chinese at this stage received what amounted to a formal intimation of impending hostilities, in the form of a combined manifesto and apologia from Palmerston to the Emperor's Minister of State, setting out what the force had arrived to do, and why. It began by reminding the Emperor that commercial intercourse between Britain and China had existed for over a century; and that during this time British subjects, trusting in the Chinese government's good faith, had established themselves as merchants in Canton. But certain Chinese officials had committed unprovoked outrages against them, on the excuse that some of them were dealing in contraband opium, a commodity liable to confiscation. The British government had no objection to the Chinese making such a law, and agreed that British subjects should obey it; 'Her Majesty does not wish to protect them from the just consequences of any offences which they may commit in foreign parts'. But her Majesty could not allow them to be treated with injustice, or with violence; and they had been subjected to both.

What had been done was unjust, Palmerston claimed, because the Chinese government, having made the law, had not enforced it impartially. The law against opium had been allowed to become a dead letter, the Emperor's subjects breaking it with impunity; until suddenly, without sufficient warning, the authorities had put it into force with the utmost vigour and severity. Even then, the British would not have complained if the Chinese government, after giving notice of its intentions, had contented itself with confiscating all the opium it could find in Chinese possession. But it had seized peaceable British merchants, the innocent with the guilty; imprisoned them in their Factory; and threatened them with death by starvation, until the opium was handed over. It was for this that the British government was demanding satisfaction.

The nature of the satisfaction was set out in the terms which Palmerston privately instructed Elliot to demand, when he had compelled the Emperor to send a plenipotentiary to treat with him. The Chinese were to be called upon to cede 'one or more sufficiently large and properly situated islands', where British merchants could live and work. Provided, however, that the Chinese were prepared to guarantee the security of the merchants and the freedom of commerce in certain ports other than Canton, 'the British government would not object to such an arrangement, and would in that case forego the permanent possession of any island on the Chinese coast'. The Chinese, though, must compensate the merchants for the confiscated opium, and for any bad debts, as well as making good the costs of the expedition.

Elliot was also instructed what to do about the future of the opium traffic. This, Palmerston had realised, presented a diplomatic problem. When Charles Elliot's initial request for military intervention had reached Calcutta it had been forwarded to Whitehall because, as the directors of the Company hastened to make clear, what had happened at Canton was not the Company's concern, but they added that presumably it was 'quite out of the question to suppose that the British government

would be justified in compelling the Chinese to eat opium';
an intimation to Palmerston that he would be wise to play
down the government's, and the Company's, connection
with the drug. Palmerston took the hint. Nothing was said
about opium either in the formal communication to the
Emperor or in the projected peace terms. Privately, Elliot
was told 'to endeavour to make some arrangement with
the Chinese government for the admission to China as
an article of lawful commerce'. But 'in bringing this matter
before the Chinese plenipotentiaries', Palmerston went on,
'you will state that the admission of opium into China as
an article of legal trade is not one of the demands which
you have been instructed to make upon the Chinese
government'. The plenipotentiaries must not be given the
impression that they were under any compulsion to legalise
it; they were simply to be told that they would be wise
to, as the British could not put down the opium traffic,
'because even if none were grown in any part of the British
territories, plenty of it would Be produced in other countries, and would then be sent to China'. In addition, the
Chinese should be reminded of the revenue which they
could expect to get from licensing the drug.

The Convention of Chuenpi

As the senior representative of the British government in
the east, Lord Auckland found himself in general control
of the expedition; and mindful of the need to preserve

the Indian revenue, in his instructions to Elliot he emphasised the importance of retaining the goodwill of the
Chinese, whose patronage would be needed if the aim of
opening up China to foreign trade was achieved. Only
government property and ships should be attacked; care
must be taken neither to harm the civilian population, nor
to interfere with its trade. Lord Jocelyn, who went with
the Elliots as their military secretary, was to confirm in
his *Six Months with the Chinese Expedition* that this had
indeed been the intention; the Chinese people were to be
conciliated at every opportunity. But 'those who are at all
acquainted with a military force', he observed, 'and with
the wants and necessities of an army on active employment
and a country in a state of resistance, must be aware of
the difficulty of carrying out such an idea'. It was made
the more difficult because contrary to expectation the
mandarins in general received the invaders with courtesy;
it was the people who turned out to be hostile. The fiction
'so industriously circulated throughout India' of the way
the Chinese hated their Tartar oppressors, Jocelyn reported,
'appeared, so far as we had an opportunity for judging,
to be without the slightest foundation'.

The attitude of the Chusan mandarins was of pained
surprise. They had never done any harm to the British;
why were they being held responsible for wrongs alleged
to have been done far away in Canton? 'We see your
strength', they told the emissaries who had come to tell
them to surrender, 'and know that opposition will be

madness; but we must perform our duty.' There was little they could do, in the way of effective resistance; but some junks and a few antiquated shore cannon opened fire, to be quickly silenced by the guns of the fleet. Their duty performed, the chief magistrate, the head of the police and the warden of the jail committed ritual suicide: and British officers, coming ashore, found nothing more serious to face than the problem of preventing their men from becoming drunk on looted liquor. 'Loot' was a Bengal word for plunder, which was to come into currency in the English language as a result of this expedition. The attempt to distinguish between the imperial government's supporters and the populace had broken down when it was learned that the white flag, first hoisted at Amoy on the way north so that Palmerston's letter to the Emperor could be delivered, had been fired on (not surprisingly, it was later realised, as the white flag was not known as a flag of truce in that part of China), and there was usually some similar excuse. The dwellings of the Chinese were entered and stripped. 'Silks, fans, china, little shoes, crutches and paint-pots – the articles of a Chinese lady's toilette – lay tossed in a sad and tell-tale melee', Jocelyn recalled about one house he had seen, 'and many of these fairy shoes were appropriated as lawful loot'.

Leaving a garrison on Chusan, with the indestructible Gutzlaff installed as Chief Magistrate, the Elliots sailed on north to their main objective, the mouth of the Pei-ho river, a hundred miles below Pekin. By the time they arrived, in August, the Emperor had realised that military resistance would be futile; and he despatched the supplest of the Court's diplomatists, Ch'i-shan (to the British, Kishen), to negotiate. Lin, inevitably, was made the scapegoat. 'You speak of having stopped foreign trade,' the Emperor wrote to tell him that August; 'yet a moment later, admit that it is still going on. You say you have dealt with offenders against the opium laws, yet admit that they are still at large. All this is merely an attempt to put me off with meaningless words. Thinking of these things, I cannot contain my rage'. A month later, Lin heard that he had been sacked.

As it happened, Lin had just recommended the policy which the Emperor now decided to adopt. Lord Amherst, Lin recalled, had been diverted from his intention in 1816 by judicious flattery. If the Emperor promised an enquiry into British allegations, and sent a high official to Canton to conduct it, 'this will impress them with the entire justice of our Heavenly Court's procedure, increase their respect for us, and deprive them of all excuse for their conduct', as well as 'dispersing their teeth and claws'. The Emperor realised that he was left with no other choice; and the obvious go-between was the elderly aristocratic Kishen, who greatly impressed Westerners with his appealing manner (his features being 'undoubtedly the most noble, the most gracious, and the most spiritual', that Evariste Huc, the French traveller, had ever seen), and his diplomatic finesse ('in the presence of a Mettemich or a

Talleygrand' Gutzlaff felt, 'he would have commanded respect'). Even John Francis Davis, who complained that Kishen would make promises innumerable, without keeping one, conceded that his 'great tact, his imperturbable suavity, and perfect command of temper, were extraordinary'.

'Let us all adjourn to Canton', Kishen told the Elliots when he met them on August 30th, 'where it is so much easier to ascertain the facts in dispute'. The Emperor, he assured them, was graciously inclined. He had come to understand how provoking Lin must have been; and 'loving as he does, strangers from afar, you may rest assured of his vast condescension'. Charles Elliot (his cousin the Admiral played little part, and illness soon compelled him to withdraw from the negotiations) was impressed. He had not fancied the idea of going in force to Pekin. Better terms might be extorted there, he had already explained to the Foreign Office; but only at the risk of toppling the dynasty, with unfortunate consequences for the British. He was relieved when the Emperor appeared conciliatory. 'So far as I can judge', he wrote to tell Matheson (the merchant in whom he reposed most confidence), 'the Court has deliberated upon peace or war, and decided peace is the wisest course'. It had, but not the peace which Elliot had been instructed to obtain. When the fleet sailed south again in September, leaving a garrison on Chusan, Kishen could share the jest with the Emperor; though the barbarians were bold and defiant, 'and scarcely amenable to reason, nevertheless they soon became well-disposed on receiving words of praise'.

Kishen had another reason to feel confident that their ruse would work: disease was ravaging the occupying force on Chusan. From a total of around four thousand troops, one in ten died. But, like Lin, Kishen had made a fatal miscalculation. The serious news from Chusan, coupled with reports of barbarities inflicted on Britons captured when their ships went aground – men and women were put in irons, confined in cages, three and a half feet by three feet by two feet, and exhibited in market places – served to remind Elliot that he could not afford to allow negotiations to drag on. When Kishen told him that cession of an island to the British was out of the question, Elliot decided he had no alternative but to resume hostilities; and he took the easiest option. Early in the new year of 1841 the batteries protecting the Bogue were attacked and destroyed, heralding what was obviously going to be a British advance with Canton as its objective. Having no force then capable of offering resistance, Kishen had to give way. On January 20th the first phase of the war ended with the signing of the Convention of Chuenpi; the ban on trade was lifted; and British ships and British merchants returned to Canton.

The terms of the convention reflected Elliot's conviction that Auckland's advice had been sound: the Chinese people should be conciliated, in the peace settlement as well as to the preceding hostilities. He had been told to take an island; and as Chusan had shown itself to be dangerously unhealthy, he settled for Hong Kong. He had been told to secure compensation, and he demanded an indemnity of six million dollars which would more than cover the value of the confiscated opium. He also insisted that in future the British representative must be able to deal directly with the Viceroy; no more negotiations through the Hong, no more petitions. But he deliberately refrained from exacting the full complement of demands which had featured in Palmerston's instructions, because he felt that any further humiliation of the Chinese would jeopardise future relations between China and Britain.

Reading the Chuenpi terms when they reached Whitehall the following Easter, Palmerston was outraged that Elliot should have taken it upon himself to modify his proposed settlement, particularly in view of the ease with which the Emperor had been compelled to accept defeat. 'After all', he had written to tell Elliot a few weeks before, 'our naval power is so strong that we can tell the Emperor what *we* mean to hold, rather than that *he* should say what he would cede'. All Elliot had held was Hong Kong, 'a barren island', Palmerston complained 'with hardly a house on it'; and that only on a form of leasehold, like Macao. The sum Elliot had secured as an indemnity would not even be sufficient fully to compensate the merchants; and he had failed to secure a promise to pay either the expenses of the expedition, or the Hong merchants' debts. 'You have disobeyed and neglected our instructions', Palmerston wrote in barely concealed fury; 'you have deliberately abstained from employing as you might have done the force placed at your disposal, and you have without any sufficient necessity accepted terms which fall far short of those which you were instructed to obtain'. Had Elliot obtained full success in his negotiations, he would have been applauded for obtaining his objectives peacefully. But he had not done so. 'You will, no doubt', Palmerston concluded,

by the time you have read thus far, have anticipated that I could not conclude this letter without saying that under these circumstances, it is impossible that you should continue to hold your appointment in China. Being convinced that I cannot, consistently with my public duty, continue to place in your hand the public interests with which you have been charged, I think it but right towards you to take the very earliest opportunity of telling you so.

Palmerston was often curt in his despatches; but he rarely allowed his anger to carry him away, as on this occasion. Why was he so enraged?

There appear to have been two main reasons: one being that Elliot had missed the significance of the proposal to forgo the idea of an island base, provided that the ports were opened up. Although Palmerston had allowed Jardine to advise him, on this issue they were not in agreement. An island base was all-important to Jardine Matheson; to Palmerston the ports were more attractive, for a reason which he expressed in a letter to Auckland that winter. 'The rivalship of European manufactures', he explained,

> *is fast excluding our productions from the markets of Europe, and we must unremittingly endeavour to find in other parts of the world new vents for the produce of our industry. The world is large enough and the wants of the human race ample enough to afford a demand for all we can manufacture; but it is the business of the government to open and to secure the roads for the market. Will the navigation of the Indus turn out to be as great a help as was expected for our commerce? If it does, and if we succeed in our China expedition, Abyssinia, Arabia, the countries on the Indus and the new markets of China, will at no distant period give a most important extension to the range of our foreign commerce.*

Although Palmerston could not openly avow that he was sending the expedition to China to compel the Chinese to accept free trade, the letter suggests that this had been his firm intention. He had already shown, in the rebuke which he sent Elliot for stopping the use of the steamship *Jardine* as a Canton/Whampoa ferry, that he believed the government had no right to interfere in commercial enterprises even if they were being carried on within foreign territory (the Canton river) against the expressed wishes of the authorities. And in the opium debate he confirmed that he still held this view; when Graham quoted Palmerston's despatch, telling Elliot it was incumbent upon him to be 'very careful not to assume a greater degree of authority than that which you in reality possess', Palmerston was heard to say 'Hear! Hear!' He believed that if Britain could get into China before the other nations – as she would be in a position to do even if, as he proposed, they were allowed equal facilities in the ports – she would be able to take advantage of her long experience there to pre-empt the bulk of the China trade with Europe. His assumption had been that rather than cede any territory, the Emperor would prefer to permit the ports to be opened up. But he had neglected to make this sufficiently clear to Elliot. Elliot, doubtless advised by Matheson, took the view that, as he explained to Auckland, access to the ports would simply give hostages to an irritated Chinese government; 'with what may be taken to be a certainty, the impatience of our own merchants, and the perfidy of the Chinese, will rapidly produce new troubles'. He had therefore settled for Hong Kong, not so well placed as Chusan but, on the evidence of the previous summer, much healthier. And he had accepted Kishen's proposal for a Macao-type lease because Kishen had told him there would be no other way to justify the deal to the Emperor. His crime, though, in Palmerston's eyes, was not really the choice of island, nor the leasehold on which it was obtained. It was the fact he had not held out for the ports.

The Select Committee on Compensation

The main reason for Palmerston's wrath, though, was that Elliot had failed to press for the full indemnity. As Elliot told Auckland, he saw no reason why compensation for the earlier debts of insolvent Hong merchants, which Jardine had persuaded Palmerston to include in the demands, should be demanded. Arrangements for the honouring of such debts had been made, and kept. If the Chinese government were compelled to pay, they would certainly call upon the Hong to put up the money, which the Hong would regard, rightly in Elliot's estimation, as a breach of faith. The amount he had secured from Kishen, he felt, was sufficient. It would be best for Her Majesty's government 'to keep and improve what they have got, and to leave all details of indemnity, all expenses of the expedition to be made good out of the growing advantage of extending trade'. And so far as trade was concerned, Elliot's optimism had quickly been justified. But the fact that it was flourishing, and that sales of opium were more profitable than they had been before the confiscation, did not make the merchants any the less determined to get the maximum compensation for past losses from the government; and the government was not in a position to refuse, having trapped itself by setting up the committee of enquiry.

With Abel Smith in the Chair, and a majority of its members supporting the government, what followed was less an enquiry into the merchants' rights to compensation (though Gladstone did his best) than a forum in which they vindicated their conduct along the lines Samuel Warren had laid down in his treatise. Some witnesses went further, maintaining that no illegality had been involved. 'If the Chinese could have seized my opium in the course of smuggling it on shore', Captain John Thacker, a merchant who had arrived in China shortly before the confiscation, argued, 'I should have no right to ask for any interference on the part of the British government', but the opium was 'not at all in the power of the Chinese; they had taken improper and illegal methods to extort it from me; and I thought I had, therefore, the right to protection'. The main objective, though, was to show that the traffic, whether or not it had been illegal in the eyes of the Chinese, had been sanctioned and deliberately encouraged by the British government. 'We have no doubt', Alexander Matheson (James's nephew) told the committee,

that an effort will be made to vitiate our just claims, on the plea that the opium trade was a contraband trade, and therefore not entitled to the protection of England. But this argument, if brought forward, is at once answered by the fact that the whole question of opium, and the Company's monopoly of it on the Bengal side, had been the subject of an enquiry by a Parliamentary Committee at the time of the renewal of the Charter; and that it was with the fullest information before them that the parliament of England sanctioned the continuance of the said monopoly, and a consequent encouragement of the opium trade.

The sessions, which ended early in June, did not satisfy the Tory minority. The Committee, they suggested, 'feeling that the matters which have been referred to them involve some grave issues of public policy, which the House is more competent than your Committee to entertain', should lay the evidence before the Commons, 'submitting the whole case to that mature consideration which, from its importance, both to individual interests and to the national character, it well deserves'. As this would be tantamount to an invitation to the Commons to debate the subject, the majority voted the proposal down, substituting a single phrase; 'Your Committee feel that they shall best discharge their duty by laying before the House, without any observation on their own part, the evidence which they have taken'; a clear invitation to the government to consider the issue closed. The government, consequently, no longer had anything to fear from parliament on the China issue. When in July Gladstone made a final effort to awaken the conscience of the House in a speech against the motion to defray the initial costs of the expeditionary force, Hobhouse simply reminded him that Wellington had been heard to say the news from Canton 'made every drop of blood boil in the veins'; and Palmerston contented himself with facile gibes at Gladstone's expense. By that time, it was safe to assume, the expeditionary force must be menacing Pekin; the Emperor would be forced to give way; and as Elliot had been instructed to obtain an indemnity sufficient to meet the merchants' entire claim, the British taxpayer would not have to be called upon to meet any of the costs of the confidently-expected resounding victory. The news of the Convention of Chuenpi, however, when it reached Whitehall the following Easter, revealed that not merely had Elliot failed to make the victory resound, he had also left an alarmingly large sum for the British taxpayer to meet. In view of the select committee's implied acceptance of the merchants' claims, to back out of paying them would hardly be feasible; and to have to raise it in taxation would be humiliating as well as politically unwelcome. There was only one way out, Palmerston realised: another expeditionary force, and another plenipotentiary, with, instructions to compel the Emperor to accept the original terms, and pay the full costs of both expeditions.

Melbourne had his doubts. He had already shown in the Lords debate that he was not entirely happy with the course events had taken; and in particular he was concerned that his government was so connected with the cultivation and export of opium, though he had excused the traffic on the ground that if Britain did not conduct it, others would. Now, he was again worried. If hostilities were resumed, would not the Chinese believe that Britain had never intended to abide by the Convention of Chuenpi? In that case, the loss of goodwill might more than offset the value of the extra payments. Palmerston, however, had astutely won Queen Victoria over to his side. 'The Chinese business vexes us much, and Palmerston is deeply mortified at it', she wrote to tell the King of the Belgians; '*All* we wanted might have been got if it had not been for the unaccountably strange conduct of Charles Elliot . . . who completely disobeyed his instructions and *tried* to get the *lowest* terms he could.' And with the help of an elaborate tabulated account, contrasting what Elliot had been told to do and what he had actually done, Palmerston was able to convince his colleagues that they had no alternative but to accept his plan.

Elliot, inevitably, was to be given no chance to justify himself. Auckland had encouraged him earlier to use his own initiative; 'you may do pretty much as you like', he had written in the autumn of 1840, 'and I trust you will do so.' Now, Auckland hastened to disclaim responsibility: he had 'never agreed with him'; Elliot had been 'greatly misled'. Elliot was denied even the courtesy of being the first to hear the news that he was being replaced; on July 24th he had the humiliation of reading the news in a Canton paper. Palmerston's despatch, upbraiding him for his disobedience, and relieving him of his post, did not arrive until a week later.

Good reason though Eliot had to feel aggrieved, the blow must have been to some extent cushioned by the course events had taken since the signing of the Convention of Chuenpi. On hearing the terms, the Emperor had immediately repudiated them. Kishen was recalled in disgrace, and after some desultory hostilities the Chinese managed by May 1841 to build up a sufficiently menacing force for Elliot to feel compelled, once again, to order the evacuation of British subjects from Canton. After they had left the Factory was invaded and burned down. By the threat of sacking Canton in retaliation, Elliot was able to compel the Viceroy to agree to a cease-fire, and to pay an additional indemnity of six million dollars, but the forces at his disposal were not strong enough for him to sail north again to compel the Emperor to accept the Chuenpi terms. His dismissal might have been unfair; but the arrival of the successor, Sir Henry Pottinger, released him from what had become an intolerable situation.

The Treaty of Nanking

Sir Henry Pottinger was a bluff, down-to-earth Ulsterman in his early fifties, who had made a reputation for himself in India by showing he could get on well socially with difficult native princes, yet be ruthless with them if the need arose. His instructions were not substantially different from those which Elliot had received; but he had the advantage over Elliot that he knew he must settle for nothing less, and could expect to be congratulated if he secured more.

Pottinger's general strategy was similar to Elliot's of the year before. His expeditionary force was to move north-wards, to threaten the Emperor more directly than by an attack on Canton, But the campaign was carried out at a more leisurely pace. The aim on the way was to show the Chinese in the ports which were to be opened for foreign trade who was the master, by demolishing their defences, before reassuring them by providing a just and efficient administration. No mercy was to be shown in battles, General Sir Hugh Gough, in command of the land forces, decided; but there would be no looting after them.

From the start, an attack on Amoy at the end of August 1841, the scheme proved unworkable. No sooner had the defenders fled than Chinese looters came out in great numbers. If any Chinaman was going to get the stuff, the British soldiers felt, why shouldn't they? Chusan was taken again, followed by Ningpo; a town, Fottinger had told Palmerston in a despatch, which it would give him 'considerable satisfaction' to see looted, as prisoners of war had been cruelly treated there (a notion which Gough vetoed, on the ground that the townspeople had agreed to surrender without resistance). And at Ningpo, as the campaign had begun late, it was decided to settle down for the winter, counter-attacks mounted by the Chinese being easily beaten off.

Again, though, good resolutions broke down under stress, leading to reprisals and counter-reprisals. The Chinese became adept at picking up stragglers, whether on marches or in brothels, and carrying them away for execution. Ningpo, spared during the winter, was sacked in retaliation before the troops left in the spring. A Chinese provincial Viceroy, too, decided to enjoy a revenge for the earlier campaign by making an example of the first Englishman to fall into his hands; and when Captain Stead unwittingly brought his ship into a harbour after the British force had left, the Viceroy celebrated by having Stead tied to a post and publicly flayed alive. When the British heard what had happened, the town where Stead had been taken was given over to the reprisals deemed appropriate.

On the resumption of the advance in the spring, the resistance encountered became more fanatical. In his account of the campaign, Lieutenant Alexander Murray of the Royal Irish described how he saved a Chinese soldier from being shot out of hand; whereupon 'the ungrateful fellow, instead of being pleased at his escape, deliberately began to cut his throat with a short sword, or knife'. Murray also paid a tribute to the enemy, who had no chance against enormously superior fire-power; 'far from their great losses being a proof of the cowardice of the Chinese, I take it to be a strong proof of their courage; for if cowards, they would have taken very good care that we should never have got within reach to them'. The respect which their bravery won, though, was short-lived. Cornered in a house at the end of a gorge, three hundred Chinese refused to surrender. When they were eventually overwhelmed, only fifty were left alive, most of them wounded; but admiration for the resistance they had offered vanished when the soldiers found the body of a man from their regiment whose face had been mutilated with his own razor. And so the savagery and the slaughter continued, as the expedition pushed on up the coast, taking Shanghai in June. Two months later Gough was preparing to attack Nanking when the news was brought that

Imperial Commissioners had arrived from Pekin, with powers to negotiate a settlement.

During the lull in the campaign, Pottinger had received the news that the Melbourne government had fallen in the summer of 1841; Peel had succeeded as Prime Minister, and Lord Aberdeen had taken over from Palmerston as Foreign Secretary. The change made no significant difference to the terms Pottinger was instructed to demand. Even before the Tories had come into office Lord Stanley, the future Prime Minister, had suggested to Peel that a motion condemning Elliot's Chuenpi Convention would meet with 'pretty general support'; There were not likely to be any serious objections within the party if Palmerston's policies were quietly adopted. For safety's sake, in a despatch to Pottinger, Aberdeen excused himself for not being explicit on the ground that the government did not even know whether he had as yet reached China, let alone whether he had already carried out Palmerston's instructions. The only modification he proposed to make to them was to allow Pottinger a measure of flexibility in assessing the amount which the Chinese were to pay as compensation for the confiscated opium. 'You will, of course,' he was told, 'exact such sums as the resources of the Chinese government and the means at your disposal for enforcing compliance seem to justify'; but to get them, Pottinger was not to 'break off the negotiation, or indefinitely prolong the war'.

Pottinger decided to take no chances of suffering Elliot's

fate. Effectively there were no negotiations; the Treaty of Nanking, signed on August 20th, represented the Chinese plenipotentiaries' acceptance of the terms he laid down. China was to pay twenty-one million dollars within three years as compensation to the merchants and indemnity to the British government. The ports of Amoy, Fuchow, Ningpo and Shanghai, in addition to Canton, were to be opened to foreign trade, the Hong losing their monopoly, and consular representation being recognised, with the right to communicate on terms of equality with the appropriate Chinese authorities. In addition, Hong Kong was to be ceded to Britain. By retaining it, Pottinger explained in a despatch, he was aware that he was exceeding his instructions; 'but every hour I have passed in this superb country has convinced me of the necessity and desirability of our possessing such a settlement as an emporium for our trade, and a place from which Her Majesty's subjects may be alike protected and controlled'.

Pottinger had not thought of China as 'this superb country' at the time he arrived. At first he had tended to treat its inhabitants as if they were savages; a view which led him, as one of his officers put it, to measures of 'somewhat an indiscriminable nature'. But since then, he had encountered and come to know the Chinese plenipotentiaries. Elepoo was by this time old and frail, but Kiying, the dominant partner, was an even more remarkable character than Kishen; an accomplished diplomat, with a shrewd appreciation of Pottinger's difficulties as well as his own, and also at ease with him socially, able to indulge in familiarities. From any of the British merchants, Pottinger would have thought them presumptuous. In Kiying, he found them delightful. The guests at one of the formal banquets in Nanking were to be astonished at the spectacle of Pottinger standing with his mouth open while Kiying, 'with great dexterity', lobbed sugar lumps into it. Kiying, though, was left under no illusions. The British terms were not negotiable; all that he could hope for was to secure a greater measure of British co-operation in making the necessary arrangements to see that they were smoothly carried out.

When the news of the Treaty reached England in the autumn of 1842 (steam had greatly reduced the time it took to transmit despatches), the Tories' only concern was to try to capture as much of the credit for it as possible. Stanley suggested a *feu de joie*; Peel agreed that 'there was never better reason for one'. The submission of the Emperor of China, *Blackwood's Magazine* claimed, had been obtained in spite of Palmerston's failure to give Elliot proper instructions; and it would give the reign of Queen Victoria a distinction 'far beyond most of her predecessors'.

The Reckoning

After the *feu de joie*, the reckoning. The new government had no intention of paying out any more in compensation than it had to. While Melbourne had been in office, the merchants knew their cause was well enough represented at Westminster to be certain of getting what they asked for, or ensuring his defeat if he tried to back out. But the Tories, with their comfortable majority, had no fear of a hostile vote on the issue, and no reason to feel generously disposed to the merchants. Was it really necessary, ministers began to ask themselves, to compensate them in full? Come to think of it, how much had the opium which Lin had confiscated really been worth?

Aberdeen wrote to Pottinger, asking him for an estimate (though warning him not to make it public; if he named too high a figure it could prove embarrassing). The value of the opium, Pottinger replied, could not be ascertained, because at the time none could be sold. Small quantities were believed to have been bought in Macao for $200-$300; but in general, the local news-sheets had reported that 'the trade is entirely suspended' and 'there is absolutely nothing doing'. Elliot, too, when asked after his return to England how he had arrived at his estimate of the value of the surrendered opium, explained that it had been based merely on what it might have fetched if it could not have been sold: 'it was worth nothing, or it was worth that'.*

---

*Elliot was not to suffer for his conduct of the negotiations. Aberdeen and even Melbourne told him he had been unfairly treated; he was appointed chargé d'affaires in Texas. Later he climbed the diplomatic ladder, island-hopping from Bermuda to Trinidad and St Helena, and eventually became an admiral.

In fact, the opium would have been worth nothing had Lin not seized and burned it, as Peel would have known if he had had access to the merchants' correspondence at the time. If Lin had declined to accept the opium, Matheson had written to tell Jardine in May 1839, 'and left us burdened with so heavy a stock under the new law punishing with death any foreigner dealing in the drug, the consequences would have been most disastrous'. And for a time, the merchants had reason to fear that Peel had rumbled them; when the compensation issue was brought up in the Commons in March 1842 (by the new member for Sandwich, H. Hamilton Lindsay; giving the new member for Ashburton, William Jardine the opportunity to make his maiden speech denouncing the Chancellor of the Exchequer for his cupidity), Peel pointedly replied that enquiries were being pursued to try to find the opium's real value; a broad hint that if the merchants made nuisances of themselves, they might find themselves worse off.

They were making nuisances of themselves, again, in China. Impressed by Kiying, Pottinger had been anxious to restore friendly relations with the Chinese as quickly as possible; but the merchants, he found, refused to co-operate. They, and their wives, tended to behave as if the Chinese did not exist, except in the capacity of servants. And they made no effort to impose any discipline on their ship's crews. Hardly was the Treaty signed than a riot, provoked by some sailors, led to some of the Canton Factories again being burned, and lives endangered. The reaction of the merchants was to demand additional compensation. Pottinger did not see why they should get it, when they themselves were at fault. Could they, he asked them, claim 'that you have in any single iota or circumstance striven to aid me in my arrangements, by endeavouring to dissipate and to soothe the very excitement and irritation of which you so loudly complain?' But most of the merchants had come out for the same purpose as William Bolts had joined the East India Company, to make their fortunes as quickly as they could; they ignored the plea. As the most lucrative trade in which they were engaged was contraband, they did not care what the Chinese thought of them.

Peel and Aberdeen were as reluctant as Palmerston to intervene. They were not concerned with the merchants' behaviour; they had simply been waiting until the indemnity was paid over, to ensure that funds were available to pay the compensation. As soon as it was secured, Peel announced that the merchants would get the six million dollars they had been promised (in spite of the fact that it was far more than the opium was even nominally worth; a court case in Calcutta had assessed its value as $200 a chest: the government was now offering $320). So far from expressing their gratitude, the reaction of the merchants' spokesmen in the Commons was to denounce the sum as miserably inadequate. 'A more unjust offer,' Sir Thomas Wilde complained, 'never was made than that which was now attempted to be forced upon individuals whose property had been sacrificed for public interests'; and Abel Smith thought the settlement would 'lower the national character, be injurious to the parties concerned, and ruinous to the interests of the trade with China'. When Peel reminded them that the sum the government was offering had been named by 'the noble Lord, then the Secretary for Foreign Affairs', Palmerston explained that he had not meant it 'arbitrarily as the value', but only as 'a sort of general guide'. The merchants, he claimed, had not only sustained a very grievous injury from the government of China; they were now being very harshly dealt with by the government of Great Britain.

As his biographer Jasper Ridley observed, Palmerston's attitude had been very different a few years earlier, when he had wanted the Russians to give up their claim for a war indemnity from Persia. 'The British government certainly can never admit the equity of principle upon which the exaction of such payments is made to rest', he had told Prince Lieven. 'When a powerful state gets into war and is, as it must be, victorious, it seems unjust that the beaten party should in addition to its own losses in the war be crushed by the overwhelming weight of a pecuniary burden from which it has no adequate means of relieving itself'. To Ridley, the whole opium war episode irresistibly recalled what Florence Nightingale was later to say of Palmerston: 'he was a humbug, and he knew it'. But the merchants got the six million dollars he had promised them; and in addition, half as much again to compensate them for the Hong's bad debts. Jardine's advice to Palmerston, to include that claim in the Treaty, had paid off.

7

BALANCE SHEET

It will never be possible to make a clear-cut attribution of responsibility for the opium war because we cannot do more than speculate about men's motives, let alone about whether they have been aware of them at the time they have been taking their decisions. But it is possible, in the light of the available evidence, to scrutinise the excuses which were put forward at the time or have been suggested since, to try to assess their validity; beginning with those which were on the list Palmerston drew up and sent to the Elliots, for delivery to the Emperor's Secretary of State. Here the blame was put exclusively on Commissioner Lin. Without provocation and without due warning, Palmerston claimed, Lin had ended the system of connivance by which opium had been allowed into China. He had seized British property. He had menaced British citizens with starvation, and even death, if they did not give way to his unjust commands. And he had demanded the sacrifice of a British subject following the Kowloon affray, as well as threatening death to many more by poisoning the wells.

The Case Against Lin

To Palmerston's contention that the Chinese had failed to give reasonable warning of their intention to abandon connivance, the 1840 Blue Book itself at first sight provided a detailed refutation. Elliot's despatches showed that the merchants had been warned at least three years earlier, and frequently thereafter; and that by the autumn of 1837 smuggling by the Chinese in and around the Canton estuary had virtually stopped. Samuel Warren actually cited this stoppage as evidence that the British government could not avoid the responsibility; knowing that British merchants were carrying the opium up to Whampoa, it had not ordered them to desist. Why, then, did Palmerston claim that the Chinese authorities had not given notice of their intention?

It seems likely that the idea was put into his mind by one of the pamphlets which came out shortly before the debates, by H. Hamilton Lindsay, in which Lindsay claimed that the Viceroy, Teng, had smashed the smugglers only to secure a monopoly for himself and his family, which he had then proceeded to exploit by running the opium from Lintin to Canton in his own boats under the viceregal flag. Lindsay had worked for the East India Company; but the experience he had gained on the prospecting voyage of the *Lord Amherst* had prompted him to go into the opium business for himself, and in 1836 he had urged Palmerston, in a published 'open letter', to send a force to seize a base on some island off the Chinese coast. His new tract, *Is the War with China a just one?*, was published as part of the Canton merchants' campaign to win public and parliamentary support; it was cited by Radical speakers in the Commons debate; and when Jardine gave evidence to the Select Committee on compensation, he followed Lindsay's line, insisting that it had not been the British merchants who took over the trade when the Chinese smugglers were put down, but Teng. When questioned by Gladstone, who pointed out that this version did not square with Elliot's despatches, Jardine explained that Elliot had been at Macao, and was consequently less well informed about the traffic in the Canton river. 'It was so well known that every Chinaman could point his finger at the flag and tell you, "that is the Viceroy's boat".'

That Teng could have carried on the smuggling in so blatant a fashion without Elliot hearing about it in Macao was highly improbable; but it is only since the letters that Jardine and Matheson were writing in the 1830s have been made available for inspection that it has become possible to test the truth of the story, for it is inconceivable that they would have made no mention of the Viceroy's activities in their frequent and detailed accounts of the state of the opium market. Their correspondence shows that the Canton authorities' drive to suppress smuggling began even earlier than Palmerston's critics in the 1840 debate realised. In March 1835 Jardine wrote to warn Jamsetjee Jejeebhoy, the Parsee whose firm looked after the Indian end of the opium business, that he had never known such difficulty in effecting sales; 'the Viceroy has given so much encouragement to the mandarins, who made the extensive seizures some time ago, that small captures are made every two or three days'. Even while legalisation was being considered, in 1836, the campaign was not called off; that November Jardine reported that the Canton dealers were 'under a good deal of alarm', fearing a complete stoppage of the traffic. By the following January, their fears had been realised; trade through Canton was 'completely at a stand'. From then on, its difficulties were continually being referred to in his letters – and in Matheson's; that autumn, Matheson described to the firm's London agent the strenuous efforts the Chinese had been making to suppress the trade. So far from the Viceroy benefiting from the stoppage to monopolise the opium, Jardine expressed the opinion in February 1838 that the Chinese authorities would have to take some new course of action to deal with the British ships because their smuggling meant that the authorities were 'deriving no advantage from the trade'. The opium market, he wrote in a further letter four days later 'is in a state that cannot be described. No regular smuggling, nor mandarin boats running'. There was irregular smuggling, though, in British ships; in direct contradiction to what he was to tell the Committee, Jardine described it in a letter the following month, saying that prices were improving a little because of the way British ships were carrying opium to Whampoa in spite of the risk and expense. When, a few days later, the Viceroy went on a visit to another province, Jardine described how some government preventive officers seized the chance to make a few thousand dollars smuggling, and opium prices staged a recovery, But on his return Teng issued a fresh warning that he proposed to proceed against the smugglers who were collecting the drug from foreign ships in Whampoa. In the autumn, seizures were made there; the price again began to fall; and as no other smuggling route to Canton remained open, from this time on no opium could be sold in or around the city.

The fleet of boats monopolising the opium trade under the viceregal flag, in short, was the product of Lindsay's imagination: stimulated, as Gladstone broadly hinted in the Commons debate, by the fact that Lindsay was 'a very respectable man, but largely concerned in the opium trade'. Presumably because this line offered the merchants a better chance of securing full compensation than the one Warren had taken, Jardine had accepted it. So the unfortunate Teng, who like Lin was disgraced and sent into exile by the Emperor, was thereafter smeared as a rogue by the British; 'a crafty, cringing, self-interested man', as W. D. Bernard described him in *Voyages of the Nemesis*, who 'derived immense sums from opium', a view accepted by many later writers, even the ordinarily charitable Maurice Collis in his *Foreign Mud*.

The second charge against Lin was that he had exceeded his legal rights by confiscating the opium from the British. If he had waited until it was in Chinese hands, the argument ran, he would have been perfectly entitled to seize it, and to inflict whatever penalties Chinese law imposed, but he had not waited. As a backbencher, P. M. Stewart, assured the Commons in the 1843 debate on compensation 'not a single chest was within the power or jurisdiction of the Chinese authorities', and so long as it was British property, to seize it must be deemed a hostile act.

This argument was originally derived from a harangue Jardine had addressed to his fellow merchants before leaving Canton in January 1839 (leading Lin to assume that the 'iron-headed old rat' must have fled; but his retirement had been impending for some time). Canton society, Jardine claimed, held a high place in his estimation;

> *yet I also know that this community has often heretofore and lately been accused of being a set of smugglers. This I distinctly deny; we are not smugglers, gentlemen! It is the Chinese government, it is the Chinese officers who smuggle, and who connive at and encourage smuggling; not we.*

Again, though, in the light of the Jardine Matheson correspondence the claim that British merchants were not smuggling can only be regarded as window-dressing. Whether the drug was actually put ashore by British ships, or taken off them and put ashore by the Chinese, was irrelevant when the operation was conducted within Chinese territorial jurisdiction. The only question was whether it did not also, as Elliot suggested, amount to piracy, the opium clippers being well armed, and their captains not hesitating to use the threat of force, and if necessary force itself. And when the British merchants began carrying the drug up to Canton, fighting off Chinese protection vessels – a method which Jardine himself described in a letter as 'very disgusting' – even the pretence of legality was set aside.

As if aware they had a poor case in law, Lin's critics tended to concentrate on a particular aspect of the confiscation. 'It should not be too often repeated', the Bombay merchants claimed in an address to the British Chambers of Commerce in November 1839, 'that the great mass of this property was not in Chinese waters, and therefore not contraband, at this time; it was not seized nor physically nor legally seizable by the Chinese government when given up'; and Alexander Matheson made the same complaint to the Select Committee on compensation. But this was really an ingenious piece of deception. The bulk of the opium handed over came from Lintin, and the merchants were pretending it did not count as Chinese territory, for a reason which Alexander Graham had given in his 1840 pamphlet. Vattel, he pointed out, had laid down that in international law a nation could not claim authority unless it were capable of causing the authority to be respected, which China, in the case of Lintin, had clearly been unable to do. Thomas de Quincey took the same line in an article in *Blackwood's* that spring, even to the point of admitting that the British, confident of their strength, did not content themselves with intercepting contraband in the course of landing, 'but *having power to sustain the claim*, go somewhat further; they make prize at sea of cargoes which are self-demonstrated as contraband'. It was an oddly Machiavellian line to take; but in any case, it was based on a misconception. The opium had been brought in from Lintin or from outside Chinese waters voluntarily, because the merchants realised they would get more from it in compensation, assuming that Elliot's pledge was honoured, than they could hope to get from taking it away and trying to sell it elsewhere. Yet the belief remained that Lin had committed a breach of international law; W. D. Bernard was to cite it in the list of accusations he used to justify his description of Lin as 'the Robespierre, the terrorist, the reckless despot'.

Whether or not Lin had the right to confiscate the opium, he had no right, the third accusation against him ran, to put British lives in jeopardy by a blockade designed to starve them into submission; 'an act of atrocity that no usage, no custom, no respect to popular prejudices in China, ever would, or ought to allow England to endure, much less to sanction', Stephen Lushington told the

Commons, 'A grievous sin – a wicked offence – an atrocious violation of justice, for which England had the right, a strict and undeniable right, to demand reparation by force if refused peaceable applications'.

If England had that right, it was odd that she had not invoked it on the earlier occasion which Lin had actually used as his precedent; the time that supplies to Macao had been cut off in 1808 until Admiral Drury withdrew his forces. So far from the Chinese authorities being denounced on that occasion, Sir George Staunton had expressed the view that they had shown 'a degree of placability and forbearance' for which few people would have ventured to hope. And Lin had been similarly forbearing. He had made clear to the foreigners in the Factories that if they obeyed the laws, they would be in no danger of starving. Nor were they: the blockade, to judge from Hunter's and Forbes's recollection, was regarded as a lark. The fact that there were no longer Chinese servants to do all the chores, Hunter recalled, meant that—

> they were compelled, in order to live, to try their own skill, in cooking, to make up their own rooms, sweep the floors, lay the table, wash plates and dishes! It may be supposed that it produced discontent, complaints and impatience. Not at all; we in the Suy Hong – and it was the same with our fellow-prisoners in the other factories, with few exceptions – made light of it, and laughed rather than groaned over the efforts to roast a capon, to boil an egg or a potato.

Hunter's boss made such a mess of boiling rice (it resembled glue) that he was relegated to cleaning silver, and eventually to sweeping the floors; his successor, after 'boiling the eggs till they acquired the consistency of grapeshot', had to lay the tables. Every day they met in the square to discuss their experiences, considering them great fun. In Whampoa, too, the beleaguered ships' crews had felt no alarm, as Surgeon Paterson of the Indiaman *George IV* recalled a year later in a letter to *The Times*. The officers enjoyed a round of dinner parties—

> *distinguished by an abundance of hilarity and capital cheer that would have gratified the most fastidious* bon vivant. *Who furnished, pray, the turkeys, mutton, capon, etc., as well as the rich selection of fresh vegetables which graced the tables? The barbaric and inhospitable Chinese government. So far from the British in Whampoa entertaining any apprehension of their personal security, as has been alleged in parliament and in other high quarters, I distinctly and most confidently declare, that no such idea could ever have entered the head of any individual but the veriest poltroon.*

Up to the point that the British left Canton, in fact, Lin's behaviour to them had been so obviously beyond reproach that it was difficult for all but the most sycophantic of government supporters to display him as a monster. It was what he had done later – the threat that the wells would be poisoned, and the demand that a British subject should be handed over to be tried, and presumably

executed, for murder – that was exploited most energetically in the debates. The *Lady Hughes* episode was recalled,
and the attempt to arrest Dent, the implication being that
he might well have paid the same penalty if the other
merchants had not stopped him from giving himself up.
The cause of the war, Wellington told the Lords, could
not be opium, because all the opium had been surrendered;
it had arisen out of another set of circumstances, 'and first
of all, a claim for the surrender of Englishmen to be put
to death, because a Chinese had lost his life in an affray'.
But homicide cases had been discreetly settled since the
Lady Hughes case (which de Quincey took some of the
heat out of, in his article, by disclosing that the unfortunate
gunner had not been some young British tar cut off at
the outset of a promising career, but an elderly Portuguese).
And so far from the Chinese authorities having ordered
the arrest of Dent with a view to executing him, one of
his partners assured the Commons Select Committee that
they had wanted to take him in only because they knew
him to be a very kind-hearted man; they felt sure he would
break down if he saw his old friends, the Hong merchants,
in cangues and chains. If anybody had had to be handed
over following the Kowloon affair, admittedly, he would
have been lucky to escape execution; but there was every
excuse for Lin's anger, in view of what the sailors had
done on their drunken spree.

'Foreign Devils'

Palmerston's formal case against China cannot, therefore, be regarded as a convincing explanation for the decision to send an expeditionary force; and the fact that it was timelessly supplemented by other arguments suggests this was uneasily appreciated at the time. In general, they were designed to prove that Lin had strained an already unhappy commercial relationship to breaking point. Lin's aggression, Alexander Graham asserted in his pamphlet in support of the merchants, 'does not stand alone – isolated and unprecedented aggression on their part; but is, on the contrary, merely the last of *a series of wrongs and insults* by which our commercial intercourse with China has been from time to time characterised'; a view echoed in the parliamentary debates, when government supporters did their best to prove that the expedition was necessary to redress the wrongs perpetrated by a 'barbarous and uncivilised people', as Hobhouse described them in the Commons.

The descriptions of China and the Chinese written in or about the period by merchants, missionaries and travellers present a very different picture. There were, admittedly, a few features of the Chinese way of life which Westerners could cite as barbarous, such as the use of torture to secure confessions. But on balance, in the opinion of most responsible British and American merchants, they were a remarkably civilised people; not surprisingly, Marjoribanks reminded the Commons in 1833, when it was remembered they had built wonderful cities and splendid edifices at a time when Britons were still staining themselves with woad. In important respects, Elliot thought, the Chinese were 'the most moderate and reasonable people on the face of the earth'. Even John Francis Davis, who was to become more critical of them following his return to China after the war, when they were distinctly less friendly to foreigners, was high in his praise of their society in his 1836 book. He was particularly impressed by the fact that where there was poverty it was only because the population was too heavy for the land to sustain, 'and not from any fault in the distribution of wealth, which is perhaps far more equal here than in any other country'; the consequence, he thought, of the importance accorded to the family tie, 'in which they perhaps beat our economists.' Although physically they were generally strong and healthy, he was impressed by the way they rated learning and literary accomplishment more highly than physical or military prowess; and he cited Sir George Staunton's opinion, attributing their moral and political standing—

to the regard paid to the ties of kindred; to the sobriety, industry and intelligence of the lower classes; to the nearly total absence of feudal rights and privileges; to the equal distribution of landed property; to the indisposition of the government to engage in schemes

of foreign warfare and ambition; and to a system of penal laws
the most clearly defined, comprehensive and business-like of any,
at least among Asiatics.

Nor could it seriously be argued that the Chinese reserved their civilised ways for themselves, treating foreigners with disdain. 'Wherever we went', Lindsay had written in his description of the *Lord Amherst's* exploratory voyage, 'we found the people anxious, beyond our hopes, for inter-course with us; and I declare that we met with more kindness and civility from the Chinese during our voyage than travellers could expect or experience from any civil-ised nation in the world'. The authorities, too, were scrupulously careful to ensure that visitors received adequate protection. 'Should a foreigner get into a distur-bance in the street', Hunter recalled, 'it was generally safe to say it was his own fault; the Chinaman went to the wall'. In China, Jardine admitted, 'a foreigner can go to sleep with his windows open, without living in dread either of his life or his property, which are well guarded by a most watchful and excellent police'. Until the December 1838 riot, Elliot assured Palmerston, he had believed there was 'no part of the world in which the foreigner felt more secure' than in Canton. Even in that riot, as the *Chinese Repository* commented, the mob had been more noisy than dangerous; little damage had been done compared to what might have been expected anywhere else. And when the British merchants returned to Canton after the hostilities they found that their property, which had been left with the Hong merchants, was there; and it was handed back to them.

How, then, was it possible for pamphleteers and politicians to portray the Chinese as uncivilised? Chiefly, to judge by the references to it, because of the language in which Chinese edicts referring to foreigners were often couched, an extraordinary mixture of bombast and menace. But this, as was pointed out by opposition M.P.s in the Commons debate, was largely a consequence of Morrison's translations, which had made them sound much more sinister than they really were; for example, the description of the foreigners as 'barbarians'. The Chinese term could be used derogatorily; but it also happened to be the standard designation for people who were not citizens of the Empire. The use of opprobrious expressions to describe people of other races, or religions, was in any case widespread, as the French traveller C. S. Sonnini had noticed: 'the Turk described the European by no other epithet than that of *infidel*; the Egyptian Mussulman, still coarser, treats him merely as *dog*', these terms being 'indiscriminately employed by persons who had no intention of offering an insult'. 'Aliens', with its dual sense, neutral and disparaging, might have been the closest approximation to the Chinese usage; certainly it would have been less misleading than 'barbarians'.

Similarly 'fan-quae', 'foreign devils', sounded offensive, but the expression had originated, innocently enough, from the fact that the Portuguese in Macao looked like the stock Chinese idea of a devil, which was not far removed from the English idea; when Commissioner Lin paid his first visit to Macao in 1839, he noted in his diary that he now understood why the Portuguese had been called 'devils'; it was the way they shaved, leaving a beard with a curly tuft. 'Fan-quae' had come to be used, Too-good Downing insisted from his experience in China in the 1830s, 'without intention to insult'. As for the description of Napier as the 'Eye', Staunton pointed out that Morrison must have known the correct translation from the Chinese was 'head or principal person', because that was the translation he had put in his own dictionary. As such expressions had been exploited to create bad blood, Staunton felt, translations of this kind could not be too severely reprobated.

There was also a simple explanation, according to Captain Bullock, one of the combatants in the London war of the pamphlets in 1840, for the 'childish arrogance' of the language used by Chinese officialdom. He agreed it was often ludicrous; but it was not meant to be offensive, only 'to impress upon all parties concerned the immense importance of his sacred majesty'. The Emperor had to rule over a vast population, with the additional handicap that his dynasty were usurpers; and this had led to an exaggerated insistence upon respect and reverence for the Dragon Throne. His subjects, it was felt, must perpetually be reminded that their country was the centre of the civilised world, 'the Middle Kingdom', to which all others were tributary; and that their emperor was *the* Emperor, the representative on earth of the divinity.

Kow-tow

It was this belief that had led to the continuance of the practices that riled Palmerston: the refusal to grant diplomatic recognition to representatives of foreign countries, and the insistence that foreigners must communicate with the authorities only by means of a petition. It was irritating, too, to know that these indignities were unlikely to be removed unless the British government was prepared to send an emissary who would perform the kow-tow before the Emperor, and perhaps not even then. The former President of the United States, John Quincy Adams, Chairman of the Senate Foreign Affairs Committee (who had been Secretary of State at the time when the sailor from an American ship was executed by the Chinese, and had evidently experienced something of Palmerston's frustration) thought that this was the real reason for the decision to send the expeditionary force to China. The Chinese Empire, Adams told the Massachusetts Historical Society in the winter of 1841, held all other nations to be tributary barbarians: an 'enormous outrage'. He went on:

> *It is a general but I believe altogether mistaken opinion that the quarrel is merely for certain chests of opium imported by British merchants into China, and seized by the Chinese government for*

having been imported contrary to law. This is a mere incident to the dispute; no more the cause of war than the throwing overboard of the tea in the Boston harbor was the cause of the North American revolution.

The cause of the war is the kow-tow! – the arrogant and insupportable pretensions of China, that she will hold commercial intercourse with mankind not upon terms of equal reciprocity, but upon the insulting and degrading forms of relation between lord and vassal.

This view has been echoed recently by Edgar Holt, arguing that the expedition was sent to end China's assumption of superiority: 'the opium crisis, though it clearly provoked the actual outbreak of hostilities, was and remained incidental to the real struggle, which was to last for twenty years, for the abolition of the kow-tow, both literally and metaphorically'. But the notion that the desire for the abolition of the kow-tow literally promoted the conflict is not supported by a study of contemporary sources. If the humiliation Amherst had suffered half-a-century before had really still rankled, more use would surely have been made of it by the merchants in their propaganda, and by M.P.s in their speeches. As for the metaphorical kow-towing – the need to petition, and to maintain indirect communication with the authorities through the Hong – they certainly preoccupied Palmerston to the exclusion of more urgent matters, but there is no indication that he regarded them as a justification for the campaign. It was the war which gave him the opportunity to get rid of them, rather than their existence which gave him the opportunity to make war.

Bullion

One other argument was freely used to show that the blame for the war should be placed on the Chinese. They were indeed worried about the inflow of opium, the contention was, but not because it was a pernicious drug. On the contrary, Indian opium was highly valued by those who smoked it. What had alarmed the authorities was that it spoiled the market for opium produced in China, because the Chinese poppy cultivators could not compete; and that it caused a drain of silver from the Imperial Treasury. 'The fact is,' Palmerston assured the Commons, winding up the China debate, 'this is an exportation-of-bullion question, an agricultural-interest question.'

The source for this view was the petition the Calcutta opium merchants sent to him in 1839. 'Like other half-civilised nations which understand not the principles of political economy', it ran, 'the Chinese consider the export of bullion as injurious to their well-being'; a point emphasised by Samuel Warren. It was a curious argument, though, for Palmerston to adopt, as his own government and its predecessors considered the export of bullion extremely dangerous to their own wellbeing, as the correspondence between the Council in Calcutta and Westminster endlessly reveals; the fear of being unable to pay for China tea without drawing on reserves was never far from British ministers' minds. For a member of a government which supported the corn laws, too, it came oddly to criticise the Chinese for wanting to protect their agricultural interest. But there is no evidence, in fact, that the Pekin authorities wished to protect the Chinese opium industry. On the contrary, when it had become known in the early 1830s that poppy was being grown, they had promptly banned it, apparently successfully. They *were* worried by the loss of specie – and with good reason; it put a premium on the coinage with which the peasants were supposed to pay their taxes, and at the same time devalued the copper coins which they used for ordinary transactions, causing discontent. But though the drain of silver had doubtless alarmed the government, Elliot felt certain that it was 'the manner of the rash course of traffic within the river' which had contributed most of all 'to impress the urgent necessity of arresting the growing audacity of the foreign smugglers, and preventing them from associating themselves with the desperate and lawless of their own large cities'.

'This black and envenomed poison'

There remains to be considered Thomas Arnold's explanation of the cause of the opium war: that it was to maintain the smuggling of a demoralising drug, which the Chinese wanted to keep out, but which the British were determined to force upon them. On this hypothesis the growth of the opium traffic smuggling had been successfully hidden from the Emperor until the 1830s, partly because it was so profitable to the mandarins, partly for 'face'. But its rapid spread, coupled with the evidence contained in the memorials, had decided him to act; and from 1835, there had been a sustained effort to end the traffic, which in turn had compelled the merchants to demand, and the British government to use, force, to ensure that it continued.

There was little attempt at the time on the British side to deny that opium addiction was a serious problem in China. The notion that opium smoking might not really be so deleterious to health or morals, which was to become one of the stock defences of the traffic later in the century, was rarely heard in the 1840s (though there was a disposition to suggest that it was no worse, and might have less sinister consequences, than drinking spirits). Reliable evidence of the effects is admittedly lacking; the absence of any statistical apparatus made subjective estimates the only available source, and they were largely guesswork. In his *China*, the missionary W. H. Medhurst surmised that the average consumption of opium by those who smoked it was around one tenth of an ounce a day; and if this was correct, there would have been around three million regular smokers. But it was not the smoker who took the same limited amount every day who was the main cause of concern. It was the man who took increasing quantities:

In proportion as the wretched victim comes under the power of the infatuating drug, so is his ability to resist temptation less strong; and, debilitated in body as well as mind, he is unable to earn his usual pittance, and not unfrequently sinks under the cravings of an appetite which he is unable to gratify. Thus they may be seen hanging their heads by the doors of the opium shops, which the hard-hearted keepers, having fleeced them of their all, will not permit them to enter; and shut out from their own dwellings, either by angry relatives or ruthless creditors, they die in the streets unpitied and despised . . . No man of feeling can contemplate this fearful amount of misery and mortality, resulting from the opium trade, without an instinctive shudder.

The more responsible merchants shared Medhurst's views. 'To any friend of humanity,' Marjoribanks thought, it was 'a painful subject of contemplation, that we should continue to pour this black and envenomed poison into the sources of human happiness – the misery and demoral- isation are almost beyond belief. Any man who has witnessed its frightful ravages and demoralising effects in China must feel deeply on this subject.' G. Tradescant Lay, who had re-entered the controversy, agreed. London, he claimed, had no spectacle so degrading as the Canton opium smoker, with the 'lank and shrivelled limbs, tottering gait, sallow visage, feeble voice, and the death-boding glance of his eye'.

Nor was it simply the effect the drug had on those who became addicted to it that disturbed the Chinese government. Its effects on society in general were also destructive. Here, admittedly, it was opium's illegality that was responsible; prohibition created the same problems as it was to do in the United States a century later. Everybody who handled or took the drug became a lawbreaker; and once in that category, there was a strong temptation to make as much as possible out of the drug by selling it, or by taking bribes to let it through, or by blackmail. The rewards offered by the authorities for information leading to arrests led to a tribe of informers who, according to Gutzlaff, became 'both murderous and unscrupulous; whoever had a grudge against his neighbour, denounced him as a transgressor of the laws against the drug'; and as the excuse of 'searching for opium' gave officials the opportunity to rob honest traders, thousands of innocent people became the victims of injustice. Lin himself admitted, when he arrived in Canton, that it had everywhere become 'a common topic of conversation that this searching would give rise to injury, seizures of property, connivance, falsehoods bribes and similar abuses'. But all this, as Charles King put it in a letter to Elliot, had risen because 'the British merchants, led on by the East India Company', had been carrying on the trade in defiance of the laws of the Empire, and of the best interests of the Chinese people.

This cause has been pushed so far as to derange the currency, to corrupt its officers, and ruin multitudes of its people. The traffic has become associated, in the politics of the country, with the axe and the dungeon; in the breasts of men in private life, with the wreck of property, virtue, honour and happiness. All ranks, from the Emperor on the throne to the people of the humblest hamlets, have felt its sting. To the fact of its descent to lowest classes of society, we are frequent witnesses; and the Court gazettes are evidence that it has marked out victims for disgrace and ruin even among the imperial kindred.

The Merchants

There is no reason, then, to doubt that the Chinese author-ities desire to end the opium traffic was genuine, and that their effort failed only because the British were determined that it should not be ended. But how, in that case, should the responsibility be apportioned for the policies the British had followed?

Unquestionably the country ship merchants had provided the opium supply, and increased it by bringing in Malwa, to disrupt the Company's policy of restricting production. They had introduced hundreds of thousands of Chinese to the drug, first from Lintin and later through the development of the coast trade. Refusing to accept the Supracargoes' authority, too, they had embarked on a campaign of deliberate provocation, not caring what offence they gave to the Chinese. Soon after he became Superintendent, Elliot described them as *a class of people who can never be left to their own devices among the natives of this country, without the utmost risk to the safety of this trade, and to the respectability of the national character. I never put my foot out of doors that I do not observe evidence of a growing dislike upon the part of the common people to our countrymen. It is the fashion of the young men particularly to treat the Chinese with the most wanton insult and contumely, and if this folly be not checked we shall have ugly matters to deal with.*

Even before he left China in 1837 Toogood Downing had noticed the signs of growing resentment against foreigners in Pekin, and felt that one of the chief reasons was 'the encouragement given by them to this forbidden trade'. Looking back over the conflict of 1844, Forbes expressed his conviction that what had wrecked the old system of connivance was the British merchants' greed; 'in order to get nearer to the market, and save the expenses of the store ships, they sent opium to Whampoa in small craft under the British flag, and even to Canton itself'. And Hunter, quoting Elliot's view that the Chinese had taken the unprovoked initiative in aggressive measures against British life, liberty and property, objected to the word 'unprovoked'. Elliot's despatch, he complained, had 'contained not a word of the provocation given by foreigners in continuing the condemned traffic under constantly repeated injunctions against doing so' – a criticism which Elliot, in a calmer moment, accepted; 'all these desperate hazards have been incurred', he wrote, 'for the scrambling and, comparatively considered, insignificant gains of a few reckless individuals, unquestionably founding their conduct on the belief that they were exempt from the operation of all law, British or Chinese'.

On another level, too, it is easy to show that the responsibility for the war lay principally with two of the merchants, Jardine and Matheson. It had been Matheson who pioneered the smuggling of Malwa from Damaun, and, later, the coast trade; Matheson, too, who orchestrated the Canton merchants' defiance of the Supracargoes in the early 1830s, and employed the most obstreperous of them, James Innes. With Jardine, Matheson had organised the lobbying campaign in Britain from 1836, perhaps the first and certainly one of the most successful of its kind. And it had been Jardine who advised Napier, and whose advice the Foreign Secretary took when planning the expedition, as he himself was handsomely to acknowledge. Writing to Abel Smith after hearing the treaty of Nanking had been signed, Palmerston said it had been mainly due to the information which he and Jardine had provided

that we were able to give our affairs, naval, military and diplomatic, in China, those detailed instructions which have led to these satisfactory results. It is indeed remarkable that the information which we procured from yourself and various other persons whom we consulted in the autumn of 1839, which was embodied in instructions which we gave in February 1840, was so accurate and complete that it appears that our successors have not found any reason to make any alterations in them . . . The conditions of peace imposed upon the Emperor are precisely those which we had instructed our plenipotentiaries Elliot and Pottinger to obtain. There is no doubt that this event, which will form an epoch in the progress of the civilisation of the human race, must be attended with not unimportant advantages to the commercial interests of England.

It was not strictly true that the Nanking terms were precisely those which the plenipotentiaries had been instructed to obtain. There was one significant difference. Palmerston had said that they should secure either the ports or an island, and Pottinger had secured both; the island being Hong Kong, in spite of the fact that Palmerston had specifically objected to it, when he heard Elliot had included it in his Chuenpi terms. Being primarily concerned with opium, the opening up of more ports to the legal trade was of little direct importance to Jardine Matheson; the existence of a secure base for their operations, on the other hand, was essential. 'If the lion's paw is to be put down on any part of the south side of China,' a writer in Matheson's *Canton Register* had urged in 1836, 'let it be Hong Kong!' The Portuguese, he went on, had made a mistake; 'they adopted shallow water and exclusive rules. Hong Kong, deep water, and a free port for ever'. Chusan would have been acceptable to them, had not the high incidence of disease among the troops during the Elliots' campaign put it out of the running: Jardine and Matheson had then decided it must be Hong Kong. Before

Pottinger left London, Jardine took care to brief him. 'I have had two or three conferences with him of a very satisfactory nature', Jardine wrote to tell James Matheson. 'On Friday he dined with me, no one present but Alexander Matheson, until John Abel Smith joined us about ten . . . I intend to send him a few hints on paper through the Foreign Office tomorrow.' It was to James Matheson's house that Pottinger went as soon as he arrived in Hong Kong; and with Matheson that he corresponded while he was away from the island. It is impossible to be certain that it was Jardine's and Matheson's influence which induced him to exceed his brief and include the cession of Hong Kong in the peace terms; but the inference is hard to resist.

Government, Company and Council

Important though their contribution was, however, Jardine, Matheson and the opium merchants in general cannot be regarded as responsible for the war. They were the guerrillas; the militant wing of the British colonialist movement. They could at any time have been brought to heel by the British government, or the Council in Calcutta; even by the abject Sir George Robinson at Lintin, if he had been so instructed. They were not disciplined because it was not in the interests of the British government or the Calcutta Council that they should be.

In matter of speculation, Alexandre Dumas was to

remark a couple of years after the war in *The Count of Monte Cristo*, man proposes, money disposes. It is never easy to assess how far the needs of commerce and revenue are paramount in decision-taking; but it can at least be shown why the governments had to attend carefully to them, in the case of opium. The expansion of the traffic from the beginning of the century to the outbreak of hostilities can be simply presented in a graph, showing (very roughly) the rise in the number of chests of the drug sold by the Company, the great bulk of which went to China.

Neither the British government nor the East India Company, therefore, could have tried to pretend that the exportation of Indian opium to China was a trifling matter. Their defence had to be that it was none of their business. Though the Company's opium was involved the Company, they claimed, had nothing whatsoever to do with the contraband traffic, as the opium and consumption of the drug lay exclusively with the Chinese. And if it were decided as a matter of moral principle that drugs ought not to be manufactured except for medical uses, it would have been futile to try to suppress opium production in India (even if that were feasible) as the only result would be the ruin of the India poppy cultivators without any benefit to the Chinese, who would have obtained the drug from other sources.

The first of these propositions hardly needs refuting in view of the abundant evidence that the Company was involved, directly or indirectly, in all stages of the traffic, from the advances to the cultivators to the book-keeping in Canton. Even David Owen, having unaccountably came to the conclusion that the evidence he had unearthed for his *British Opium Policy* in some way justified the Company's policies, had to qualify its spokesmen's stock argument; 'the Company's official interest in its narcotic production', he wrote, 'ceased with the auction sale' – his qualification being the insertion of the word 'official'. *Un*officially, the Company's interest was maintained right through to the point of sale to the Chinese. Although the opium was auctioned in Calcutta to independent merchants, they were permitted to buy it only on condition they took it to China; and they took it in the Company's chests, because the Company did not care to have spurious imitations sold in its name, and because the Chinese smugglers wanted to be sure it really was the Company's product (the fact it was the Company's was not necessarily a guarantee of quality, but it meant that a refund might be obtained if serious adulteration were found). The Company went to considerable trouble to ensure not merely that its opium was manufactured to suit Chinese tastes, but even that it was wrapped in ways likely to attract them; in 1821 experiments were made with different types of packaging, to see which the Chinese customers preferred. For the British government to insist that 'it had no knowledge of the existence of any but the legal trade', was, therefore, as Gladstone commented, 'a miserable equivocation'.

Its second claim, though, that it was the Chinese demand for the drug, rather than the Company's need to sell it to them, which was responsible for the massive increase in sales – that it was a pull from the consumer, rather than the push from the vendor – is harder to refute, backed up as it was with so much evidence that the traffic had been greatly facilitated by the connivance, and sometimes the active assistance, of the Chinese authorities.

Was corruption the cause of the spread of the drug habit, or did the spread of the drug habit breed the corruption? The weight of contemporary testimony suggests that the Chinese were not easily corruptible. In their commercial dealing, the Company and the merchants found the Hong to be trustworthy. Their integrity, Hunter thought, was 'unsurpassed by the mercantile classes of any other country'. Jardine agreed; business in Canton was 'conducted with unexampled facility, and in general with singular good faith'. The complaint of corrupt practices was ordinarily made only about the mandarins, or those who worked for them; and this was chiefly because every transaction made had to be lubricated by the payment of the required amount of 'squeeze'. The use of 'squeeze', though, was not inherently corrupt. Everything depended on the integrity of the official; and according to Davis, the Chinese officials were generally men of surprisingly high calibre. Senior administrative and judicial posts, he had found, were with few exceptions filled by men who had been selected on a basis of merit, and who had given evidence in examinations of superior learning and talent, 'without regard to birth or possessions'; and he quoted a friend's opinion that the reason so huge a country was so peaceable was that the fairness of the method of selection gave 'every person in China (with the exception of menial servants, the lowest agents of the police, and comedians) a solid reason to be satisfied with the system'. Ordinarily, it was ambitious men who overturned governments; in China, Davis remarked approvingly, 'there is a road open to the ambitious, without the dreadful alternative'.

This was in striking contrast to the British system, by which advancement could as a rule be obtained only through influence and wealth. To secure a parliamentary seat, even after the passing of the Reform Bill, required both. Writing to Peel in 1841 to beg him to include her husband in his government, Mary Anne Disraeli actually boasted that £40,000 had been spent, due to her influence, on winning Maidstone from the Whigs; and she pledged it as a safe seat to the Tories for the future. As for jobs in the East India Company, they were distributed exclusively through the patronage enjoyed by the directors.

In Britain, though, the corruption was at source. Having acquired a post, the occupant was then expected to behave according to the conventions, rejecting bribes. 'Squeeze' appeared to the British, when they encountered it, in China, as bribery; and it was a weakness of the system that it very easily became bribery, wherever a local mandarin was needy or greedy. In Canton, though, 'squeeze' was usually applied with care and dexterity. The Company Supracargoes would find that the amounts demanded were put up only when, say, some incident had given offence to the authorities; it was the Viceroy's, or the Hoppo's, way of indicating displeasure. But the opium traffic had disrupted the system; partly because it was so lucrative to all concerned that higher 'squeeze', when demanded, could easily be paid; partly because it was conducted on behalf of the East India Company, on whose trade Canton so heavily depended. The Hong merchants owed their livings to the continued trade, in tea particularly; so did the tea growers; so did the mandarins, whose income was largely dependent upon how much 'squeeze' they could safely take from the Hong. All concerned had consequently been prepared to bend imperial regulations, with a view to preserving this harmonious and very profitable relationship.

The existence of corruption in China led easily to the next assumption: that the reason for the opium traffic was the demand that existed there, which the mandarins exploited; and that if the Company's product had not been available to satisfy it, the opium would simply have been imported from other sources, leaving the Chinese no better off, and British India the poorer.

What would have happened if the Company's opium had never been exported to China cannot now be estimated with any certainty; but there is some evidence that the opium-smoking habit might never have taken hold. The

Chinese, foreign observers were agreed, were an unusually temperate people. They took large quantities of tea, and enjoyed smoking tobacco; but what would now be described as 'hard' drugs were virtually unknown. Rice wine was sometimes taken with meals, and a liquor distilled from rice at celebrations; but drunkenness was rarely seen. In the opinion of R. Montgomery Martin, who lived in Hong Kong in the 1840s, the Chinese were the most sober, as well as the most responsible, people on earth. Why, then, had some of them taken to opium? Martin thought it was because the Manchus had tried to impose an alien rule of law, with the help of despotism which 'destroyed public energy and private enterprise, leaving to the wealthier classes no other source of enjoyment than what may be temporarily, but dearly, obtained from sensual indulgence'; and opium happened to offer them 'a transient pleasure and oblivion of woes, which was difficult to resist'. Such alienation has often been blamed for the spread of drug cults in more recent times, and it is at least a plausible hypothesis that the dreamy pleasures which the Chinese smoker came to expect from his pipe provided him with a solace he could not get from alcohol. But a distinction has to be made between the firm demand which comes from habit and addiction, and the flexible demand which is aroused by curiosity. When the merchants began to prospect along the coast, they found plenty of interest in the prospect of securing supplies of opium; but the interest was not keen enough to impel Chinese smugglers to come to Lintin from afar. Although curiosity simplified the task of selling the drug in new places when supplies exceeded the amount of demand that habit and addiction had established in the Canton region, there is nothing to suggest that it would have been impossible for the Company to continue to restrict production, and therefore consumption, if its monopoly had not been broken by the Damaun traffic. Doubtless its opium would have been supplemented by supplies from Turkey, and possibly from Chinese sources; but they would have been used only to stretch the supplies from Bengal.

With most commodities, where there is sufficient purchasing power and freedom of choice, demand creates supply. With illegal drugs it is often the availability of the supply that creates the demand. The reason is that the difference between cost price and selling price is so great that it is worth the producers' while to 'push' their product in order to increase the number of potential customers, which they would not be able to do, or would not bother to do, if the profit margin were small. The figures suggest that the Chinese could be persuaded to take as little or as much of the drug as the Company cared to send. During the first decade of the century, when the Company was restricting output, they remained perforce content with their 2,500 chests or so a year, supplemented by sporadic imports from Turkey. It was only when Malwa began to add to the flow, and they absorbed it, that the Company realised that even though there might be temporary gluts, they could be induced to purchase ever-increasing quantities; a realisation that encouraged the abandonment of the policy of restriction. As the Company's later directives to the Canton merchants showed, the amount of opium sent to China was from that time on determined by the amount produced, regardless of the demand. That this was a policy consciously decided upon in Calcutta is clear from St. George Tucker's comments. Since joining the Court of Directors, Tucker reminded his colleagues on it in 1841, he had

> uniformly and steadily opposed the encouragement given to the extension of the manufacture of opium; but of late years we have pushed it to the utmost height, and disproportionate prices were given for the article in Malwa. We contracted burdensome Treaties with the Rajput States, to introduce and extend the cultivation of the poppy. We introduced the article into our own districts, where it had not been cultivated before, or where the cultivation had been abandoned; and we gave our revenue officers an interest in extending the cultivation in preference to other produce much more valuable and deserving of encouragement.

Under Cornwallis and his successors, Tucker recalled, the plan had been very different: to circumscribe production, and even to eradicate it from some districts:

> How fatal have been the consequences of a departure from this wise and humane policy! Is there any man so blind as not to perceive that it has had a most injurious effect upon our national reputation?

If a revenue cannot be drawn from such an article, otherwise than by quadrupling the supply, by promoting the general use of the drug, and by placing it within the reach of the lower classes of the people, no fiscal consideration can justify our inflicting upon the Malays and Chinese so grievous an evil.

Although Staunton shared Wellington's view that the Chinese must be punished for what Lin had done he, too, blamed the Company's opium policy for the outbreak of the war. If the traffic had been left to look after itself, he told the Commons in 1843, 'if it had not received an extraordinary impulse from the measures taken by the East India Company to promote its growth, which almost suddenly quadrupled the supply, I believe it never would have created that extraordinary alarm in the Chinese authorities, which betrayed them into the adoption of a sort of *coup d'état* for its suppression'.

The conquest of Sind

The third argument, that if the Company had stopped buying and selling opium, the Chinese would have obtained it from other sources, was freely used by the merchants and their spokesmen; and it was adopted by Palmerston in his speech in the China debate. If British merchants were forbidden to deal in opium, he pointed out, the Americans would be waiting to carry it to China; doubtless using clippers which had formerly been British, but which

THE OPIUM WAR

their owners would simply switch to sail under the American flag.

It was certainly true that the merchants engaged in the opium traffic would have taken American registration the moment it became more convenient. Some of them had done so, during the 1839-40 trading season, in order to continue collecting tea from Whampoa. But the taking-over of the entire traffic would not have been as simple as Palmerston implied, because of American public opinion. By 1838 Olyphant and Co, alarmed at the way British merchants were bringing consignments of the drug to Whampoa, was warning its Boston office of the danger that the Chinese might retaliate by cutting off the legal trade with America as well as with Britain (Lin in fact did, though he removed the ban when the Americans signed the pledge to bring in no more opium); and at the time that the Tories were preparing to exploit the situation in China to embarrass the Melbourne government the Senator for Massachusetts, Caleb Cushing, was preparing to needle President Tyler's administration on the subject, and also to try to win some cheap popularity for himself. He had been disturbed, he told the Senate in March 1840, to hear that the British were regarding the Americans as their allies in the traffic. 'God forbid', he said, 'that I should entertain the idea of co-operating with the British government in the purpose it has, of upholding the cupidity and violence and high-handed infraction of all law, human and divine, which have characterised the operations of the

British, individually and collectively, in the seas of China'. The idea would no longer be entertained, he hoped, 'that she will receive aid or countenance from the United States in this nefarious enterprise'.

Cushing's righteous indignation might not be taken seriously in Washington, where he came to be known as a man who had 'voted for every bill and then justified every veto'; no doubt there were others, too, who shared John Quincy Adams' view, that the Chinese needed to be humbled. It is hardly conceivable, though, that American public opinion would have sanctioned a massive take-over by their merchants of the opium traffic into China; and assuredly the congress would not have sanctioned the despatch of an expeditionary force to compel the Chinese to accept it. The American merchants would not have cared to run the risk both of courting unpopularity at home and of losing their right to conduct their legal trade through Canton. Nor, if the Americans (or anybody else) had tried to take over the opium traffic, would they have found supplies readily available. When in the 1840 debate, Macaulay had decried the notion that if Britain co-operated with China, the opium traffic could be stopped and asked if the opposition were suggesting that Britain should pay the expense of a preventive service for the whole coast of China, he was answered by Gladstone with another question. 'Did the Rt. Hon. Gentleman opposite know that the opium smuggled came exclusively from British ports?' No preventive service would have been required;

'it was a matter of certainty that if we had stopped the exportation of opium from Bengal, and broken up the depot at Lintin, and had checked the growth of Malwa, and had put a moral stigma upon it, we should have greatly crippled, if indeed we had not entirely extinguished, the trade in it'. Gladstone was right. The Company had never had much difficulty in regulating poppy cultivation in Bengal; and though Malwa presented more of a problem, as production could not effectively be controlled in the native states, it would be a threat only so long as there was an outlet to the Indian Ocean, which smugglers could use. By the 1840s the Portuguese possessions had been cut off, by British occupations. Sind, which had retained its independence, alone offered the smugglers a possible outlet But there was a simple remedy: occupy Sind.

The conquest of Sind had been mooted in 1819, but had met with strong opposition from Sir Charles Metcalfe; and in spite of frequent complaints that the smugglers could not be controlled until the region was in British hands, his influence had prevailed until he left India in 1838 to become Governor of Jamaica. In a perceptive memorandum, warning that though Sind and Afghanistan had retained their independence 'the spirit of interference would no doubt soon find cause for the exercise of its withering and mischievous influence even in those states'. Interference had already been proposed: the Indian Ocean, he sadly remarked, 'our exterior boundary to the south, is almost the only power that has altogether escaped that suggestion'. Hardly had Metcalfe left when his forebodings were fulfilled. The decision was taken to reverse his policy and invade Afghanistan, ostensibly to protect the frontiers of India from the Russian menace. Kabul fell in 1839, and the usual rejoicings followed. But the venture was to end in the worst disaster ever to befall British arms. Two years later an uprising compelled the British to retreat; some 16,000 men and women tried to reach India; and there was only one survivor. Another victory was urgently required, to deflect public wrath in Britain; and Sind happened to be the only available victim. This was embarrassing, as the inhabitants had proved loyal allies; they had allowed the British force to march through to Kabul, and made no attempt to take advantage of the subsequent catastrophe. Napier, however, insisted that there would be disaffection; and in any case, the warriors of Sind were a danger. How little danger they really represented was revealed when with a force of only 3,000 he was able without difficulty to assume control of the whole basin from Sukkur to the sea.

The need for a quick, cheap victory was the immediate reason for the annexation of Sind: an act of aggression, St. George Tucker bitterly complained, foisted on the Company (which had to pay for it) without consultation. Behind the move, though, he felt sure, was the determination of the Council in Calcutta to close the smugglers' remaining route. This was not on account of the inroads they had been making into the Bombay traffic; it was to enable the Council to put up the Bombay transit duty without the risk of diverting supplies of Malwa into illicit channels. Naturally this was not stated at the time; but the duty immediately went up from £12 to £20 a chest; in 1845, to £30, and in 1847, to £40.

The occupation of Sind meant that it would no longer be possible for the British to claim that they could not control the supply of opium to China. With so vast a territory to police, it would not have been possible to prevent some smuggling; but the amounts which could have reached China from India would have become negligible compared to the 1830s. And as the Chinese did not care for Turkish opium, there was no other comparable source. The rising price, due to scarcity, would eventually have stimulated production elsewhere; but that would have taken many years. The 'if we don't send it, others will' argument, therefore, had little validity.

Divide and Rule

The available evidence, therefore, indicates that Thomas Arnold's instinct was correct when he put the blame for the war on the British Government's determination that the Chinese should continue to accept opium from India, whether as a legal importation or as contraband. But this is not to argue that the East India Company can be acquitted of responsibility – as David Owen, for one, felt that it could, at least as far as its Council in India was concerned. 'There can be no reasonable doubt', he claimed, 'that the course of action which the British government followed was charted in Canton and London, not Calcutta. The break with China was intended to serve interests other than those of Indian opium'. Interests other than the Council's were indeed being served by the opium traffic, but this did not necessarily mean that the Council had no share in the charting of the action's course. The continuing prosperity of the traffic was every bit as essential to the Council for its revenue, as it was to the Treasury for its excise duty and its bullion reserves. All three, however, felt it wise not to let themselves be formally identified with a policy which involved the smuggling of a deleterious drug into the territory of a friendly nation, in defiance of that nation's laws and of conventional morality. And it was mainly to prevent such identification that a colonial structure had evolved which amounted to an elaborate hierarchy of irresponsibility.

Theoretically, the Company ran India. But the Company was itself still controlled, as Buckingham reminded the Commons in the 1833 debate, by its shareholders:

a body fluctuating between 3,000 and 5,000 individuals, including men, women and children; the two latter predominating in number over the former, and each and all having no other interest whatever in the prospects of the country than just to secure their fixed dividend and nothing more . . . And yet to such a body was still to be confided the future government of India – a body so changeable that it was never composed of the same materials for any two days following, some selling out their stock, and some buying in, every day of the week, and no other qualification than being a stockholder being required to form part of this governing body.

The idea of committing the government of an Empire containing a hundred millions of souls to the management of a joint stock company, Buckingham went on, whose only interest was in dividends, was so preposterous 'that if it were now to be proposed for the first time in this House, no language would be adequate to describe the astonishment which its bare announcement would excite'. And it was entirely unnecessary; 'there was not in the world a more intelligent, high-minded and generous set of men', he felt, than the Company's administrators in India; they could with advantage have been recognised as colonial civil servants. But the British government could not afford – financially or morally – to grant them that recognition. Had India been prosperous, capable of paying for its administration, there would have been no problem. But to hold on to India meant the need to exploit every available source of revenue, including opium; and it was therefore better, for British governments' peace of mind, that the country should appear to be run as a commercial enterprise, though still ostensibly for the benefit of the inhabitants. So it had created 'a screen interposed between the government and the people', as St. George Tucker described it; retaining effective control of policy, but keeping itself in a position to leave the Company with 'the discredit of measures of which we may have disapproved'.

This could be likened to the parallel 'divide and rule' method by which territories were won, and then held, by playing off rival forces within them – Hindu and Moslem, in India; thereby acquiring an empire apparently with the consent of the people. But commercial divide and rule worked as it were vertically; from government down. Just as policies for which the British government did not care to avow the responsibility could be attributed to the Company, so the Company, for its own protection, had perfected the system by which it could claim to have no part in the opium trade, while in fact controlling it. Government, Company and Council were all part of the conspiracy to deceive.

Political Economy

It is doubtful, though, whether they would have been able successfully to maintain the deception had it not been for the assistance of a formidable ally: political economy. Waiting to be tapped in Britain was Arnold's mood of righteous indignation: the Evangelical fervour which so recently had helped to sweep away slavery in countries under British rule. The anti-slavery campaign, though, had been supported by political economists. The gospel according to Adam Smith, Mill, Malthus and Ricardo, laying down that there must be no interference with the mechanism of supply and demand, applied to labour as well as to goods; and slavery constituted an interference with the right of the individual to dispose of his labour in the open market for the best price he could command. But the political economists in general, and Ricardo in particular, wasted little time on moral judgments. Their philosophy was encapsulated in Gresham's Law, that bad currency drives out good. There was no point, they argued in insisting that bad currency ought not to drive out good, or in passing laws to try to stop it driving out good; as well might Canute's courtiers expect him to stop the incoming tide. Governments, therefore, must not waste their time trying to regulate trade, even if the trade happened to be in a dangerous drug. Had not Edmund Burke, whose *Thoughts on Scarcity* had been one of the earliest attempts to make political economy serve political ends, defended the state's right to be morally neutral in relation to spirits? They were abused, he had claimed, only by the dregs of the population who, in any case, if they could not intoxicate themselves with gin, 'would most likely resort to opium, or some other stupefying drug'. The same argument was to be adopted by the government's defenders in the 1840 debate, though they switched it the other way round; deprived of opium, they claimed the Chinese would resort to spirits, whose effects were just as bad, or worse.

The political economists went further. Economic laws,

they insisted, applied also to smuggling. They did not dispute a government's right to discriminate between commodities, classifying some as essentials, which the people should have, and others as luxuries, or poisons, which people would be better off without. But they pointed out that it was beyond the power of any government to *ban* goods in the second category. All that a government could do was impose duties on them; high enough to bring in revenue (thereby laudably reducing the amount the state would need from the taxpayer) but low enough to make smuggling unprofitable.

Political economy provided the government with a fig-leaf. What was regarded as immoral in ordinary life, ministers could argue, was legitimate in commercial affairs. This in fact was the argument which Lord Lansdowne used introducing the Lords' debate on the Company's charter in 1833, when he boasted of the knowledge of political economy which the British had shown 'when twenty years ago we first discovered that a wholesale system of prohibition was injurious, and when we imposed duties on articles in its stead'; if the Chinese wished to stop opium being smuggled into their country, they had only to follow the British example and legalise it. The opium merchants were also well aware of its potential value to them. In 1831 the *Canton Register* offered a prize to the writer of a book which would illustrate 'the great principles of Political Economy, applicable to the errors and abuses which may exist in China'; realising that it provided them with what amounted to a blanket dispensation for smuggling, they often cited it in their memorials and petitions. They did not, admittedly, like to be described *as* smugglers; but that was because the term, whatever it might connote to the political economists, still had sleazy associations for the public in general; not so much moral as social. Men who had planned on their return to England to acquire parliamentary seats did not care to be bracketed with the kind of buccaneer who arrived in a boat from France to roll barrels of brandy into Cornish coves. Yet the opium merchants did not feel that the traffic they were engaged in was morally wrong. When asked by the Commons committee in 1840 whether they had been unaware of any moral objections, Jardine's reply was that if the houses of parliament, 'with the bench of bishops at their back', thought it inexpedient to do away with the trade, he did not think it was necessary for a merchant to worry. If the Chinese wanted opium, that was their affair.

Political economy was also used to justify the methods which the Council used to keep down the price it paid the producers of opium. The basic proportion, based on the teachings of Malthus and Ricardo and elaborated upon by Ricardo's disciple J. R. McCulloch, was that cultivators, whether tenants or peasants, had no right to more than a bare living for themselves and their families. If they earned more, it could be taken from them by the landowner in the form of rent, or the state in the form of the land tax, and if they objected, they might be evicted, and another tenant brought in. To the argument that this was manifestly unjust, the political economists' reply was that nobody was compelled to become or remain a cultivator. That the alternative for many families might be starvation was not disputed; this form of culling was necessary, Malthus explained, to prevent over-population where resources were limited. Where the Council was not in a position to fix the price to be paid to the opium producer, it could use the land tax as its way to appropriate any surplus income the poppy cultivators might otherwise have enjoyed. Where it could fix the price, as in Bengal, it could still cite political economy in justification, by presenting Mill's theory that monopoly control was justified where the objective was revenue, not profit. Either way the opium producers could be relentlessly squeezed, with political economy as the excuse.

Palmerston

In Palmerston, there happened to be a Foreign Secretary who was a devoted adherent of the political economists, as his despatches continually revealed. He was forever emphasising that the British Government neither had nor wanted to have any control over commercial operations, even when they involved breaking the laws of the country concerned. Contraband, to him, conjured up a picture not so much of rogues criminally defying authority, as of authority criminally denying the benefits of legitimate trade to its subjects. According to Sir Charles Webster, he often referred to smuggling as the great medium for the exchange of goods between the countries of the world.

How much thought Palmerston gave to protecting the British merchants connected with the opium traffic from interference can be gauged by the way in which he tinkered with the wording of the instructions which were given to Napier, about what his attitude should be to the merchants who were exploring along the China coast with a view to finding new markets for opium. The original draft ran:

It is not desirable that you should encourage such adventures, but you must at the same time by no means check them. You have no powers to interfere, and your conduct must be consistent with the knowledge of that fact.

Dissatisfied, Palmerston altered the draft's wording:

It is not desirable that you should encourage such adventures, but you must bear in mind that you have no powers to interfere to prevent them.

And there was to be yet a further change, in the final printed version:

It is not desirable that you should encourage such adventures; but you must never lose sight of the fact that you have no authority to interfere with or to prevent them.

It was these adventures – particularly when they were undertaken up the Canton river, as well as along the coast – that precipitated the war, as even Palmerston's colleagues could not deny. The interruption of peaceful relations with China, Melbourne admitted in the Lords' debate, 'has been occasioned by the opium trade': and in his memorial to the Emperor Pottinger described it as 'the immediate cause of the war.' But a question remains: can Palmerston's defence – that he was taken by surprise by the sudden change of Chinese policy from connivance to suppression, and that if Lin had only shown reasonable patience, there would have been no need to send the expeditionary force – be accepted?

The evidence of the 1840 Blue Book made this defence difficult enough to sustain; but had the Foreign Office files from which it was compiled been available to the opposition, they could have torn it apart with even less difficulty. Certain relevant documents had been omitted: the most important of them being a detailed memorandum from the Board of Trade to the Foreign Office in 1833, pointing out that the Act depriving the East India Company of its monopoly required to be implemented not simply by the appointment of Superintendents and staff, but by the introduction of trade regulations, courts to enforce them, and funds to finance them. That Palmerston was aware of the risk of letting the existence of these recommendations become public knowledge is clear from a note he made in the margin of the despatch which Sir George Robinson sent him in 1835, complaining that Elliot had some important official document relating to China whose contents he would not divulge; fearing that it must be the recommendations, Palmerston called for an enquiry into how Elliot had got hold of a copy. Had they been printed in the Blue Book, they would have convicted Palmerston of culpable negligence for failing to do anything about them. But the Blue Book discreetly began with the appointment of Napier, two months after they had been received by the Foreign Office.

Other omissions included the exchange of barbed memoranda between Robinson and Elliot, which would have shown that the hopelessly unsatisfactory nature of the Superintendent's status had already become obvious by 1835; and proposals which Elliot had sent Palmerston in 1837 for remedying the situation by providing him with the authority he required to control British subjects. And the fact that Elliot had received no reply to his frequent appeals for clarification of his powers was ingeniously disguised; two short despatches which Palmerston had sent to him were brought forward a year, when they were printed in the Blue Book, giving the impression that his answers had been sent in good time, when in reality they had not reached China until after hostilities had broken out.

How far Palmerston himself was responsible for this fudging of the records is impossible to decide with any certainty; particularly as certain documents which might have given dues were at some point abstracted from the Foreign Office files, and have not been recovered. But it seems likely that he decided deliberately to deceive parliament, by editing the Blue Book himself. And though his failure even to try to implement the Board of Trade's recommendations, until it was too late, may have been due partly to ignorance of the situation in China and partly to indolence, it also seems likely that it reflected his determination to do nothing which might jeopardise the opium traffic. This policy of letting things slide had the advantage for him that it would work either way. If the Chinese continued to connive, the traffic could continue to flow; if they tried to stop it, they would provide the pretext he needed to use force to compel them to accept the opium, legally or illegally.

For obvious reasons, Palmerston could not admit that this was what was in his mind. Elliot and Pottinger had to be instructed to say that the British government 'by no means dispute the right of the government of China to prohibit the importation of opium into China, or to seize and confiscate any opium which, in defiance of prohibition duly made, should be brought in by foreigners or by Chinese subjects into the territories of the Empire'. Finding this instruction in the files, Professor Costin took it to be unmistakable proof that the war 'was not one, as has been sometimes said, to force the Chinese to trade with the British in opium'. But Palmerston did not care to risk the obloquy of compelling the Chinese to accept opium against their will. If legalisation appeared as one of the terms of the Treaty of Nanking, it would inevitably have been attributed to British compulsion; a version that the Chinese would doubtless have encouraged even if they had decided that legalisation was in their own interest. A safer approach was to wait until the Treaty was signed, and then put pressure on them to legalise the drug in the course of the detailed negotiations which were to follow about how the treaty ports would be administered. This was the course Pottinger took. Palmerston's instructions, he explained to the Chinese plenipotentiaries, were to emphasise what would be the consequences if the ban was maintained:

> *Experience has shown that it is entirely beyond the power of the Chinese government to prevent the introduction of opium into China; and many reasons render it impossible that the British government can give the Chinese government any effectual aid towards the accomplishment of this purpose. But while the opium trade is forbidden by law it must inevitably be carried on by fraud and violence; and hence must arise frequent collisions and conflicts between the Chinese preventive service, and the parties who are engaged in carrying on the opium trade. These parties are generally British subjects; and it is impossible to suppose that this private war can be carried on between British opium smugglers and the Chinese authorities, without events happening which must tend to put in jeopardy the good understanding between the Chinese and British governments.*

If the Chinese did not legalise opium, in other words, they would be recreating the circumstances which had led to the war. Should there be another, Palmerston's implication was, theirs would be the responsibility. That he should have felt bound to spell out the consequences in this way confirms that, as the Chinese plenipotentiaries suspected, legalisation was his aim.

On the evidence, then, it seems clear that Maurice Collis's conclusion – 'though mixed up with a dispute over opium which led to it being called the opium war, the real object of the operation was to force China to trade in a modern way' – while a correct appreciation of Palmerston's long-term strategy, tells only part of the story; easily the most important branch of the trade being in opium. He cannot have been under any illusion that the opening of the Chinese ports would lead to a massive demand for British goods. Had there been any such demand, it would long since have been manifesting itself in Canton, where the Hong merchants had been using every inducement to promote British goods, without success: imports were hardly higher than they had been at the turn of the century. Doubtless Palmerston sincerely believed that if China were opened up to Western influences, trade would eventually pick up; but in the meantime, what was vital was to keep the opium supply line open, to keep the administration in India solvent and to pay for China's tea.

In a sense, it was really the Tea War. To the British people, as Sir George Staunton reminded the Commons in one of his homilies in 1833, tea had come to be 'nearly equivalent to a necessary of life'; and to the Treasury no less essential, as the revenue from the tea duty brought in three to four million pounds a year, enough to pay nearly two-thirds of the cost of maintaining the entire civil establishment, including the Crown; a revenue raised 'with greater facility and certainty, and with less pressure on the people, than is the case with any other tax of equal amount'. Up to a point, therefore, there is substance in Hsin-Pao Chang's contention, in his *Commissioner Lin and the Opium War*, that any commodity would have served; that it might have been the Molasses War, if molasses had happened to be in demand, rather than opium. But there would not have been the same pressure of demand, as there was for a drug of addiction. It was the fact that the opium the Chinese liked to smoke came only from India, and that smokers became so dependent on it that they were prepared to pay heavily for their supplies, even at the risk of the cangue and the bamboo, that mattered. And only an addictive drug could have been marketed at a price high enough to provide the Company with so huge a profit margin (between 300-500 per cent, the Calcutta merchants claimed in the 1839 petition to Palmerston), ensuring a revenue of between one million and two million pounds a year. It had to be a drug, obtainable only from British India, for the Council, the Company and the British government all to be satisfied.

The Sorcerer's Apprentice

The first opium war came about not through any deliberate imperialist aim, but as the unforeseen end-product of developments in India: Clive's victory at Plassey, which brought the Mogul Empire under British rule: the destruction by William Bolts and the others of Bengal's economy, leaving opium as the Company's only profitable trade commodity; and the decision to keep opium production as a state monopoly, which left the administration dependent upon its revenue. So long as production could be restricted, the effects on China were not serious; but the decision to try to incorporate Malwa within the Company's monopoly, and the failure of that policy, had led inexorably to the uncontrolled increase in supply. With any other commodity so rapid an expansion of the traffic would have brought about its own remedy, by saturating the market; but China was so huge and so heavily populated that the merchants had been able to tap fresh sources of demand. But they had to create the demand; they had to 'push' the drug. As the traffic was illegal, the figures tended to be untrustworthy where they were available; but the picture that emerges from Jardine's and Matheson's correspondence is of dwindling profit margins as the turnover increased in the 1830s; and this in turn meant that the revenue which the Council obtained from each chest of opium produced was all the time falling. The Company had to run ever faster, in terms of production, in order to stay in the same place, in terms of revenue. Obviously this was not planned, either by the Company or the British government. It was the consequence of a misguided colonial policy, based on a fallacious interpretation of an undigested economic theory. And it had led inexorably to war in a way which, Lord Sandon suggested in the 1840 debate, could only be likened to Greek drama 'where, from the very first, they felt that disaster and calamity must arise'.

To compare it with Greek drama was to invest it with too much nobility. The story of the Sorcerer's Apprentice might have been more apt; or the analogy F. S. Turner was to make in his *British Opium Policy*, published forty years later. The government, he suggested, became addicted to their revenue like a Chinaman became addicted to the drug: beginning 'with a few whiffs, very pleasant, very refreshing'; progressing until he realises that it will be dangerous to get too dependent, but cannot bring himself to do anything about it; and eventually reaching the stage when it becomes an absolute necessity; 'the only anxiety now is to get a constant supply'. Just as, in desperation, the addict does not hesitate to commit a crime to ensure that he gets his supply, the British government had gone to war with China, to maintain its revenue; the reactions of the Chinese, provoked beyond endurance, providing the excuse for those who, like de Quincey, were embarrassed by the opium traffic but determined that it should not hold up the grand imperial design. 'It is obvious that we are now arrived at a crisis in which some powerful impression is indispensable', as he put it, 'in order not only to make the further progress which is challenged by our position in Asia, but to continue our hold on the progress which is made already'; a complacent expression of that ugly brand of chauvinism by which the commission of a rash or foolish act by an adversary cancels out all the multitude of rash and foolish actions that have goaded him into it.

The Chinese contribution to the drama was largely negative: the adoption of a policy likely to end in war, and certain to ensure losing it, because it was based on ignorance of Western ways, and contempt for Western military resources. The premise on which the policy was based was sensible: that foreigners, and particularly the British, were not to be trusted. As Buckingham reminded the Commons in the 1833 debate, when the Chinese had observed the ways of the East India Company in India,

landing first upon the coast as humble traders, and soliciting, as a matter of grace and favour, the grant of a small spot of land whereon to erect factories for the sale of goods, and afterward, under various pretences, possessing themselves of the whole country as sovereigns, was it to be wondered at that they should regard the Company as a set of designing adventurers who would insinuate themselves first, into the ports of China, then into the interior, and afterwards assume the dominion of the whole country?

But having come to that conclusion, the Chinese ought to have reasoned from it that they must be able, if necessary, to defend themselves. They had not done so. They were incapable of doing so; China had become, in Collis's words, 'the mummy of a once vital and marvellous civilisation'. To this extent, the first opium war can be regarded as the consequence of a clash of two cultures – as Fairbank described it, and as Hsü has argued recently in his *Rise of Modern China*. Opium, Hsü believes, was the immediate, but not the ultimate, cause of the war; it would have been bound to erupt anyway, eventually, owing to the incompatibility of Western commercial ideas and needs with Chinese self-sufficiency. The evidence suggests he is right; except that in all probability, war would have come sooner, rather than 'eventually'. To pay for their tea, the British would have had to find some excuse to impose terms even earlier; perhaps by sending Napier out backed by an expeditionary force. Nor would it have saved the Chinese if they had opened up their ports before they were compelled to, as Collis felt they should have done, allowing Western ideas as well as

Western goods to flow in. In the event, the opening up of the ports following the Treaty of Nanking was to afford the Chinese no protection. Britain and China were to remain on the verge of war for the next fifteen years, until the affair of the lorcha *Arrow* once again precipitated hostilities, and led to the despatch of another British expeditionary force, and further demands.

The beneficiaries

The opium war, in fact, settled nothing, except that the opium traffic would continue to the benefit of those who profited from it. 'Whatever their imbroglio with Commissioner Lin may have cost British opium dealers', Owen thought, 'the days of plenty that followed recompensed them many times over'. Admittedly Jardine Matheson, who had pioneered the coast trade, now faced greater competition owing to the improved facilities which would be offered to hitherto less enterprising firms by the use of the Treaty ports. But they would have faced even keener competition if the opium trade had been legalised; and they were so well established, particularly as they were able to settle and build in Hong Kong, that they had little need for concern. Matheson could afford to retire. He stopped off on his way back to England to be entertained by Jardine's old friend and business partner in the opium enterprise, the Parsee merchant Sir Jamsetjee Jejeebhoy, knighted for his services to British India, who in gratitude for Matheson's services in their mutual enterprise presented him with a fine service of plate. And Jardine's death in 1843 saved Matheson the trouble of finding a seat in the Commons; he took over Ashburton, and in due course received a baronetcy.

The East India Company was the other beneficiary, in that the Treaty ensured that its source of revenue would not be interrupted. Alarmed by the prospect that what had happened at Canton might lead to a campaign against the opium traffic in Britain, the Company in 1840 considered dropping the Calcutta opium monopoly and instead, imposing an export levy on the Bombay model. But if the monopoly were abandoned, it was pointed out, the competition among merchants to buy opium would encourage the cultivators to demand, and get, a better price, which would reduce the revenue. In the circumstances, it was decided, there could be no change in the system.

Apart from the fact their supplies of tea were guaranteed, the British people could expect no benefit from the war; and even before it was over, it had begun to dawn on some British merchants that they had been the victims of a confidence trick, played upon them by the Canton merchants. Opening up China to British trade was all very well in theory: but what trade would be opened up? The answer was the opium trade, because it was extracting so much of the purchasing power that could have been used to buy other British goods. According to Jardine, opium was retailed in China at around $100 a lb.; which meant that close on five hundred million dollars was being taken annually from the pockets of the consumers. How much of that amount would otherwise have gone to purchasing British manufactured goods is impossible to estimate; but without opium's competition, the state of the legitimate trade through Canton would surely have been very much healthier. Elliot had made this point in one of his

despatches to Palmerston in 1837. It was, he felt, suscep-
tible of proof 'that the gradual diversion of British capital
into other channels of employment than this would be
attended with advantageous circumstances'. But here again,
political economy had intervened. One of its tenets was
that capital could not profitably be diverted by state action;
it must be left to find its own level. The fact that it *was*
being diverted by the state in India, operating its opium
monopoly, was simply ignored, because the success of that
operation in terms of revenue could not comfortably be
fitted in with the dogma; and British Chambers of
Commerce had allowed themselves to be persuaded that
Matheson, Lindsay, Warren, Graham and the other
spokesmen of the Canton and Calcutta opium merchants
were speaking on behalf of British merchants, too. Fry's
Facts and Evidence ought to have been a warning, but its
humanitarian tinge did not appeal to them; and it was only
in 1842 that commercial doubts began to surface. That
summer, over two hundred British merchants signed a
memorial to Peel claiming that even if, as a result of the
war, opium were to be legalised:

> the trade would inevitably undermine the commerce of *Great Britain*
> with China, and prevent its being, as it otherwise might be, an
> advantageous market for our manufacturers. It would operate for
> evil in a double way; first, by enervating and impoverishing the
> consumers of the drug, it would disable them from becoming
> purchasers of our productions, and second, as the Chinese would

> then be paid for their produce chiefly as now in opium, the quantity
> of that article imported by them having of late years exceeded in
> value the tea and silk we receive from them, our own manufacturers
> would consequently be to a great extent precluded.

Events were soon to show that the petitioners' diagnosis
was correct; but they were rebuffed. They were even, by
a final irony, condemned as heretics for their presumption
in disputing the teachings of the political economists. What
right – a junior minister, W. B. Baring, asked in the
Commons – had they 'to deprive the Hindu from
competing with us in fair commercial rivalry in the ports
of China? How far would it be consistent with the honour
and duties of a Christian kingdom to put down this competition, free and equal competition of trade, by the exertion
of our supremacy over a subject race?'

The victims

It was, in fact, the Indian cultivator, Hindu or Moslem,
who was being deprived: not by state interference with
the opium traffic, but by state intervention to compel him
to grow poppy without gaining any advantage from his
crop, apart from a bare living. It was a short-sighted policy,
because by making it impossible for the peasants to earn
a disposable income, the Company destroyed the chance
to revive the flourishing economy which it had found
when it first came to trade with Bengal. And the poppy

growers, as Crawfurd had pointed out, were the hardest hit, because theirs was traditionally the best land, producing the finest crops. In every case where its cultivation had been increased, a Company opium agent told the Commons committee in 1832, it had been substituted for other produce which had been grown from time immemorial; and in the 1840 Commons debate Staunton expressed his regret that instead of being devoted to the cultivation of 'so pernicious an article', the most fertile land in India had not been used 'to produce that which was beneficial to man.'

The effect of the Treaty of Nanking was to ensure that the best land would continue to be used to grow poppy; that more land would continue to be appropriated for that purpose; and that the price paid for opium would remain low. This, coupled with the weight of the land tax, the salt tax and other duties, insured that the peasants would be kept down to the subsistence level. What this meant had already been vividly illustrated by Buckingham, Rickards, Crawfurd, and other writers who had shown that in Bengal, as in Ireland, the use of taxes and rack rents to soak up all the purchasing power of the peasants was a recipe for economic stagnation, punctuated by famine. As far back as 1812 David Macpherson had explained in his *History of the European Commerce with India* that it was foolish to cite political economy as a justification for the Council's policies, because it was pointless to prate of the necessity of free trade when there was no trade to be free; a warning echoed the following year by Wellesley who, though careful to insist that he did not undervalue the science (as its supporters already insisted it was) of political economy, expressed doubt whether India's economy was ripe for it. But such views had gone against the prevailing tide; and they had been ignored. Not that Wellesley would have had any notion what alternative economic and social policies to adopt. In any case, he shared the prevailing illusion that however appalling the condition of the natives they would have been even worse off without British protection. 'He would say, and he was borne out by the facts', he told Parliament, 'that no government had better fulfilled its duties to the people whom it governed than that of India'. The situation of the natives had been meliorated and improved: 'in every instance, their wants and comforts had been attended to'. This, after sessions in which witness after witness had described the dire poverty into which the Indians had sunk. And so it had continued, and was to continue; an endless flow of cant, while the peasants starved.

Albion Perfide

There was one other casualty of the opium war: Britain's good name. Melbourne had foreseen the possibility; he had felt great concern and regret, he told the House of Lords in the China debate, that 'a system should exist which, in the eyes of the world, identified the government of this country in some degree with the propagation of the evils arising from the use of opium'. By that time, denunciations of Britain's involvement had already begun to appear abroad. 'The proud escutcheon of the nation which declaims against the slave trade,' the Rev. Howard Malcolm, an American missionary, had written in his *Travels in South-East Asia*, published in Boston in 1839, 'is thus made to bear a blot broader than any other in the Christian world'; the precursor of many such attacks. Even the Comte de Montalembert, devoted admirer though he was of Britain and her institutions, could not defend her opium policy; he was to describe the enforced production of the drug in India as 'a shame to England, and a scourge to China'. It was not so much what Britain had done that was castigated; it was her politicians' cant that rankled. Writing to thank Gladstone for his speech in the Commons debate, Baron Bunsen told him that at least it would help England's friends abroad to hold their ground against the attacks of her numerous enemies, 'all throwing that question in our face, as proving the humbug and hypocrisy of all the pretended Christian professions and works of the English nation'. And in 1843 Balzac, observing in *An Inventors' Tale* that the common notion of an Englishman had up to that time been 'noble-hearted', suggested that the reverse would be closer to the truth: 'the English flaunt their perfidiousness in the face of the whole world.'

Albion Perfide was the reputation that was to haunt England throughout the century, and indeed up until 1940, when her reputation in Europe was at last for a time redeemed. A hundred years earlier, there was only a handful of M.P.s who had taken a stand on the moral issue; and the two who had taken it most effectively in the Commons, Gladstone and Herbert, were both silenced by their acceptance of junior ministerial posts in Peel's 1841 government. The news of the Treaty of Nanking, however, aroused *The Times* to suggest that the moment had come for Britain to extricate herself from her involvement with opium. Some moral compensation, an editorial argued, was owed to China 'for pillaging her towns and slaughtering her citizens in a quarrel which could never have arisen if we had not been guilty of an international crime'. Peel had no love for newspapers, but he owed a debt to *The Times* for ceasing to support the Whigs in the 1830s, and sustaining him in opposition. It was also to become the most influential newspaper in history, not lightly to be disregarded.

Nor, as time was to show, was it safe to ignore another critic of the Treaty, a member of the Tory party in the Commons. Lord Ashley had already made a reputation as a humanitarian, fighting for the better care and protection of lunatics, children in factories, and chimney sweeps; but his interest had been in domestic issues, and he had not spoken in the 1840 debate, though he had voted with his party. 'Intelligence of great successes in China', he wrote in his diary on November 22nd, 'I rejoice in peace; I rejoice that this cruel and debasing war is terminated'.

But, he went on, 'I cannot rejoice – it may be unpatriotic, it may be un-British – I cannot rejoice in our successes; we have triumphed in one of the most lawless, unnecessary and unfair struggles in the records of history'. Three days later, when he heard of the terms which had been imposed at Nanking, he added that the peace was as wicked as the war; 'we refuse even now to give the Emperor of China relief in the matter of the opium trade'. And it was to be Ashley who, at William Fry's prompting a few weeks later, took up the campaign against Britain's involvement in the opium traffic; a campaign which was to continue to harass governments for the rest of the century.

Acknowledgments

My thanks to Matheson and Co., for permission to examine the Jardine Matheson archives, now at the University Library, Cambridge; to the staff of the Archives Section at the Library; to the staffs of the Public Record Office, of the British Library, and of the London Library; to the long-suffering Bill Grundy, who has read my typescripts more often than he cares to remember; and to Asa Briggs and Bernard Levin, who somehow found the time to read the proofs. I am indebted to them for a number of suggestions.

Bibliography

To avoid the necessity for detailed source references I have ordinarily indicated the authorship of quotations in the text; but for students of the period who may require more precise chapter-and-verse references a copy of the book, containing them, has been deposited in the Library of the School of Oriental and African Studies in London.

For the sake of brevity I have omitted the standard biographies and memoirs of the statesmen of the period, except when I have quoted from them in the text.

The place and date of publication given here refer to the edition consulted, which was not necessarily the first edition.

Unpublished

The Jardine Matheson archives: University Library, Cambridge.
Foreign Office files, China (F.O./17): Public Record Office,
London

Published Hansard Parliamentary Papers

1783 IV (first series). Reports from the Select Committee on
the East India Company's affairs

1812 VI Papers relating to the Company's Charter 1812-13
VI-X Correspondence relating to the Company's Charter

1813 XXV Further correspondence

1820 II, III Reports, minutes of evidence, etc. of the Select
Committee of the Lords on foreign trade

1821 VI, VII Further reports

1831 VI Papers relating to China and the Company's affairs

1831-2 X (parts one and two) Minutes of evidence, etc., of the
Select Committee on the Company's affairs XI Further papers
on the Company's affairs, and the opium monopoly

1838 XLI Papers on the establishment of a court of judicature
in China

1840 VII, Reports, etc., from the Select Committee on the trade
with China

XXXVI Correspondence relating to China, 1834-40

1857 XLIII Papers relating to the opium trade with China, 1842-56
(There are many more Parliamentary Papers in the period
touching on the subject; many others, too, in the second half

of the century which contain references to, and information about, the events leading up to the opium war. But the above are the main sources.)

Books, pamphlets, articles

Adams, John Quincy 'Lecture on the war with China' (reprinted in the *Chinese Repository*, May 1842)

Allen, Dr Nathan *The Opium Trade*, Boston, 1850

Anon, *An Inquiry into the Monopolies of the East India Company*, London, 1830

Auber, Peter *China*, London, 1834

(Barrow, John) 'On Chinese Commerce' (*Quarterly Review*, January 1830)

(Barrow, John) 'Free Trade to China' (*Quarterly Review*, January 1834)

(Barrow, John) 'China' (*Quarterly Review*, July 1836)

(Barrow, John) 'Chinese affairs' (*Quarterly Review*, March 1840)

Bell, Sydney S. *Answer to Samuel Warren's 'The Opium Question'*, London, 1840

Bolts, William *Considerations on Indian Affairs*, London, 1772

Bruce, C. A., *Report on the Tea Plantations of Assam*, Calcutta, 1839

Buchanan, Francis *An Account of the Districts of Bihar and Patna in 1812*, Patna, 1936

Buckingham, J. S. *Autobiography*, London, 1855

Bullock, T. H. *The Chinese Vindicated; or, Another View of the Opium Question*, London, 1840

Checkland, Sydney, *The Gladstones*, Cambridge, 1971

Chinese Repository, The, Canton, 1830-42

Colebrooke, H. T. *Remarks on the Present State of Husbandry and Internal Commerce of Bengal,* London, 1804

Crawfurd, J. *Chinese Monopoly Examined,* London, 1830

Crawfurd, J. *An Appeal from the Inhabitants of India to the Justice of the People of England,* London, 1839

Davis, John Francis *The Chinese,* London, 1836

Davis, John Francis *China during the war,* London, 1852

De Quincey, Thomas 'The opium question with China' (*Blackwood's Magazine,* May 1840)

Downing, C. Toogood *The Fan Qui in China 1836-7,* London 1838

Eatwell, W. C. B. *On the Poppy Cultivation,* Calcutta, 1851

Ellis, Henry *Journal of the Embassy to China,* London, 1818

Forbes, R. B. *China and the China Trade,* Boston, 1844

Forbes, R. B. *Personal Reminiscences,* Boston, 1892

Fry, William Storrs *Facts and Evidence Relating to the Opium Trade with China,* London 1840

Graham, Alexander *The Right, Obligations and Interest of the Government of Great Britain to Require Redress from the Government of China for the Late Forced Surrender of British-owned Opium at Canton,* Glasgow, 1840

Gully, Robert and Captain Denham *Journals Kept During a Captivity in China in the Year 1842,* London, 1844

Gutzlaff, Charles *The Life of Taou Wwang,* London, 1852

Heber, Reginald *Narrative of a Journey through the Upper Provinces of India,* London, 1828

Hill, J. Spencer *The Indo-Chinese Opium Trade,* London, 1884

Hue, Evariste *The Chinese Empire,* London, 1855

(Hunter, W. C.) *The Fan-Quae at Canton,* Shanghai, 1911

Jefferson, John *A sermon occasioned by the death of the Rev. Robert Morrison*, London, 1835

Jocelyn, Lord, *Six Months with the Chinese Expedition*, London, 1841

Kaye, J. W. *Sir John Malcolm*, London, 1851

Kaye, J.W. *The Administration of the East India Company*, London, 1853

Kaye, J.W. *Henry St. George Tucker*, London, 1854

Kaye, J. W. *Life and Correspondence of Lord Metcalfe*, London, 1854

Kaye, J. W. *Papers of Lord Metcalfe*, London, 1855

Lay, G. Tradescant *Trade with China*, London, 1837

Lay, G. Tradescant *The Chinese as They Are*, London, 1841

Lindsay, H. Hamilton, and the Rev. C. Gutzlaff *A Voyage to the Northern Ports of China*, London, 1833

Lindsay, H. Hamilton *Letter to Viscount Palmerston on British Relations with China*, London, 1836

Lindsay, H. Hamilton *Is the War with China a Just One?* London, 1840

Loch, James 'Dr Tennant's Indian reactions', *Edinburgh Review*, July, 1804

Macaulay, T. B., *Essays*, London, 1892

McCulloch, J. R. *Principles of Political Economy*, London, 1849

MacPherson, David *The History of the European Commerce with India*, London, 1812

Malcolm, Sir John *A Memoir of Central India*, London, 1832

Martin, R. Montgomery *China, Political, Commercial and Social*, London, 1847

Martin, R. Montgomery *British India*, London, 1862

Matheson, James *The Present Position and Prospects of the British Trade with China*, London, 1836

Matheson, Donald *What is the Opium Trade?* Edinburgh, 1857

Medhurst, W. H. *China*, London, 1840

Morrison, John Robert *A Chinese Commercial Guide*, Canton, 1834

Murray, Alexander *Doings in China*, London, 1843

Ouchterlony, John *The Chinese War*, London, 1844

Phipps, John *A Practical Treatise on the Chinese and Eastern Trade*, London, 1836

Raffles, Sir Thomas Stamford *History of Java*, London, 1817

Rickards, R. *India*, London, 1829

Shuck, Mrs Henrietta *Scenes in China*, Philadelphia, 1852

Shuck, J. Lewis *Portfolio Siniensis*, Macao, 1840

Sirr, Henry *China and the Chinese; the Evils Arising from the Opium Trade*, London, 1849

Stanley, A.P. *Life of Dr Thomas Arnold*, London, 1844

Staunton, Sir George *Miscellaneous Notices Relating to China and our Commercial Intercourse with that Country*, London, 1822

Staunton, Sir George *Remarks on British Relations with China*, London, 1836

Staunton, Sir George *Observations on the Chinese Commerce*, London, 1850

Thelwall, Rev. A. S. *The Iniquities of the Opium Trade with China*, London, 1839

Thelwall, Rev. A. S. *Memorial*, London, 1858

Tod, James *Annals of Rajasthan*, Oxford 1920

The Trial of Henry St. George Tucker esq, London, 1810.

Tucker, Henry St. G. *Memorials of Indian Government*, London, 1853

Turner, F. S. *British Opium Policy*, London, 1876

Vansittart, Henry *A Narrative of the Transactions in Bengal*, London, 1766

Vattel, Emerich de *The Law of Nations*, London, 1834

Verelst, Harry *A View of the Rise, Progress and Present State of the English Government of Bengal*, London, 1772

Warren, Samuel *The Opium Question*, London, 1840

Wheatley, John *A Letter . . . on the Latent Resources of India*, London, 1816

Young, George *A Treatise on Opium*, London, 1753

Secondary sources

Ascoli, F. D. *Early Revenue History of Bengal*, Oxford, 1917

Bastin, John S. *The British in West Sumatra, 1685-1825*, London, 1965

Beeching, Jack *The Chinese Opium Wars*, London, 1975

Beveridge, Henry *History of India*, London, 1904

Birdwood, Sir G. *Report of the Old Records of the India Office*

Blake, Clagette *Charles Elliot*, R.N., London, 1959

Brown, Robert *The Opium Revenue and Indian Finance*, Glasgow, 1891

Chang, Hsin-pao *Commissioner Lin and the Opium War*, Harvard, 1964

Colebrook, Sir T. E. *Life of H. T. Colebrook*, London, 1873

Collis, Maurice *The Great Within*, London, 1941

Collis, Maurice *Foreign Mud*, London, 1969

Cornwallis, Lord *Correspondence* (ed. C. Ross), London, 1859

Costin, W. C. *Great Britain and China, 1833-60*, Oxford, 1937

Crafts, Dr and Mrs Wilbur *Intoxicants and Opium in All Lands and Times*, Washington, 1906

Davies, A. Mervyn *Warren Hastings*, London, 1935

Davies, A. Mervyn *Clive of Plassey*, London, 1939

Dennet, Tyler *Americans in Eastern Asia*, New York, 1941

Dikawar, R. R. *Bihar Through the Ages*, Bombay, 1959

Dodwell, Henry *Warren Hastings: Letters to Sir John MacPherson*, London, 1927

Durga Parshad, I. *Some Aspects of Indian Foreign Trade, 1757-1893*, London, 1932

Dutt, Romesh *The Economic History of British India*, London, 1902

Eames, James B. *The English in China*, London, 1909

Eitel, E. J. *Europe in China: the History of Hong Kong to 1882*, Hong Kong, 1895

Elvin, Mark *The Pattern of China's Pasty* London, 1973

Fairbank, John K. *Trade and Diplomacy on the China Coast 1841-54*, Cambridge (Mass.), 1953

Feiling, Keith *Warren Hastings*, London, 1954

Forster, John W. *American Diplomacy in the Orienty* Boston, 1903

Furber, H. *Henry Dundasy* Oxford, 1931

Gardner, Robert B. *The East India Company*, London, 1871

Greenberg, Michael *British Trade and the Opening of China, 1800-47*, Cambridge, 1951

Hallward, N. L. *William Bolts*, Cambridge, 1920

Hamilton, C. J. *Trade Relations Between England and India, 1600-1896*, Calcutta, 1919

Holt, Edgar *The Opium Wars in China*, London, 1964

Hsü, Immanuel C. Y. *The Rise of Modern China*, New York, 1970

Kuo, P. *The First Chinese War*, Shanghai, 1935

MacKenzie, A. *A History of the Mathesons*, London, 1900

Melbourne, Lord *Papers* (ed. LI. C. Saunders), London, 1889

Morse, Hosea Ballou *International Relations of the Chinese Empire*, London, 1910

Morse, Hosea Ballou *The Chronicles of the East India Company 1635-1834*, Oxford, 1926

Owen, David *Imperialism and Nationalism in the Far East*, London, 1930

Owen, David *British Opium Policy in China and India*, New Haven, 1934

Panikkar, K. M. *Asia and Western Dominance*, London, 1953

Philips, C.H. *The East India Company, 1784-1834*, Manchester, 1961

Ramsbotham, R. B. 'Revenue, administration of Bengal, 1765-86' (in the *Cambridge History of the British Empire IV*, Cambridge, 1929)

Redford, Arthur *Manchester Merchants and Foreign Trade*, Manchester, 1934

Ridley, Jasper *Lord Palmerston*, London, 1970

Rosselli, John *Lord William Bentinck*, London 1974

Rowntree, Joshua *The Imperial Drug Trade*, London, 1906

Scott, J. M. *The White Poppy*, London, 1969

Teng, Ssu-yu, and Fairbank, John K. *China's Response to the West*, Cambridge (Mass.), 1954

Thompson, Edward *The Life of Charles, Lord Metcalfe*, London, 1937

Thompson, Edward, and G. T. Garratt *Rise and Fulfilment of British Rule in India*, London, 1934

Victoria, Queen *Letters* (ed. A. C. Benson), London, 1907

Waley, Arthur *The Opium War through Chinese Eyes*, London, 1958

Watt, George *A Dictionary of the Economic Products of India*, London, 1892

Webster, Sir Charles *The Foreign Policy of Palmerston*, 1830-41, London, 1951

Weitzman, Sophia *Warren Hastings and Philip Francis*, Manchester, 1929

Williams, S. Wells *The Middle Kingdom*, New York, 1883

Woodruff, Philip *The Men Who Ruled India*, London 1954

Wright, H. R. C. *East Indian Economic Problems of the Age of Cornwallis and Raffles*

ENDEAVOUR INK

Endeavour Ink is an imprint of Endeavour Press.

If you enjoyed *The Opium War* check out
Endeavour Press's eBooks here:
www.endeavourpress.com

For weekly updates on our free and discounted eBooks sign up
to our newsletter:
www.endeavourpress.com

Follow us on Twitter:
@EndeavourPress